D0531700

Holly
Hagan

521 790 25 4

Holly Hagan

NOT QUITE A GEORDIE

My Autobiography

With Elissa Corrigan

JOHN BLAKE

Published by John Blake Publishing Ltd,
3 Bramber Court, 2 Bramber Road,
London W14 9PB, England

www.johnblakepublishing.co.uk

www.facebook.com/johnblakebooks ▪
twitter.com/jblakebooks ▪

First published in hardback in 2014
This edition published in paperback in 2015

ISBN: 978 1 78418 336 3

All rights reserved. No part of this publication may be reproduced, stored in a
retrieval system, or transmitted in any form or by any means, without the prior
permission in writing of the publisher, nor be otherwise circulated in any form of
binding or cover other than that in which it is published and without a similar
condition including this condition being imposed on the subsequent purchaser.

British Library Cataloguing-in-Publication Data:

A catalogue record for this book is available from the British Library.

Design by www.envydesign.co.uk

Printed in Great Britain by CPI Group (UK) Ltd

1 3 5 7 9 10 8 6 4 2

© Text copyright Holly Hagan 2015

The right of Holly Hagan to be identified as the author of this work has been
asserted by her in accordance with the Copyright, Designs and Patents Act 1988.

Papers used by John Blake Publishing are natural, recyclable products made from
wood grown in sustainable forests. The manufacturing processes conform to the
environmental regulations of the country of origin.

Every attempt has been made to contact the relevant copyright-holders,
but some were unobtainable. We would be grateful if the appropriate people
could contact us.

I want to dedicate this book to you, Mam. I love you so very much.

Contents

NOT QUITE A GEORDIE

INTRODUCTION

'I'm fake, I'm flirty, I've got double FFs...
and I want to be famous!'

For as long as I can remember I've always wanted to be a 'somebody'. I've always felt like I had all the ingredients to be a ready-made star; all you needed to do was add water. Or, in my case, vodka!

But I couldn't inherit fame from my parents, and I didn't really possess any special talents. I always knew that if I wanted to get my name out there then I would have to become a 'man-made' celebrity created by the media, similar to my idol, Katie Price.

I've always admired Katie, not just because of her looks but also her ability to market herself well. Nowadays, that's all that seems to count. She's rebellious in a way that appeals to people. They can't get enough of her and that's something I've always strived for.

Of course I didn't know when I was younger that I would wind up on a reality TV show, but as soon as I saw an opportunity to be a part of that world I grabbed it with both hands. All my life I've been a fan of those American TV shows, so much so that I even nicknamed my boobs 'Heidi' and 'Audrina' after the two stars of the reality series, *The Hills*.

So when I heard the concept for a new series featuring people from my area, the north-east of England, I knew I'd found my calling. This show was to be my way to fame and fortune. I could feel it. And luckily for me, the stars aligned just at the right time. I was picked to be one of the eight new housemates on the new, no-holds-barred reality show called *Geordie Shore*.

Back then I didn't know it but life would never be the same. I was about to launch a career in the media spotlight, but it came at a cost: I had to give up the right to privacy and share intimate details of my life as entertainment for the masses. Nothing was off limits, not even sex.

My life was to be offered up to millions to be commented on, critiqued and even ripped apart. And when I wasn't parading on TV, I was expected to tweet about myself round the clock, like a lifelogger. No part of me could be kept hidden in the dark anymore. For me, it's like there's no distinction between public and private.

It's not for everyone. There is much more to life than fame and just because I chose this lifestyle, that doesn't mean you should, too. I'm not a role model and never wanted to be.

But even though I have laid myself bare on TV, quite literally, you only get to see Holly from *Geordie Shore*, the man-made celebrity edited by a production crew. You don't really know who I am or where I've come from, which is why I've decided to write this book.

If you've seen me on the show, one thing you'll already know is that I'm brutally honest. I will not hold back when it comes to speaking my mind, so don't expect me to sugar-coat anything now. Everything I'm about to tell you is the truth, the way it actually happened, even the parts I'm embarrassed to admit.

You might think you know what I'm about from watching all seven series of *Geordie Shore,* but you only see what we allow you to see. I'll tell you straight up what goes on behind the scenes, how much is fudged for the audience and what I really think of the other housemates.

My story isn't exactly a pretty one. In fact, it should come with an 18-rating. There's violence, cruelty, sex and a lot of swearing. But stories that are not pretty have a certain value, I suppose.

Everything, as you well know – having lived in this world long enough to figure a thing or two out for yourself – can't always be sweetness and light. Even in my tender twenty-one years on this earth, I've been through and seen more things than most people my age. I've travelled to all corners of the earth and had a mint time doing it.

So leave your prejudgements at the door because I'm inviting you to get to know me, the real me, and perhaps then you can make your own mind up because what you see is not what you get. I'm fake, I'm flirty and I have got double FFs, but I'm not quite like you see onscreen. I'm not quite famous and I'm not always the boozy, promiscuous lass you'd expect. And I'm not quite a Geordie. In fact, I'm not a Geordie at all!

Happy reading,
Love Holly x

Chapter One

WHERE IT ALL
BEGAN

Since I signed my life away on a reality show, it seems nothing can ever be private again. Not that I'm complaining – I knew exactly what I was getting into before I etched my autograph on the contract. With that in mind, I suppose you're going to want to know every last detail about what led me to star in one of the most outrageous TV shows ever made. How I, Holly Victoria Hagan, was plucked from obscurity to be cast in the hugely successful series *Geordie Shore*.

But first of all, let's start at the beginning.

I wouldn't say I've had a privileged childhood, but I was given the best upbringing my parents could provide. My mam, Vicky, and my dad, Barry, are your typical, hard-working northern types. They met in a nightclub called The Madison, a very popular spot in the late eighties. Locals affectionately called it 'the Madhouse' or 'Mad Dogs', which gives you an idea of the kind of place it was.

Mam was just a tender twenty-year-old when she was spanking the planks in The Madison most Saturday nights. She would be out with a gaggle of her glamorous friends, boogying round her handbag, knocking back spritzers and eyeing up the local Teesside talent.

It was on one of these nights my mam first spotted my dad. She was instantly smitten because he was quite the catch, back in his heyday. He was 6' 2", with big broad shoulders, a rugged exterior and a canny attitude all the ladies loved. He was standing over by the ladies' toilets, so my mam kept walking past, hoping he would notice her, but he never even batted an eyelid. Poor Mam! Not even at ten to two, when you'd cop off with any woman who wasn't taken, she didn't get a look. Although, don't get me wrong, my mam was never a ten-to-two boiler. Tall, busty and blonde, she used her assets to their full potential. She was a real looker – to borrow a phrase from *Geordie Shore*, 'a worldie'.

It wasn't until three weeks later when my dad, Barry, was back down at the Madhouse with a group of his pals that he and Mam first made contact. Legend has it, he kept making eyes at her all night. Mam was flattered because she'd fancied him ever since she'd first seen him. This bit of eye flirting carried on for a while, with neither of them making a move to go and speak to the other. God, it makes me cringe to even think about my parents flirting!

Although oblivious to Mam at the time, there was another strapping hunk vying for her attention (remember this part because it becomes very important later in the book). His name was John and was equally good looking as my dad. Tanned, blue-eyed, with a muscly frame and a wicked smile, John wasted no time in making a move on Mam by asking her friend if he could dance with her. My mam's friend had to politely decline on Mam's behalf because, unfortunately for John, she only had eyes for Barry Hagan.

Dad was twenty-one, already married and had a one-year-old baby, my half-brother, Leon. But my mam had no clue he was otherwise taken at this point – she just knew him as the local Middlesbrough hunk. It was only a while later that she learned the full extent of his background and marital status.

John, who was obviously gutted not to get a dance with the hottest chick in town, politely stepped aside like a gentleman and let my mam go for her man. Which was good news for me because without John stepping aside that evening, Holly Hagan might never have been born.

From that night on, my mam and dad were inseparable. They fell in love, and as a result, Dad ended his relationship with his wife at the time. By all accounts, it was a messy, tough time and one I cannot even begin to fathom so I'm not going to. I wasn't there, and that kind of business was between the adults back then. It's not for me to start commenting on it now.

My dad and mam moved in together shortly after Dad's split from his wife and like any young couple in love, they worked hard, enjoyed being together and made plans for the future. They were serious about each other, so much so that three years later, they decided to have a baby. They told me they had wanted a child for so long and eventually, after a year of trying, my mam broke the good news to my dad: she'd finally fallen pregnant.

Mam had always wanted a little girl, but back then you

couldn't tell which sex your baby was going to be, so it was a nice surprise for her when, on 7 July 1992, the midwife presented her with a newborn girl.

She was in labour with me for seven hours and twenty minutes. By all accounts it was a fairly easy birth – well, as easy as giving birth can get.

My mam and dad immediately fell in love with me. A seven-pound six-ounce bundle of joy and there wasn't a dry eye in the house as they all wept tears of happiness over the new addition to the family. There were four of my relatives in the room when I was born and I was the only one who wasn't crying! Odd how I never cried when I was born, but as you'll come to learn I've shed a lot of tears throughout my lifetime.

As soon as Mam held me for the first time, she knew at once what she wanted me to be called: Holly Victoria Hagan. Little Holly Hagan… It's funny because when my mam's cousin came to the hospital to see me for the first time and found out they'd named me Holly Hagan, she said, 'That sounds like a famous person's name.'

Mam and Dad were like any other young couple with a baby. They lived together and were totally devoted to me. I was a pretty good baby, too – I slept through the night, I was responsive to my mother's wishes and I only ever whinged when it was absolutely necessary.

Neither of my parents had come from money, so they had to graft for anything they wanted. When I was born, they were living in a council house in a run-down housing estate in Middlesbrough called Grove Hill. Grove Hill's only other claim to fame is that the footballing legend Brian Clough also grew up on its rough streets.

Mam was twenty-three when she had me, which seems so young by today's standards. She'd been working at Greggs, the bakers, ever since she was sixteen, but had to give up when she had me.

To support his new family, my dad had to work away, down in Essex on a construction site, and return back up north at the weekends. It was hard for my mam because she was, in effect, a single mother. There were a lot of young girls and single mams living on the same street, which was good for Mam at the time because they all helped each other out (my mam was one of the few living on the street actually to have a partner). Even though the area was a rough place to live, the people who lived there were the salt of the earth. It was a close-knit community and everyone knew each other.

The other mams would jokingly call my mam 'the posh one' because she came from a place called Thornaby-on-Tees, which was a lot more upmarket than Grove Hill. It never bothered Mam though, and it's not like they ever held it against her; they just used to playfully take the mick. Mam always tried to fit in with them by going on nights out and round to each other's houses, something the other girls appreciated. It's one of the best qualities my mam has, the ability to get on with literally anyone she comes into contact with.

Mam went back to working at Greggs when I was eighteen months old. She had always been a worker and genuinely enjoyed getting out there and earning her own money. She enrolled me in a private nursery, which was expensive and she got no help to pay the fees, but with both my parents' wages, they could afford it. But their relationship was beginning to show signs of strain. They were spending hardly any time together because Dad would be down south five days a week. Mam worked on Saturdays, which is when he would look after me, and then my dad would be out with his mates of a Sunday down the pub before he would go back down to Essex again.

Thinking about it now, it's a wonder how they managed like that for so long. It was as if they were living completely separate lives. It can't have been easy on either of them, especially Mam, who had to juggle work and looking after a child.

We stayed in that house in Grove Hill until one day, when I was three, we were burgled. My dad was still working away and it was really scary for Mam. She was a young woman on her own looking after me and some scumbag decided to rob from our house while we were asleep. It's the lowest of the low, if you ask me, but in Grove Hill, that's what life was like. It wasn't uncommon to hear of someone being burgled round there on a weekly basis.

The final straw came when Mam heard a commotion outside the window of our house. She looked out, expecting to see another domestic going on between the neighbours, but instead she saw a car on fire with three screaming people inside. Having someone torch a car with people still inside is not something you want on your doorstep and that, coupled with the burglary, really shook her up, especially as Dad wasn't around. It was horrific and the next day she started making plans to move. She would be leaving her friends and neighbours behind, but what choice did she have?

The house we moved into wasn't very far away, but it was in a slightly safer location. It was still a hellhole if you ask me, but it was marginally better than the last house. The new neighbours were much older than my mam and most of them had saved up enough money to buy their council house. It was a lot quieter and there were no single mams with kids running around, but Mam seemed to be a lot happier there, and it was where I spent the majority of my childhood. Although a step up from the last house, I was still very much aware that it wasn't a nice place to live. I wasn't allowed to play out or even step foot outside the front door for a second without an adult being there.

When I was four, I was enrolled at the local school, St Joseph's RC primary in Middlesbrough, which gave my mam a little more time to be able to work. Mam was craving a change: she was sick of coming home from Greggs each day smelling like pastry, having to wear those embarrassing hairnets and deal with rude customers. Her relationship with my dad was getting worse, too. So when she saw an advert in the paper for an assistant at Vision Express she applied for the job and a few months later was given a position in the Middlesbrough branch. The change she needed at the time, it gave her more confidence and she could work longer hours and earn more money.

At school I made a best friend, a girl called Laura O'Callaghan. Soon we became inseparable and, being an only child, she was like a sister to me. We were so close. After school, while my mam was working, I would go to her house. Laura's mam didn't work and so my mam paid her a little bit of money each week for making my tea. It was a situation I was happy with: I got to see my best friend, and Mam was happy because I was being looked after by someone she trusted.

But my mam would never palm me off with just anyone, she was always very careful about who she let into my life. My nana, Olwyn, was like my second mam and all through primary school I would spend the majority of my time round at hers. Every Saturday she would take me swimming, and she actually taught me how to swim. It's funny, the inconsequential things you remember from your childhood, but when I think about those swimming lessons, I always remember the smell of sausage sandwiches. My nana would get me one straight after swimming and she'd use the 50p from the clothes locker to buy me a chocolate bar. The little pleasures make up so many of my memories, and every time I get a whiff of a sausage sandwich it will always remind me of Saturday swimming with Nana.

Sometimes on the weekends Nana and her partner, Alan, whom I absolutely adored, would take me to this place called Beamish in Durham. An open-air museum you could walk around, showcasing what everyday urban life was like in the early twentieth century, it was like stepping into another world. I thought it was awesome. We'd spend all day there, playing with the livestock, riding the trams and buying 'ye olde' traditional sweets from the gift shops.

I always have such happy recollections of my time there, especially with Alan. Like a big, cuddly, gentle giant, he had an amazing, fun personality and my face would be hurting by the end of a day because he'd made me laugh so much. Unfortunately, he died a few years ago and I was totally gutted. He was really special to me, and I'll always treasure fond memories of us climbing all over the Beamish steam trains.

There are moments when I wish I could roll back the clock and remember more from those early years, but I can't really. The one piece of advice I'd give anyone is to treasure the small things in life because you come to realise that they were the big things you'll always miss and you can't get that time back.

Anyway, I loved being with my nana and every Christmas we would always go round to her house because she cooked the best turkey dinner you could imagine. When I say 'we', I mean Mam and me because my dad was hardly ever there on those special days. When I look back at all my old Christmas photos, I seem happy amongst all my toys and the bits of shredded wrapping paper, my smile beaming from ear to ear. Mam and me around Nana's Christmas tree, but I've rarely got a photo with my dad in it and that does make me sad.

Regardless, our Christmases were brilliant. My mam would always save up to make sure I wanted for nothing, even if it meant getting into debt. She couldn't go to banks, so she was relying on lenders like Provident and Shopacheck to make sure I had the easiest life possible – she wanted me to have the best of everything and not to miss out. It's only as I've got older that I realise how much Mam did sacrifice for me, although at the time I never really understood it and she was very good at making sure I was oblivious to our financial situation. No matter what it took to get me something I wanted, she would always try her best for me.

Most of the early years kind of merge into one, except for one year when I was five years old and my parents almost split for good. Two days before Christmas my dad had left my mam. They'd had a massive row and he went back down to Essex for work. I could tell he and Mam had been on a rocky road for a good few years. Although I know they must have had some blazing rows, they both shielded me from the arguments. I never really witnessed any of the fall-out from their relationship; they were always so careful not to have a slanging match in front of me.

But kids are more perceptive than parents think and I could tell their relationship had changed from when I was younger. It was like they couldn't stand being around each other now. I know my mam was still deeply in love with my dad, but it was just too much for her to take. She knew she deserved better, but she didn't know how she would cope without him. Now, she'd say my dad had done her a favour because she would never have been strong enough to leave him but back then, when he finished the relationship and told her he was spending Christmas away she was devastated.

Mam never said a word to me at the time. I never knew where or why he went. All I knew was that Dad had left us at the best time of the year, and I was gutted. I caught my mam crying about it. She never knew I'd seen her but that vision of her wiping the tears away always stays with me. It's only as I've grown up and Mam has explained the situation that I can fully appreciate how much pain she must have gone through.

At the time, she would plaster on a smile and never let on how much she must have been hurting. She really did keep it together. In some ways, I wish she had told me more of what was going on, and then in other ways I'm glad I didn't know. She says she never wanted me to think of my dad as anything but a great guy, even though she could have slagged him off to high heaven. But she chose the moral high ground, which shows a tremendous amount of courage and strength.

That year, I'd asked Father Christmas for a desk, so of course my mam saved up so she could buy it for me. She'd been hiding the flat-pack desk under her bed for a couple of weeks, hoping Dad would fix it up on Christmas Eve. Of course when he left us, Mam had to muster up the energy and do it all herself. She told me she sat there in the living room, reading all the instructions over and over again before she started the assembly. Then she spent hours scrabbling around for a screwdriver, but couldn't find anything that even resembled any kind of DIY tool. In the end, she had to make do with a butter knife and patience. She sat up for hours, crying and sobbing, trying to build this desk.

It was like an analogy of her life at the time, too. Life as she knew it had been flattened and it was up to her to build it back up again, whatever way she could, for me. It took hours of persistence, of getting it wrong, of putting pieces in the wrong place, against a heavy heart and painful sobs, but eventually she did it.

Mam built that desk and it had been a lot more difficult than if Dad had been around, but she did it. The same went for our lives: it would take time for her to rebuild everything that had been flattened, but with patience and persistence she eventually got there. I remember opening my desk on Christmas Day and being so happy about it. It was the exact desk I'd asked for, the best desk I'd ever seen! I unwrapped all my other toys and placed them away carefully in my shiny red desk.

Even though I would have loved Dad to be there, I know love and relationships are a ridiculously knotty issue, especially when kids are involved. I kind of hoped he'd have wanted to stick around for a couple more days to watch his daughter open her presents, but then what was he supposed to do? Leave on Boxing Day, in the middle of Christmas or even at the start of the New Year? No, I'm old enough now to appreciate that nothing in life is easy and affairs of the heart are never black and white. I'll never know the full story of what went on with Mam and Dad. To be honest, it's not really my business and

I don't want to know. Those are their lives, not mine. All I care about was how they were with me and you know what? I couldn't have asked for better parents. Despite them not being together, they did everything they could for me and that's all that mattered.

Chapter Two

TURNING
THE CORNER

Even though my dad had left that Christmas when I was five, my parents did get back together for a short while but it was clear by all accounts that the relationship had broken down. And two years later, when I was seven years old, they officially split.

My mam and dad were never married, even though they were engaged for several years, but when they separated it was almost like they were divorcing. I know so many kids blame their parents' divorce on their problems and that's something I don't necessarily agree with. It's only a tragedy if you let it affect you, and I didn't. All things considered, I came to terms with it really well. The real tragedy would have been for them to stay unhappy together for the sake of me. I wouldn't have wanted that because I look at them now and see how happy they both are, now that they've moved on from each other. No one ever died from a break-up.

My dad left with literally just his clothes. He didn't own a spoon in our house; Mam had bought everything and she wasn't allowing him to take any of it away from her. She saved all the money she could and eventually had enough to buy her own council house. She paid £18,000 for the house, which is nothing in today's current climate, but back then it was a huge sum and the deposit had taken her years to save. She made sure the house was in her name and all the furniture in there was hers, too. My mam is a smart woman. She has more common sense than me anyway, and when the time was right, three years later, she sold her council house for £62,000 and made a hefty profit for herself.

Even though Mam is a strong, steely northern lass, my dad leaving broke her heart. Their relationship had been more bad than good, but it's all she had ever known. They had been together for eleven years. When she met my dad, she'd fallen hard. She loved him so much that she had a child with him. She knew she deserved better but she had become too comfortable and familiar with her life. She didn't know any different. But now he had left her for good. It was a bitter pill to swallow, as it would be for anyone.

It was hard on my dad, too, but in a different way. I suppose for him, the only thing more unthinkable than leaving was staying; the only thing more impossible than staying was leaving. He didn't want to destroy anything or anybody; he just wanted to slip quietly out the back door, without causing any fuss or consequences. If only life could have been that easy! The last thing in the world he wanted was to upset me and sometimes I think he feels guilty for leaving. But I don't want him to do that: honestly, hand on heart, I think it was the best decision for all involved. He wasn't happy and why should anyone spend years like that? Imagine the guilt I would have felt now that I'm older, knowing my dad sacrificed his happiness for so long.

No, unlike some other bratty kids, I'm big enough to say that I prefer my parents apart. And I don't want it to come across as if my dad was a real bastard or anything. Like I said at the beginning, I'm only comfortable speaking with brutal honesty. These are the facts of what happened and I can't change them. Also, I don't blame anyone for anything; I'm no angel and I don't expect my parents to be either.

And I love my dad to pieces. He is the best father I could imagine. I don't think we've ever had a disagreement or an argument once in my life. We've been best mates ever since I was born and he's one of the funniest men I know. My dad has always been able to admit when he's wrong; it's one of his best attributes. I know I can call him up any time of the day or night and ask his advice. He's been through a lot, has my dad, and because of his experience he has given me a realistic and positive example of how to deal with the world.

The first time my mam had to see my dad after the split was at my first Holy Communion. I was seven and a half at this point and they'd been separated for almost six months. Mam is a Catholic. She doesn't take her religion that seriously, but she always preferred me to attend a Catholic school because they are usually smaller in class size. I never really had much time for religion, but the idea of getting dolled up and walking to the front of the church with everyone looking on appealed to me. While I only have a few small memories, the whole day was bittersweet. It was great to see my dad again. I'd been so excited to see him and show him my flowing white dress but I could tell Mam was nervous – she kept fussing over herself and me. She spent ages getting ready. She had her nails done and she made sure she smelled divine by splashing on her favourite Baby Doll perfume by YSL. She looked an absolute knockout though, and I'm sure that was the point. To show Dad what he was missing.

It must have been tough for Mam. All her emotions were still raw. She was still very much in love with him, but she kept it together that day. They both did. My dad was great fun and he was so proud of me. I was delighted he wanted to be there on my special day despite how awkward it might have been for him. That was always the good thing about my parents. They did everything for me and, if they had to be in each other's company, no matter how they felt about each other, they would set their emotions aside and just get on with it.

I used to hear a few people saying I was from a broken family, something I never agree with. Family is not determined by pieces of paper like marriage certificates or divorce papers. Families are made in the heart. For me, my family wasn't broken, it was just extended. It wasn't like my dad had gone to Essex and forgotten about me, he would regularly come back to Middlesbrough just to see his little Hunza Bunza (his little nickname for me). He would take me out at the weekends and we would have such a laugh together.

He'd sometimes take me to see his mates play football in Sunday league matches. He didn't have to do that, but he wanted to spend every second with me when he was back home. I would sit behind the goalposts, watch the game and pretend I was a cheerleader, cheering them along.

At half time I'd always get the same snacks, so much so that my dad would just say, 'Are you having the usual, Holly?' like I was some regular boozer. My particular tipple was half a Coke and a packet of cheesy puffs to chomp on through the second half.

After the game, we'd go back to a pub called The Doormans and stay in there until late evening. Then we'd head to a second pub, The Yellow Rose, before I had to go back home again. The landlord would always have a word with my dad about having a kid on the premises past 4pm, so I used to hide under the tables until we were ready to leave. When I think back it was quite irresponsible, but at the time it was hilarious and I genuinely loved being there. I enjoyed being in adult company and my dad's mates doted on me just as much as he did.

My mam let me get involved with her mates, too, when they came round to the house. They'd be having a few glasses of wine in the living room and it would give me a chance to perform in front of them. Always a really confident child, I'd sing and dance while they all sat around laughing. I liked that my parents involved me in their lives in that way – they would never just palm me off with a babysitter unless they were going out on the razz, which was only on rare occasions.

That's how I like to look back on those times, with my mam and dad being equally happy but not with each other. It never bothered me because I would get the best of the both of them, and sometimes I think having separated parents can be a good thing.

My mam has since told me the years that followed the break-up had a profound effect on her. She became terribly unhappy and depressed. For a while she had to leave Vision Express and take some time out to be on her own. She was like that for two years and we really did struggle to get by during those times. We had virtually no money, but she did her absolute best and made sure I still had everything I needed. There were things she was willing to sacrifice and others she wasn't. Having a yearly holiday was something she refused to let me live without, even if that meant she would run herself into debt just to be able to afford it.

My dad contributed, too. Every month he would pay a small amount of maintenance. It was not nearly enough to keep up with the bills, the food shopping or any new clothes, but it was all he could spare. I told you I've never come from money, which is why I value all the money I earn for myself now. I know first-hand how hard it is for 'normal' hard-working families to make ends meet.

So, I had two parents who grafted, but in the end my mam had to start claiming benefits. She is a proud woman and had never relied on the government for anything, but during those years money was so tight that she had no other choice. And she didn't see the benefits as an excuse for her to laze about at home watching Jeremy Kyle; she just used the money for six months until she felt better and could go back to work. Mam was always a worker, and I like to think that's where I get my strong work ethic from now.

I remember her waking up one Saturday morning with a new sense of determination. It was like she really turned a corner in her life. She had decided she wanted to be back at work and to start getting her independence back again. She'd never been one to rest on her laurels, and I remember watching her as she sat down at the table and penned a letter to Specsavers asking if they had any job vacancies. She wasn't the kind of woman who would wait for a job to pop up; she would go out there and get it.

A month later she was back in work and so much happier within herself. I was young, but even I could tell: it was as if she had her sparkle back. Now she had confidence and knew what direction she was going in. It had a good effect on me, too – I was happier, knowing she was happier.

Don't get me wrong, I still missed my dad – I would literally pine for him and get upset when I knew I wouldn't be seeing him for weeks on end. And it took me a while to get used to the idea of not seeing him every weekend. While I loved spending time with my mam, Dad and me always had this special bond.

Dad had a new girlfriend called Debbie (now my stepmam), who lived down in Essex and he moved in with her shortly after he broke up with my mam. I remember the first time they invited me down to see them. Going to meet this new lady, I was incredibly nervous. I hardly knew anything about her – I didn't know what she looked like or anything. My mam had told me to be on my best behaviour for her, which of course I always was (I think she might have thought I would have got jealous or been nasty to her because she was now with my dad). I know it can sometimes be extremely difficult with kids, but it was never like that with Debbie and me.

I'd got a soap making kit for Christmas so, a few days before my trip, I made her some lavender and elderflower soaps. Debbie was so touched by my little present and it really helped us get off on the right foot. It broke the ice between us and we've always got on great ever since.

After that I would visit about four times a year. Dad would have liked to have me down more often but it was hard fitting in a trip down south around school. He would also have me for one week in the summer and then one week at New Year. The rest of the time I would visit him for a weekend every eight weeks.

When I came back from my dad's house, I would miss him so much. I would wail and scream for days, which must have been hard for my mam to see because she was the one who raised me on a day-to-day basis. She was the one struggling to keep a roof over our heads and food on the table. Mam would see the best of me, but she would also have to put up with me when I was being a stroppy child and throwing tantrums. It was almost like I didn't appreciate her. Of course I *did* appreciate her and, almost ever since I was born, we'd been the best of friends. When she wasn't working, we'd spend all our time together.

On Sundays, my mam would dress me up nicely and she would make that extra bit of effort with her hair and make-up, then say, 'Let's do some retail therapy!' We'd get the bus into Middlesbrough and have a little bite to eat – nothing like a big fancy lunch, but we would find a café and have a hot chocolate and a muffin. I really felt like one of the grown-ups when we were out on our shopping trips. Mam never treated me like a child. She always spoke to me as if I was one of her mates and we had such a great time.

We would wander round the shops, admiring all the window displays, and people-watch, pointing out funny folk, and generally have a laugh. We'd walk around the town centre, stopping at nearly every clothes shop along the way until it was time to go home. Mam might have only had ten pounds in her purse to spend on those Sunday shopping trips, but she always made sure we would buy something on our little jaunts. I know ten pounds doesn't seem like a lot of money, but even that was hard enough for her to spare at the time. Obviously anything she got would be nothing big. I was really into dolls, so she would buy me a new dolly or a teddy, or new stationery. I remember getting these coloured gel pens and everyone at school was insanely jealous – we all wanted to write our names on our exercise books with the pink one. A couple of times, I'd get a new top from my favourite shop, Tammy Girl.

I remember us going in there one time and spying this white plastic, crinkly coat on a mannequin. It sounds gross, but it was like a sixties-style mac with big white buttons. I promise you, it was absolutely gorgeous. My mam loved it, too – she made me try it on and I think she was more excited than I was. It cost a bit more than ten pounds, but she said it was worth it because it was that nice. In her own way I suppose she spoiled me, but not too much because I knew the value of money and I knew we didn't have much. I wouldn't scream and demand this and that. I was never a brat, but my mam made sure I never went without. I was her absolute world. Gone were the days of her spending money on a new flash outfit for herself; she would get more pleasure out of seeing me in a fancy new coat than buying anything for herself to wear.

Don't get me wrong, she still had her own life and she had her own friends to go out with some weekends. And when she did, I would stay in with my nana, doing puzzles and crosswords. She didn't go out very often, although now I wish she had. I would never have held it against her, but I suppose she felt guilty for leaving me while she was out, having a good time.

When I think back to how she must have felt during those years, I just can't imagine how she coped. Sometimes she would get in from a night out and because she'd had a little too much to drink, she would sit and cry about me, about my dad leaving, about her going out and enjoying herself. It breaks my heart to hear it now, because my mam was entitled to a life just like anyone else. Just because she had a young daughter, that didn't mean her life should stop. It's easy to say this in retrospect, but if I could go back now, I'd tell her not to be so daft. If I could have told her at the time, I would have encouraged her to stay out all night and get mortal, *Geordie Shore*-style. But she wasn't like me. She had responsibilities and took her role as a mam very seriously. She put herself at the bottom too much.

Plus, I genuinely loved staying with my nana. I remember one time we did a design competition in a magazine. You were supposed to colour in the girls' dresses with crayons or felt tips, but I decided to use old pieces of fabric. I didn't even have any glue, so I had to use clear nail varnish. Most kids wouldn't have thought to do anything like that, but I think it shows I've always had a creative style from a young age. My nana sent it off to the magazine. I never expected to hear anything back, but I actually won it. My photo was printed in the publication and so was my name.

My mam bought the magazine from the newsagent, flicked to the page and showed me. I loved seeing myself published for the first time. She showed everyone at work and everyone who came round to our house. They all made a big fuss and it made me feel really happy. Maybe you could pinpoint that moment as the time when I discovered my obsession with fame and my love of seeing myself in print. I adored being in that magazine and seeing how everyone had reacted, like I was important and special, was a great feeling. It was the praise and comments I craved, something that has stuck with me for years.

Chapter Three

SHOWING OFF

One word you wouldn't use to describe me would be 'wallflower'. I have to be the centre of attention at all times. Even when I was little at school, I was the one you would see and hear first, always striving to be at the front.

During a Christmas nativity play I was given the lead part as the Angel Gabriel because of my confidence and love of performing to an audience. I sang my heart out on stage because, for a girl of my age, I had a huge voice, so the teachers always picked me for the big roles. But I was only ever confident performing in front of adults. I don't know why, but when it was something to do with other kids, I would close up and become shy – I even ran away once from one kids' club. If it was a group performance in front of parents, I would dive right in. I guess I've always felt more comfortable around them.

Even when I went on holiday, I would get up and perform

for the adults. I was the most outgoing of all the children in the kids' clubs. And I remember being in Majorca when I was eight years old, and I had the biggest crush on the entertainer. This was my first ever crush on a boy and I'd blush whenever I was around him. His name was Michael and I'd wake up early every morning because I couldn't wait to hang out with him. If he ever needed a volunteer, I'd be the first one to shoot my hand up and help him out. When it came to putting on shows for the parents, I made sure I was always the star in Michael's makeshift productions.

I remember one night in front of the whole hotel Michael asked if I'd like to sing a song. Well, this really was music to my ears! Most kids would never even dream of belting out a song for a room full of strangers, but I always jumped at the chance. Picking up the microphone, I sang Anastacia's 'I'm Outta Love', complete with hip twists and head bobs – I thought I was a diva, like Mariah Carey. Honestly, if you could have seen me, you'd have thought I was auditioning for *The X Factor*.

After I finished my performance, I took a huge bow and everyone in the hotel stood up and gave me a standing ovation while Michael looked on, proud as punch, laughing and smiling. When he told me I had a great voice, I almost melted. Seeing everyone's reaction was amazing. They were clapping and cheering for *me*! I suppose I got quite an adrenaline rush. I loved that everyone was looking at me and that I had them eating out of my hand. It was a good feeling and from that day on, I knew I wanted to be in the limelight. Obviously no one could have envisioned I would end up on a reality show like *Geordie Shore*, but it was clear I craved attention on a massive scale.

From then on, anytime there was an opportunity to perform

for people, I took it. When I was ten, my mam took me to her uncle's fortieth birthday party in Ireland. He had this huge house in the countryside and the place was packed to the rafters with revellers. There was a band there and they allowed me to sing a track with them on the karaoke. I chose Christina Aguilera's 'Genie In A Bottle' because she was my ultimate singing idol and I'd been practising the lyrics to perfection.

I could see my mam at the front, laughing and clapping. She was so proud of the way I was able to get up there in front of 150 people and command the room. It's something she herself could never have done and I think in some way she admired my fearless, carefree attitude. Like at the hotel in Majorca, everyone loved my performance. I know they were all family members, and even if I'd choked on stage they would still have told me I was better than Mariah, but I was excited by the buzz I got from them.

I'd also learnt all the lyrics and the full dance routine to 'Wannabe' by the Spice Girls, my heroes at the time. I wanted to be just like them. Their crazy hair, mad clothes and their enormous platform trainers were all fashion must-haves.

One afternoon, my mam had to take me into Specsavers. Dad usually looked after me on Saturdays, but that day he couldn't and so mam's boss kindly allowed her to take me into the shop. They let me do a few little admin jobs to keep me busy, like the filing, stamping of letters and stuffing envelopes, but I didn't mind – I was having a great time.

At the end of Mam's shift, and because I'd been such a well-behaved little darling, her workmates allowed me to sing a song for them. I started off by taking centre stage in the middle of the staffroom and then went full throttle into Spice Girl mode.

Pointing my finger at an imaginary crowd, I began, 'Yo, I'll tell you what I want, what I really, really want…'

Next, I'd spin around to the other side of the room, 'So tell me what you want, what you really, really want…'

Then I'd start the full Spice Girl routine and the Mel B hands-to-the-knees' move, 'I wanna, I wanna, I wanna, I wanna, I wanna, really, really, really wanna zig-a-zig ah…'

After my energetic performance, my mam's workmates were in raptures. They couldn't believe such a big voice came from such a young girl. Mam was laughing. She was so proud of me, it was written all over her face.

I remember one of her pals clapping and whispering to her, saying, 'She'll be a little star one day, Vick! I should get her autograph now.'

Clearly I always wanted to be a somebody, I always wanted to be famous. Even at four years old, if you asked me what I wanted to be when I grew up, I would say, 'I want to be a singer, an actress, a model or a lap-dancer.'

Don't ask me how I even knew back then what a lap-dancer was because I have no idea – I just wanted a glamorous job. And I craved the extraordinary. I was greedy for an exciting life. Growing up in the north-east was tough, rough and far from glam, but still I aspired to be like a celebrity. It's not as if I could ever become a movie star, like the rich kids in LA: the only doors open to a girl like me really were singing, or dancing and performing. I remember applying for *Stars in Their Eyes*, the kids' version of the TV show. I wanted to get up on stage and be Anastacia but I never got anywhere with it. Like I've said before, my ultimate idol was Christina Aguilera – if I could have had a career like anyone it would have been hers.

I was willing to put myself out there in public to be judged, but my mam was so overprotective of me. She herself had never been very outgoing, and even though she could see how confident and comfortable I was on the stage or performing for people, she never encouraged me to pursue that type of career. Mam wasn't the pushy type. She didn't want me to be disappointed if I wasn't good enough, or to waste my time on something that was probably never going to happen. For me it would have been a dream come true to be a pop star, but I don't think I wanted it badly enough to beg her to let me follow my dreams.

Besides I never really stuck at anything for too long. I wanted to go to dance classes so I did for about six weeks before I quit. Then I enrolled in a drama school, but lost interest after five weeks. I think if my mam had seen I could stick at something for long enough, then she would have been right behind me. Although I still harboured dreams of being someone, I didn't know how my big break was going to come, but on some level, I knew it would.

Chapter Four

WEIGHING ME DOWN

I've always had an issue with my weight. Well, actually, *other people* have always had an issue with my weight. I never thought it was a problem and then one day, one comment literally started years' worth of unhappiness and low self-esteem.

I remember exactly what triggered the weight issues like it was yesterday. It happened at a school disco when I was ten years old. It was the first disco I'd ever been to and I'd been looking forward to it for weeks. My mam had bought me new clothes for it, which was a rarity because she never really treated me to fancy clothes on a whim. I'd seen a skirt in the window of Debenhams and instantly loved it. It was a pink, glittery, A-line number, which meant it stuck out at the bottom.

Mam helped me try it on and then stood back, looking at me approvingly.

'You look lovely, Hol! Do you really want it?'

'Yes, Mam, I love it,' I said, as I spun around, admiring myself in the mirror.

My mam looked at the price tag and then furrowed her brow. Back then I wasn't perceptive enough to realise she probably couldn't afford it, all I knew was that I really wanted it more than anything in the world.

'OK then, Hol, get changed, I'll treat you.'

A week later, when the school disco eventually came around, Mam was just as excited as I was and helped me get ready for what felt like my first ever night out. I had my sparkly skirt, a little camisole top and my hair was down, with pink slides in the sides. I felt really girly and cute. I don't ever remember feeling that excited before a party – I felt like a proper grown-up going out for a night on the tiles. My mam dropped me off and she arranged to pick me back up when the party was over. I walked through the same old familiar school hall, which had now been turned into a makeshift disco. There was a DJ playing party music and he'd attached flashing coloured lights that spun around to the front of his table.

The floor was covered in balloons and streamers. There was a table full of plastic cups of orange squash and plates piled high with party ring biscuits. All the boys were sliding around on their knees and playing football with the balloons, while the girls danced in a circle together. I remember strolling over to my group of mates and dancing to Girls Aloud, who were my favourite band at the time. Twirling around, I let my skirt catch the air, making the pleats spin around my body.

I loved that skirt, I really did. I felt like one of those Disney princesses attending a grand ball. Everyone else loved it, too. I had so many compliments from my friends and everyone was asking where I got it. I'd never felt pressure to look a certain way for a certain occasion before, but I knew I'd got it right with my shimmering skirt and I felt so good about myself.

Then, while I was busy singing and dancing, a girl from another class – Gemma – came over to me, wearing the exact same skirt. As an adult this would undoubtedly be a huge fashion faux pas (going to a party with the same dress on is a fashion crime), but as kids we just laughed about it.

'Is your skirt from Debenhams, too, Holly?' Gemma asked me.

'Yeah,' I replied, with a giggle.

By this point a small crowd of girls had gathered to look at our matching sequin skirts and we both started spinning around to the music. Then Gemma asked me the one question you should never ask anyone: male, female, child, grandma... anyone.

'What size is your skirt, Holly?'

'I don't know,' I said with a shrug, because I genuinely didn't.

'Mine's an aged 10, let's look at yours,' she said.

And before I even had a chance to protest, Gemma peeled down the back of the waistband to see the label.

'Aged *13*!' she shrieked in horror.

'Oh my God, Holly, yours is an aged 13!' said one girl with disbelief.

'My sister is aged 13 and she is in big school,' exclaimed another in shock.

'It's an aged 10, I'm sure,' I said, trying hard to minimise the embarrassing situation.

'What, a woman's size 10?' Gemma asked cruelly, with a snigger.

Up until that point in my life, I'd never been so humiliated. I was embarrassed because my skirt was three sizes bigger than Gemma's. And I was angry with Mam, too – why had she got me an aged 13? Obviously, I now realise this was the size that fitted me but, back then, I was so mad at her.

After those comments I couldn't enjoy the party. I just wanted to rip that stupid aged 13 skirt off me! No longer did I want to twirl around, I wanted to throw it away. My sequin dream was ruined. I was convinced bitchy Gemma and the rest of the girls would tell the boys, and they would probably bring it up again at school the next day. Then everyone would know my shameful secret and I would be mortified.

So I did the only thing I could think to do. I ran to the toilet, put my hand under the hot tap and placed it on my head to make my face flush red. When I was sure my forehead was warm enough, I ran back outside into the school hall and told a teacher I was feeling unwell. I was impressed by my craftiness, if I'm honest. She looked at me and felt my temperature with the back of her hand, like teachers always do.

'You do feel a little warm, Holly, it's not like you to be poorly,' she said.

'I know,' I lied. 'I feel really sick, I don't want to, but I think I need to go home.'

'OK then, Holly, I will call your mam. Such a shame, too – you look so pretty in your jazzy skirt,' she sympathised.

Urgh, don't mention my frigging skirt, I thought.

Mam was disappointed for me. She thought a mystery illness had ruined my big night out. I never told her the real reason I left the party early, I just said I was feeling ill and moped about so she'd believe me. I must have given an Oscar-worthy performance, too, because she kept me off school the next day, which I was delighted about. I didn't want to see any of my school friends at all. I just hoped and prayed they would have forgotten the same-skirt shambles by the time I got back there after the weekend.

Luckily, my fashion faux pas was soon forgotten and no one ever mentioned 'Skirtgate' again. I also never wore it again either – for me, my pretty pink skirt held too many bad memories. But I felt so guilty because my mam never had any extra money to spend on luxuries, and she'd seen how happy I'd been when I first tried it on in the changing rooms. She'd sacrificed the little money we had to buy the skirt and now it was shoved in the back of my wardrobe, never to see the light of day.

Those comments always stuck in my mind. From then on I started looking at all my friends' body shapes and realised I was bigger than them. It had never really occurred to me before, but I can pinpoint all my issues with my weight and body confidence back to that school disco. At ten years old, I felt like a hippo and no one should ever feel like that at such a young age, or at any age for that matter.

The funny thing was, I wasn't even big compared to some of the other kids in school. Those who were genuinely obese never got called any names because that would be too offensive, but the ones who had a bit of puppy fat like me were called fat all the time. Usually it was the boys who would taunt me the most, which completely knocked my confidence and made me self-conscious around them.

It still upsets me now when I think about how a few stupid remarks had such a profound effect on my life as an adult.

Those feelings of insecurity and inadequacy have always been at the forefront of my mind for as long as I can remember.

Chapter Five

CHANGING
TIMES

G iven my relaxed attitude to sex on *Geordie Shore*, I suppose people would probably think my mam must have had a different guy every couple of months, but nothing could have been further from the truth.

In fact, I never once saw Mam with another bloke through the whole time she was single. When my dad left, she could have gone out dating and started to enjoy other men's company, but she never let me see any of that. I mean, let's be honest, I'm not daft, I'm sure she had a few gentleman admirers because she was a proper head turner. When she went out, she always looked so glamorous. Her long blonde hair would be tousled, she'd have a decent bra on, giving her boobs a helping hand to maximise her cleavage, and a figure-hugging bodice top to make sure you could see them. Many of her friends had men coming and going into their kids' lives, but my mam was never like that. The first and only man I ever met apart from my dad was my stepdad John.

Now, do you remember the part in the beginning when I told you to remember the guy called John, who later becomes very important? Well, bizarre as this sounds, the man who asked my mam to dance on the same night she met my dad then became my stepdad.

After that evening in The Madison, my mam and John would occasionally bump into each other. Out of politeness they would both say hello, but really nothing more than that. Mam was always sociable with him because they had a few mutual friends in common but she never saw him as a love interest. He was just a nice guy and she didn't want to ruin her friendship with him by being anything more.

A couple of her friends would let slip he still fancied her after all those years so in the end she decided to give him a call and arrange to go for a drink. She didn't see any harm in getting to know him a little better. After all, she had been with my dad for eleven years and split up with him six years ago. If, after seventeen years, John Gibson still fancied my mam, surely she owed it to him to give him a shot.

Well, there must have been some instant chemistry because the pair of them spent three hours chatting about everything and nothing, just idly whiling away hours on the phone to one another. The next day, John came round to my mam's house for a coffee and never left. Instantly she knew it felt right. She must have because, before the kettle had even boiled, she called me downstairs to introduce us.

That was a big deal for her. Like I said, she had never let me meet any man in her life apart from my dad. It meant a lot to her to have my approval and luckily, I loved John. We really did hit it off straight away and we got on like a house on fire. It wasn't until I got slightly older that things began to turn sour, but more on that later.

For now, John and I were great friends. He'd come round and play cards with me for hours. We'd go shopping in the big department stores and we'd start playing hide and seek, much to Mam's annoyance. Young at heart, he was like a big kid and we would have such a laugh together. Sometimes he'd take me to McDonald's and after we got our food, we'd call up complaining they missed out half our order and get another one totally free. I know it seems daft now, but John and I would literally be falling about laughing.

Meanwhile, the relationship between him and my mam moved at lightning speed. I'd only met the guy on a Monday and by the Sunday they were engaged. Can you believe it? Engaged after a week! I've had longer relationships with a loaf of bread. It still stuns me.

John proposed one cold sunny morning in January 2005, quite out of the blue, but Mam said she just knew it felt right and so she accepted his proposal. Just as I was getting used to the idea of having a new stepdad, they decided to drop another bombshell.

At the beginning of February, my mam announced she would be renting out her house and we were moving in with John. It made sense, since they were now engaged, but still it was a lot of change to deal with in such a short period of time. If that wasn't enough stress for Mam, she set the date for the wedding, which was to be a big family affair, at the end of April. To top it all – and this was the real icing on the cake – she fell pregnant in March.

Even one of those changes in a young person's life is a lot to deal with, but having a new stepdad, a new house, a big wedding and a new baby all within the space of four months was just impossible to get my head round. Everything was moving so fast. I didn't have time to get used to the changes before something else was going on.

Life as I knew it had completely transformed. It was as if I went to sleep one night and woke up in someone else's place. I didn't even have a choice in the matter; all these big decisions were being made for me. Like it or lump it.

The only part of this new life I was looking forward to was their up-and-coming wedding. I'd never been part of a proper wedding before. I was a bridesmaid, along with six others, so I just focussed on the big day.

And I planned my whole routine to perfection. I wrote down what I had to do and at what time – I was leaving nothing to chance. Never mind Mam, it was almost like it was my special occasion, not hers. I'd organised my beauty routine with strict military precision. My hair was first, then I applied my make-up, which had been rehearsed to death, I'd cleaned my white shoes the night before and I'd just zipped on my dress. I was so organised, I was left with about an hour to spare.

As I was hanging around, waiting for the other bridesmaids to get ready, I picked up what I thought was a glass of orange juice. I drank it quickly, not wanting to have it in my hand and give some clumsy person the opportunity to knock it onto my dress. I thought it was odd the orange juice was fizzy but I downed it anyway, not realising it was actually a Buck's Fizz cocktail. Before I knew it, I was giddy and giggly. I genuinely thought it was Fanta, so I was necking it like there was no tomorrow. Before I knew it, I was mortal. My eyes were glazed over and I was hammered. My mam kept asking me if I was all right before she realised I'd knocked back way too much booze. I had to go down the aisle, half-cut, at twelve years old. Mam will be mortified I've told everyone this.

In church I sang 'Dreams' by Gabrielle. At first I was nervous about singing in front of all those people, but as soon as I got into my stride I was belting it out, confident as any West End performer. It must have been the alcohol giving me some Dutch courage. Thank God for Buck's Fizz, that's all I can say.

I have some great memories of that day. It was fabulous from start to finish but when the wedding was over, it was time for the marriage to begin. I had a new stepdad and a new family to adjust to.

I think all of that had a more profound effect on me than I first thought because, looking back now, I really did feel as though I was unimportant to my mam. As you've probably guessed from the way I talk about her, she was the closest person to me. For years it had just been her and me but now she had this whole new life away from me.

I was in that awkward teenager stage and we started to fall out all the time. It was hard on John, too, because he didn't have any kids at this stage so he didn't know what it was like to have a grown-up child or be a father figure.

My thirteenth birthday was quite pivotal because the family really made a fuss of me. They'd hired a huge bouncy castle for the garden. Hot sunshine was beating down and all the adults, apart from Mam, who was six months' pregnant, were drinking outside. I had all my friends over to play and there was a huge cake with thirteen candles. A barbecue was sizzling away in the corner and I just remember everyone having a great time. But in the weeks that followed everything started to go downhill. I don't know what happens to kids when they turn thirteen but it's almost like they get possessed for a few years by some hormonal monster. I started my periods and my whole attitude completely changed.

I don't really know why, maybe it was because I was being a typical teenager, but I began to resent John. I honestly didn't want to speak to the guy anymore. From being best friends, it was now like he was my worst enemy. And although we were living in the same house, we were acting like total strangers. We would argue over small things, like when I wouldn't wash up the plates, or pick up my wet towels, or when my bedroom would be a tip. They were never big issues and certainly nothing worth quarrelling over. The problem was my mam had always done everything for me and now this guy was having a go at me for just doing what I'd always done. And it wasn't so much what he was asking me to do, it was the way he would shout at me, trying to exercise some authority. I'm not good at being told what to do, so I would roar back at him. I'd shout, scream, swear and slam my door in anger.

I didn't hate him, but he made me feel so annoyed and irritated. I'd come home from school, throw down my school bag and just crave a little peace and quiet. But literally as soon as I'd parked my bum on the couch, he would be on at me to do something – 'Holly, take the bins out', 'Holly, this place was tidy before you came home, clean it up', 'Holly, sort out your bedroom, it's a disgrace!' Every damn day, he was ordering me around. Then he'd go on about my attitude, but it wasn't an attitude, I was just fucking annoyed! Of course, I selfishly wouldn't lift a finger, something he saw as disrespectful, and so we would have huge rows about it. But I didn't go on about the ways in which he pissed me off. Sometimes the way he would loudly walk down the stairs made me fume, but I never had a go at him although I wished he would just shut up. He won't mind me saying all this because now we get on great, it was just difficult to adjust to each other at first and even he will agree.

I can see how my total 180-degree change towards him must have upset John. It upset me, too. But what he needed to remember was that he'd come into my life after it had just been my mam and me. I felt neglected by Mam and so I took it out on John, blaming him for coming in between us. My mam would be caught in the crossfire but I was stubborn. In some ways, I kind of punished Mam for daring to have another baby by being a total bitch.

Meanwhile, my mam tried her hardest to involve me the best way she could and prepare me for when the new baby arrived. She'd ask what kind of names I liked and show me photos of her scans. Of course, I was happy to see her so happy. This was something she really wanted. I would never try and rain on her parade. But I couldn't help feeling unwanted, like an old doll that has been cast aside, ready for a replacement. Suddenly everything became about the new baby. It was as if that was the only thing going on in anyone's world.

When my sister Darci was born, I loved her, but she was too small for me to even bother with at that stage. It was only when she was a little bit older, when I would babysit, that I could really enjoy having fun with her. But when she was first born, she would cry and scream and keep the whole house awake. Honestly, she was the worst baby ever. I don't think she slept for two years! All night long she would let out blood-curdling shrieks at the top of her voice. It was so disruptive. But she was only tiny and it wasn't her fault. I still loved her unconditionally and would lay down my life for her.

Now, I could see how stressed my mam was but I kind of thought, well, if she needs help doing this and that, she shouldn't have had another baby then. She knew what she was signing up for. Although I wasn't like that all the time, I didn't mind looking after Darci as long as it was on my own terms. It would annoy me when they would ask me to take her out on a Sunday to give them a break because as far as I was concerned it was their child, not mine. I never felt like I should take any responsibility for her because it wasn't me who chose to have a child.

God, to think I was like that still makes me cringe! I was so immature, but when you are a teenager, you are so wrapped up in your own shit and so I didn't have time for anyone else. I had enough on my plate with the crap I was dealing with at school, I didn't want to come home to a screaming baby, a worn-out mother and then have orders barked at me by a man who wasn't even my dad.

My mam would ask me nicely if I would help her out but I'd just ignore her, and instead of giving me a dressing down, she just let me get away with it, whereas John was more vocal and frustrated by me. Mam was too soft – even she would admit it – and during some of those really horrible arguments, she would always take my side. At the end of the day I was still her daughter and she would defend me to the hilt against anyone.

Those rows were just awful sometimes and would always result in me screaming and crying in my room. I still wouldn't bother cleaning it, though! I know it must have been hard for John, trying to understand a hormonal teenage girl, and now I do empathise with him. All he wanted was for me to show a little respect in the house, although it never really felt like it was my house because we had moved in with John and I suppose that's where it all stemmed from.

My mam never wanted any arguments and it used to really hurt her, seeing the two people she loved most in the world arguing like mad. Just to keep the peace she'd end up doing everything round the house and looking after Darci, too. She doesn't like confrontation and would rather have an easy life.

I wished I could have just sat them both down and explained that I felt like an outsider, a stranger in my own home. I didn't feel like I was part of any family. My dad had a new life with Debbie, hundreds of miles away. Now Mam had John and Darci, and I didn't feel like I belonged there. They were the Gibsons, my dad's side was the Hagans and I was just kicking around in the middle somewhere, not belonging to either group. I guess that's why I had this overwhelming feeling of not really fitting in anywhere all the way through my teenage years.

Chapter Six

SCHOOL
FIGHT

My home life was so haphazard with Mam, John and Darci, sometimes being at school felt like my only escape. But when things started to turn ugly there, too, I felt as if I had nowhere to turn.

The secondary school I attended, Newlands School FCJ, was fairly rough. It wasn't uncommon to see pupils fighting and arguing at least once a day. All the girls hung around in a big group and it could be really bitchy. I'd had my fair share of arguments with a few lasses, but nothing so harrowing as the one when I was thirteen. I still get anxious now when I think about it. Often, when I'm feeling stressed, I have this recurring dream about what happened in the schoolyard that day.[1]

It was a balmy July afternoon and the day had started unremarkably like any other. I walked to school with my heavy

1 *I've changed all the names of the horrors in this chapter to protect anonymity.

backpack casually on one shoulder, went to my lessons, joked with my friends, got told off for wearing too much make-up and because my skirt was rolled up to an indiscreet length.

Only today was the last day of term and there was a heightened sense of excitement around the place. And when the school bell rang at 3.35pm, it summoned the end of Year 8 and a long six weeks off for the summer.

I was saying my goodbyes to everyone because back then six weeks felt like six years. I waved to my teachers, the girls from my science class and then I hugged my friend David, who it just so happened was going out with a girl called Hayley.

Now Hayley was a hard-knock sort of girl, one you definitely wouldn't want to mess with. She was the type of girl who would always disrupt your lessons selfishly because she was going nowhere in life, but she didn't want anyone else to either.

David and Hayley had been going out for a few months. It was hardly Romeo and Juliet but they seemed to be genuinely into each other at the time. I knew they were going out together, everyone in school knew it. The pair of them would be kissing all the way through lunch and leave each other covered in big spammy love-bites as if they were both marking their territory.

Anyone who really knows me knows I'm not the kind of girl who would steal someone's boyfriend – I was just giving David a harmless hug. But to an irrational hothead like Hayley that hug was like a red rag to a bull.

Hayley saw me embrace David from across the school playground. She was standing with her friends Vicky and Tina, another two girls who could more than handle themselves. Tapping them, she pointed in my direction before the three of them stormed their way towards me, like a pack of hyenas.

Hayley stood in front of me, spitting in my face and asking me what I was playing at.

'I wasn't doing anything,' I protested.

'Keep your fucking hands off my boyfriend!' she bawled.

'But… I wasn't… I swear…' I tried to get the words out but I kept stammering.

'You little slag, Holly. Go and get your own lad!' Tina screamed.

'Really… please… you know I wasn't…'

That's when I felt the first blow to my cheek: Hayley had smacked me straight in the face. It took a while to register what had happened. I'd never been involved in a physical fight with anyone before. Yeah, I'd had verbal rows but I'd never actually had anyone hit me. It was a complete shock. But before I could bring my head back up, I felt another blow to the other side of my cheek. Now I was in complete confusion – I just couldn't fathom what was going on, it was all happening so fast.

The three of them continued to hammer me with their fists. They pulled my hair and dragged me to the ground, so I was primed for a good kicking. By this time a crowd had gathered and kids just stood there open-mouthed, watching as these girls assaulted me one after the other, over and over again.

My lips went tight and my fists shook, but I was helpless to stop them. Every time I tried to get up and run away, one of them would drag me back and give me another beating. But I didn't say a word to them. I didn't want to look like a wimp. In my school, it was important that you didn't look soft so I just took what they threw at me.

David, as you've probably guessed, did nothing to stop them. He was spineless. He knew this fight was pathetic and over absolutely nothing, but he never stopped it. Instead he just stood by watching as his vicious girlfriend and her two spiteful sidekicks beat the living daylights out of me.

Eventually I did manage to get away. I ran as fast as my cumbersome backpack would allow. The trouble was, our school was down a long road and it took about twenty minutes to get to the end of the lane. They followed me all the way down the road, continuing to slap, kick, punch and throw loose stones at me.

'Come back here, you fucking slag!' one would shout.

'Hit her, Hayley. She deserves it, the fucking bitch!' yelled another.

They pushed my face into the ground and I could feel the dirt swilling round my mouth with blood. I kept thinking about my teeth, I was terrified they were going to knock them out.

And I didn't know what to do – I couldn't catch a breath. And you know what made it all worse? Practically the whole school was watching this mindless violence and not one person tried to break it up. The teachers were nowhere to be seen either. In a way I hoped they would see what was going on and try to help, but in another way, I knew I had to man up and take it.

People were shouting and jeering at me, like some bloodthirsty mob. I heard a few of them say, 'She can take a good beating', which like I said before, was really important at my school. You had to take it on the chin. Kids were laughing, while a few gutless others shouted for it to stop but never intervened. Even the older ones never thought to wade in. They just stood there, girls and boys at least three years older than us, refusing to get involved. I couldn't believe it. It still makes me angry when I think about it today. I know if I ever saw anything like that happen then I would be the first to step in and calm the situation, regardless of the consequences.

The fight only stopped when I finally got to the end of the road, where there was a row of shops. As quickly as I could I bolted inside the newsagents, safely away from danger. In there I caught sight of myself in the reflection of the fridge door and was in total shock when I saw myself: I was a complete mess. My hair had been pulled out in big clumps, I had red scratches all over my face, my nose was bleeding, my shirt had been ripped to shreds, my legs were covered in fresh bruises and my lip had been split.

I began to ache, everywhere. And not just physically. My pride had been wounded, my emotions shattered. I felt embarrassed and completely humiliated. Through deep breaths, I managed to call my stepdad, John. Naturally, he was alarmed when he heard the state I was in down the phone. He dashed out of work at lightning speed to come and rescue me.

As soon as he arrived at the newsagents, he burst through the door and gave me a cuddle. I was like a limp dolly.

'Come on, Holly,' he said. 'You don't need to cry, you're safe now.'

His kind words were comforting but I couldn't hold back the emotion.

John wrapped an arm around me and gave me a little squeeze. He was never one to be big on affection, but I knew he meant well.

'Don't cry,' he whispered in my ear. 'Calm down. Keep your chin up, Holly,' he told me, as he patted my back gently.

I don't know if it was his words or the fact that I was safe now, but I just let go and I sobbed uncontrollably into him.

Never in my life had I experienced violence like this and I just couldn't understand it.

'Shhh, Holly,' he soothed. 'It's not worth it.'

I was still sobbing when we picked up my mam and my friend Laura and they took me round to Hayley's house. At first I didn't know where we were going. Opening my eyes to stare through the cloudy, salty water, I saw her driveway approaching us. Instantly, fear struck me.

'John, what are you doing? Where are we going?'

'I'm not having some girl do this to you, Holly. Look at your face! You're black and blue!'

'No, please, John, just leave it. It will only make matters worse.'

'It will be worse if she doesn't apologise for what she's done!' he yelled.

Outside Hayley's house there were about five lads on bikes and Hayley stood in the middle of them all. It was so embarrassing.

My mam and John opened their car doors so fast and I watched as they marched up to the gang. I couldn't hear what was being said but I could see the pair of them making heated arm gestures. I just wanted the ground to swallow me up.

Hayley attempted to run off, but my mam dragged her back.

'Holly, get out of the car!' Mam shouted.

'No, John, just leave it, will ya?' I shouted back.

Hayley stood there, her face flushed red with embarrassment, and she looked like she was about to break down.

'Holly, get out of the car! Let's sort this out – Hayley wants to say something to ya,' John bawled.

Slowly I walked up the driveway, still coughing and spluttering from the upset. As I stood before her, she didn't even look me in the eye, she just shuffled from one foot to the other and looked uncomfortable. One on one she wasn't so tough.

'I'm sorry, Holly,' she said, her eyes firmly on the ground.

But I didn't know if I was supposed to answer or apologise, too. I couldn't, even if I'd wanted to – I couldn't speak, I was literally shaking.

'Now, that's the end of it! I don't want to have to come back here again,' John shouted and walked me away, back down to the car.

That night I peeled off my blood-drenched shirt and got into the bath. For the first time I could see all my bruises in full. Ugly, painful and more than skin-deep, my body was covered in them. I knew they would heal over a couple of weeks, but nothing had hurt me more than my pride.

That fight really affected me and like I said, I still have recurring nightmares about it when I feel stressed.

All during the holidays that summer, I was too scared to go into town with my friends in case I saw Hayley, her gang or their older sisters. I'm not a fighter. As I said, I'd never experienced that kind of violence in my life before. I even contemplated not going back to that school again.

'But I hate that school, and this town, and the sooner I leave, the better!' I would protest. 'I want to start over in a new place.'

I remember John sitting me down and giving me a sharp talking to, not because I needed telling off, but because he was so annoyed that I was letting these bullies win. They were getting me down to the point where I just wanted to leave the place where I grew up. It's hard to explain, but I felt like I wasn't the person I was supposed to be. I wished I could be someone else and that I would have a better life, if only things were just a little different.

At the time it was the biggest ordeal I had ever gone through and it was over something completely pathetic. If one little hug made me a slag then I'd hate to think what that made Hayley!

I'd like to tell you that the bullying with those girls stopped there, but it never did. I suppose some people will just never be happy until they've pushed you to the ground. What you must do is have the courage to stand your ground and not give them the time of day. Those girls were rude to me – shutting doors in my face, leaving nasty notes on my desk and in my locker, making fun of me when I could obviously hear them – but if I could give one piece of advice to anyone who is going through anything like what I went through it would be this: you are not alone, you are strong, you are beautiful and above all you can talk to someone.

Bullying has to stop, so please don't suffer in silence.

Chapter Seven

MENTAL SCARS

To look at me now, you'd see I'm a contented and confident young woman. I have an amazing family. I get to live out my dreams on a wild TV show, travel the world with my best friends and, for the most part, I'm popular with people. Most days, folk stop me for photographs and just want a couple of minutes of my time to chat but there's a part of me, deep inside, that is a shy, frightened and sad little girl who tells herself she's ugly and unpopular. A freak. And I suspect that no matter how successful, how old or how happy I may become, that girl will always be there, curled up inside with fear and self-loathing, because for years it's what I believed. Or rather, that was what I endured.

I wish I could tell you after the fight in the school playground things got better for me as I grew older. But they didn't, and it's the way I was treated in those vulnerable years that has caused this lasting impression on my life.

I'd had chavvy blonde highlights for a while when I went to the hairdressers one night after school and asked if she'd dye my hair a coppery colour. I actually loved it when I came out of the salon – I felt like a million dollars. And I kept catching sight of my new hair in shop windows and I was delighted with it. I'd saved for a while to get my hair dyed professionally and it cost £50 for the colour, cut and finish.

It seemed to me every time I felt good about myself, someone would find something to pick on me for it. When I got to school the next day, one of the popular boys in my class started calling me a ginger minger and fell about laughing. And then, of course, the whole class joined in. All day long I was called names because of my new coppery hair. It was so upsetting and ridiculous.

Back then I was so self-conscious. I didn't want to be individual or different, all I wanted was to blend in and get people to like me. On the way home from school that day, I went to Boots and spent another £12 on a black dye. On the one hand, I didn't want everyone to think I'd changed my hair again because of their cruel jibes, but on the other, I couldn't face another day of being picked on and called ginger.

I chose a black dye because I wanted something to cover the coppery tones, hoping the end result would be more like a brown colour. As soon as I'd bought it, I rushed home, read the instructions carefully and started to plaster my hair in the thick, creamy mixture. For twenty-five minutes I sat in the bath, waiting for the dye to rid my hair of its carroty hue, and as I did so, I could see where I'd splattered the concoction all over the bathroom. I must have got it on nearly every surface. It was all over my hands, the sink, the shower curtain, the walls, the floor, my neck, my ears, my shoulders, my hairline... literally everywhere. Mam was going to hit the roof when she saw it all. I started trying to scrub the excess off my skin, but already it had stained it to a dark grey.

Eventually when it was time to wash all the dye off, I looked in the mirror and was startled to see just how dark my hair actually was. I knew the colour on the box said black, but I never expected it to end up being quite so dark. I washed the colour out and quickly blast-dried it with my hairdryer, hoping the end result would be lighter. No such luck! I looked like Morticia Addams. The colour didn't suit me at all and made my face look ridiculously white.

My mam absolutely hated it. That was even before she'd seen the state of the bathroom! She couldn't understand why I wouldn't just leave my hair my natural colour.

Of course when I went to school the next day, I was no longer the ginger minger. No, instead the boys decided I'd turned into a Goth overnight. I couldn't win. No matter what I seemed to do, I would always get picked on. Honestly, I didn't know why I bothered. I couldn't do right for doing wrong.

At first I kind of brushed off all the comments, but then all of a sudden they started to really get me down. I probably had a year of being picked on and bullied by various groups in my class. Always, I tried to keep my head up and laugh it off, which worked for a while but then, over time, my confidence had been chipped away so much the comments started to really hurt. During school I would agonise and dissect everything they'd say to me and I would be glum. I was acting up at home, too. Lashing out at my mam because I was frustrated and angry at the way I was being treated. I never spoke of what was happening to me, though – I just thought I could deal with it by myself.

I used to go home some days, just thankful I was away from school, but most of the time I didn't want to be at home either, getting barked orders at by John. I'd sit in my room and play on MSN Messenger. I had most of my year group on my MSN and everyone would sign in when we were at home. Sometimes, I'd see someone appear online that didn't like me, and it would make me panic. I'd click my status to appear offline, so they couldn't see me just in case they started arguing with me. I don't know why they'd do it, or what kind of kicks they got out of it. The worst of it used to happen on Sunday nights. Everyone would be online and they'd be calling me all kinds of names, like a fat slag or a fucking rat, and telling me I deserved a good kicking.

Every Monday morning I'd be terrified something would kick off, like they would go through with their threats eventually. I would go to school and nothing would ever happen but all the time I would have this fear inside me. When I think back to those days now, all I can remember is for years feeling scared.

No boys in my school were ever interested in me. Instead, they picked on me, laughed at me, humiliated me. Some would say that's just playground antics and boys just do that sort of thing, but I knew then and I still know now, they genuinely didn't like me, never mind fancied me. I never got the way they acted with me. They'd be nice to me in private if we were alone, or they'd send me nice messages on MSN, but then back in the classroom amongst all the other boys they would say they hated me and that I was disgusting. It was so hurtful and confusing.

I was so young and I would cry about it all the time – I didn't know how to handle my emotions.

There was this one time, when I was chatting to a lad I was totally hooked on over the Internet. He had been so sweet in all his messages. I had liked him for ages and I honestly thought I was in love with him.

The next day I went to school absolutely buzzing; I couldn't wait to see him and throw my arms around him in front of everyone. He'd told me I was his girl and I was so fucking happy, I can't even tell you. Then when I actually saw him in the morning, he totally ignored me in front of his friends. At first I thought it was slightly weird, but you know how boys can be. Then at lunchtime, he still hadn't so much as looked in my direction, so I decided to take matters into my own hands.

I strolled right up to him and said 'Hiya' with a big beaming smile.

'What do you want?' he replied.

'Why haven't you said hello to me today?' I asked, while his friends sniggered.

'Why would I? Go away, will ya,' he said as he turned his back on me.

'Why are you being like that? What have I done?' I asked, confused.

'Just fuck off, will ya, we're chatting.'

'But why are you saying this? You were being nice on MSN last night.'

'And you think I meant any of what I said? You dumb cow, fuck off!'

With that, he shooed me away from himself and his pack of cronies.

Well, after that I was distraught. I couldn't understand why he'd been so nice the night before and now he was acting like I was some piece of shit he'd wiped off his shoe. I spent the whole rest of the day moping around, being miserable. He had embarrassed me and rejected me in front of all his mates. At that time, I'd never experienced emotional pain like it. I thought I loved this guy and to have him act like I was embarrassing him in front of his gang made me ache. I was devastated.

That evening I went home and locked myself in the bathroom. Then I looked in the mirror, at my face that was awash with tears and mascara. I stared at my image for an unusually long time, taking in all my features, one by one, trying to understand why everyone thought I was so ugly. I wished I could be thinner and prettier. I wished my teeth had been naturally straight and I didn't have to wear my braces. The more I looked at myself, the more disgusted I became with my reflection before me. It made me so mad and I had no one but myself to take it out on.

My eyes lit on a razor that was next to the bathroom cabinet. Before I knew it, I'd taken the blade out and carefully held it up to the light between my first two fingers. I twirled it around, watching how the light bounced off the smooth edge and then without a second thought, I stabbed it into my thigh and began to drag it across my skin. Then I made a deep cut and watched as the blood trickled out. It was like an instant release. I lay on the floor, crying and shaking, searching for some inner strength, but always coming up empty. My eyes burned and my mouth was dry, as I tried to suck in the air that seemed thicker. I leaned my forehead against the door, trying to figure out why I had just done it. Then I looked down at my thigh that was still dripping with blood and closed my eyes, like it was all a bad dream.

It's very hard to explain to someone how it made me feel, but all I know is it took my mind off the emotional ache. The hurt I felt at making the red tracks across my legs was enough to block out the pain of rejection by that boy. I felt so much emotionally that I didn't know how to handle what I was feeling, but after I made that first cut, after I caused myself some physical pain, it made all the internal pain fade away. It was the only way I could control it. I never wanted to kill myself or seek any attention. I just used cutting as a release from the anger I felt inside. In some ways it was a cry for help – I wanted people to see my cuts, ask me about it and realise just how unhappy I was, but then on the other hand I was so deeply ashamed of what I was doing to myself, I didn't want anyone to know. If people found out they would think I was some weirdo who got kicks out of seeing myself bleed, which really wasn't the case.

I tried not to let anyone know, but sometimes they would see the slashes on my arms if I wore a polo T-shirt. A few of my friends would ask me about all the marks and I would say that my neighbour's cat had attacked me, just to fob them off with an excuse. No one really believed me, and I hadn't done a good job of hiding my cuts. I remember in science class a boy sat next to me asked about the cuts on my arms.

'Why do you do that to yourself?' he wanted to know.

'Do what?'

'Cut yourself,' he said, pointing to the slashes.

Embarrassed, I moved my arms back towards my body and folded them in front of my chest to hide the obvious marks.

'Why don't you just do it properly and slit your wrists?' he laughed.

'Yeah, Holly, why don't you just kill yourself if that's how you feel?' said his pal to the left of him.

I wouldn't be able to run out of class so I just sat there, completely hollow and feeling sick, not really knowing what to do. When I got home, I did the only thing I knew that made me feel better. I cut myself again and again. Over and over, I made small slices on my arms and watched as the blood ran down the sink, along with my tears and any self-esteem I had. I hid what I was doing from my mam and John. I was terrified of what they would do if they ever found out. They would probably have tried to have me committed or something, but luckily they didn't know at that time.

Meanwhile, I hadn't realised how many people at school had actually noticed the marks on my arms – I presume they just didn't know how to bring it up. Self-harm is still a massive taboo subject and not one that can be casually spoken about in conversation, although one of my concerned friends did bring it up with me. She had seen the slashes appearing more frequently and asked what was happening and why I was doing this to myself. I told her about the boys in the science class, about how they had told me to kill myself and how I'd bought two packets of paracetamol to swallow so I could finally be gone from all this misery. She was obviously worried and told a teacher immediately, which I saw as a massive misplacement of trust at the time but now know that it was the right thing to do. Actually I hadn't bought any tablets, it was all a misunderstanding.

Next thing you know, I had this teacher pulling me aside

with tears in her eyes, asking about my suicidal thoughts. I kind of shrugged her off but then she rolled back the sleeves on my jumper to see my cuts, and when she saw them her face just dropped. She held a hand over her mouth and shook her head with sympathy. The overdose allegations coupled with all the slashes on my arms made her panic. She took me straight to the head teacher's office where my mam was called to come in for a serious talk.

Mam, as you can imagine, was heartbroken at being told that I had not only been self-harming, but that I was at a stage where I could potentially take my own life. She blamed herself, of course she did. And if I'm being completely honest, I did, too. It shouldn't have been for the teachers to notice I was unhappy; it should have been Mam who spotted my cries for help, but I felt she was too preoccupied with Darci now. This new little girl was taking up all her time and energy, while the old girl was pushed out and replaced.

My mam hadn't a clue what life was like for me. She always thought I was a popular girl in school, with a carefree attitude and mates in abundance. She hadn't noticed I'd become more detached from her. I would spend less and less time in the house, not telling her anything. She had no idea what was going on in my life and didn't really ask either. I felt like I couldn't speak to her anymore, we had lost that bond. In some small gnarled place inside me, I resented her for her neglect. I had taken a step back from my mother, put up a wall to protect myself and I wasn't sure if everything would ever be the same with us again.

It was pretty selfish, I know, and if I'd have got involved more with my little sister, things might not have been so strained. I get that now, but at the time I was too wrapped up in myself.

I've tried to block out much of what I went through at school because it was so upsetting. Even now, it's tough to talk about it, years on. I'm ashamed to say it, but I only stopped cutting myself when I was sixteen. I don't know why I chose to stop then, I was just happier within myself, I suppose, but for four years, self-harm was the only way I could really cope with the pressures of teenage life.

I still have the scars now. I had many very deep cuts on my legs that have scarred and were caused by me self-harming. I remember my mam once asking me how I got them and I just told her they were stretch marks. She knew about the ones on my arms, but never the wounds on my legs from the very first time I cut myself.

Sometimes I'll catch myself looking at my scars and wishing they weren't there. They are a reminder of how stupid and naïve I was when I was younger. Then other times I'll look at them and see something else: a girl who was trying to cope with some horrible feelings that she should never have had to go through. My scars show pain and suffering, but they'll always be reminders of how I survived. They are part of my history that will always be there. And while no one could question that I am a happy adult, I can't deny bullying has affected who I am now – and how I behave. There are things that happen in a person's life so scorched in the memory and burned into the heart that there's no forgetting them.

Chapter Eight

LOSING IT

At a time when young girls should be hanging onto it, everyone I knew was obsessed with turning it in. I don't know why but it stressed so many of us out at school. It wasn't just the girls, either. Guys were under just as much pressure, if not more.

Of course, what I'm referring to is our virginity. Or lack of. I was fourteen when everyone started making a big deal about sex. I'd only been having periods for a year and I was yet to lose my V-plates. Many of my school friends had lost theirs at fourteen, thirteen, even twelve. They'd come into school and regale you with the finer details of their first encounter. Some were deflowered during sticky scenarios behind a bowling alley, or they'd bled on a towel placed on a boyfriend's bed, or when they were pissed up at a house party. I'd be lying if I said I hadn't felt the pressure to lose mine and although I wasn't in a rush, it was always in the back of my mind.

I remember my first time as clear as day and I think it's because of the way it happened, and the way the guy was with me afterwards, that it's made me think of sex in an unhealthy way. People have often asked me why I am the way I am – like, why I will have one night stands on TV – and I'm being honest when I say it all stems from when I popped my cherry.

The guy in question was called Danny. I had liked him for ages and when he finally asked me out on a date, I was absolutely buzzing. He'd offered to take me to the cinema one Saturday night, which I thought was cute. It was my first ever date with a lad, too, although on that Saturday morning, I had another very important date that I absolutely couldn't miss.

For years, everyone had been telling me how much of a great singer I was and I really believed them. So much so, when I was watching an episode of *Britain's Got Talent* and up flashed details of how to apply for the next series, I scribbled down the address and sent off for a pack.

I remember when it arrived, it all felt so official. There was a big questionnaire, which I filled out. I had to send photos of myself and explain a little of my background. A few weeks later, the show invited me down to audition in Manchester.

Even though my stepdad John and I had a pretty turbulent relationship at the time, he would still do anything for me. He'd kindly agreed to take me to my audition, because he really thought I had a chance. I was ultra-nervous about singing in front of strangers. I know I've got a good voice, but I've never had any kind of formal training or lessons, which could make it great. I kind of had the feeling I wouldn't be good enough, but I thought I won't know until I try.

John woke me up at six in the morning, an ungodly hour for

me. I dressed in the outfit I'd laid out for myself the night before: a pretty top, some low-slung jeans and white trainers, because I wanted to be noticed for my voice and not my garish clobber. On the drive down, John and I had fun. He was really encouraging and told me just to try my best, that's all I could do.

When I got to the hotel where the auditions were being held, there were hundreds of people all waiting around. I queued up for what seemed like a year to get my contestant number and then waited around for another couple of hours before I was to do any singing. I had high hopes of meeting Ant & Dec and all the other celebrity judges, but the audition process is nothing like you see on TV.

I was taken into a conference room and told to sing in front of four producers. First, they asked me a few questions about myself and then told me to begin singing. I'd been preparing my song for weeks. Bryan Adams's 'Right Here Waiting For You'. The song didn't have any special meaning for me; I just thought it would show off my vocal range to the best of my ability.

I began belting it out as best I could but it didn't take the producers long to unanimously decide that I wasn't going to be the next SuBo and they quickly thanked me for coming. Of course I was disappointed and probably would have been more upset if I didn't have my date with Danny to look forward to, so I wasn't too disheartened.

When I got home I couldn't even be bothered to tell my mam about how the audition went, I'd leave that up to John. I didn't have any time to waste. As soon as I got through the front door, I jumped in the bath and started my beauty ritual. Bath, wash hair, shave legs, dry hair, tan, make-up, eyelashes, clothes, perfume and a slick of lip gloss to finish... sounds easy, doesn't it? But all that took me at least three hours and we were only going to be sat in the dark in the cinema.

When I met Danny he looked great. I kept thinking in my head how much of a great couple we'd make. I really wanted him to be my boyfriend. I would have done anything. We hit it off straight away and he made me laugh. However, we were so engrossed in each other that we failed to look at the film titles properly, and when we finally sat down to watch the film, we realised it was a Bollywood movie.

Neither of us wanted to sit through a movie with subtitles, so we sneaked out and into another screen. I can't even remember what film we watched because we didn't see much of it. We were your typical teenagers, snogging on the back seat, much to everyone's annoyance.

Afterwards, he took me for a stroll round the back of the cinema. I kind of knew what was coming, because who the fuck does that? It was a big, dirty industrial estate, hardly the local beauty spot. Neither of us talked about whether we'd done it before but I think he thought I had, although I was actually one of the last of my peers to hold onto my virginity.

We started kissing and yeah, I guess I was ready to get rid of my 'virgin' label. I just thought 'fuck it' and let him go where no one had gone before. We did the deed to the sound of busy dual carriageway traffic, and all I could think was, 'Oh, is this it, then?'

Any woman who tells you losing her virginity is enjoyable is lying. It's not enjoyable in the slightest. I've yet to meet a girl who says it was a mind-blowing experience. Mine was cold, wet, painful and in a disused car park behind a cinema. Not really the romantic candles, flowers and silk sheets set-up most of us would hope for, was it? I didn't realise quite how depressing losing it in this manner was until I started writing this book, but I suppose that's the beauty of hindsight.

I woke up the next day and thought I'd feel different afterwards, like a neon sign around my head that said 'virgin' would now be extinguished. I'd spent so long obsessing about it, so it seemed something should have changed. But I felt a little weird, too. I had only done it because I'd wanted Danny to like me. It was your classic 'girls play at sex to get love, while boys play at love to get sex' scenario.

Then I saw a text message from Danny and in it he'd asked me to be his girlfriend. I was made up because that's what I had wanted all along, but I also knew it was because I'd put out for him.

That was it. That was the pivotal moment in my life that gave me a skewed view of men and sex. From then on I was on a downward spiral with boys. I thought if they were going to want you, they would want you because of your ability to give them a good shag. And for the rest of my life, I have always thought that's the way I should be.

If I ever wanted a guy to like me, then I would hop into bed with him, no questions asked. It's not even the sex I wanted, it was the person and the best way to get that person was to use sex. If I could go back now and tell myself to do things differently, I would, but I can't. I'd tell myself, '*Holly, don't do it, you'll be respected a lot more*', or even '*Socialise with as many lads as you want, Holly, but never share your body with them*'.

Too many young people are careless with their virginity. One day they have it, the next they don't. Danny had a part of me that no one – and I mean no one – had ever had before and because of that my whole self-worth was hinged on my ability to please men. It was like sex had become a party favour. I'd watched all my friends disappear into the adult world of sex until I was one of the only ones left who wasn't in on the secret. So I'd just slept with him, given him my precious virginity – a guy I didn't love and who didn't love me.

I know how hard it is for young people and a show like *Geordie Shore*, centred around casual sex, doesn't help. Like I've said before, I'm not a role model, so don't follow my lead because I regret so many things about my past.

Some people may give you a hard time about being or not being a virgin. I know what that's like. There will always be people who pass judgement, but you've got to be true to what you believe in and not let those people stress you out. And at the end of the day, the choice to have or not have sex is yours and yours alone. My only advice to you, whether you're a guy or a girl, is to wait until you are one hundred per cent ready – that way, you'll have no regrets later.

Chapter Nine

NAILED ON

By now you'll know I was a typical stroppy adolescent, but I was never a bad girl. Yeah, I was hormonal and ridden with teenage angst but it was nothing that my mam couldn't put up with. I was rebellious in the usual ways – under-age drinking, smoking, staying out late and kissing too many boys – but I never got in trouble with the law. Except once when I was fifteen.

Mam was doing the weekly shop with my sister Darci, and I was trailing behind her, more interested in what was going on with my phone than actually helping out. I kept wandering off by myself, moseying along in my own little world. In the end, she got fed up of trying to find me and told me to meet her back home when I was done browsing.

At the time everyone was going through this phase in school, where it was really cool to shoplift. I'd been brought up to be an honest girl. My mam always told me I had to work hard if I wanted something in life and I must pay for it like everyone else. But some of the other girls in school didn't have parents like mine. They would let their kids get away with anything, whereas my mam wouldn't think twice about screaming at me and grounding me if I misbehaved.

Since everyone I knew at school blatantly shoplifted most weekends, I didn't think it would matter too much. They got away with it all the time. I knew a few girls who would steal pockets full of make-up or grab a jazzy top from a shop in the precinct and just wander out with it. Heck, even millionaire celebrities like Winona Ryder and Antony Worrall Thompson have succumbed to the temptation. I mean, how hard could it be?

My chosen loot was a French manicure nail kit. I looked up and down the aisle and carefully tucked the box in my school bag and went into the changing rooms. The funny thing about it was, I actually had the money to pay for the kit, but I just wanted to feel the thrill of stealing something. It was a challenge I'd set myself.

I strolled out of the shop, trying to act as cool as possible. Just as I was about to approach the daylight outside, as I was about to reach freedom with my pinched plastic nails, I heard all the security alarms being set off. At first I tried to look puzzled, like I didn't know why they were blasting out that stupid noise. I thought about running away but something stopped me. Fear of being a fugitive, probably. It was fight or flight and I just froze. I berated myself for even attempting to steal from a shop. Somehow I knew the one time I'd do it, I'd get caught. This just wasn't me; I'm not a thief.

Out of the corner of my eye, I saw this big, burly overweight security guard coming to grab me. He got me by the arm in front of all the other slack-jawed shoppers, who were craning their necks to get a better view. I've never been so mortified in all my life. My heart was racing, the alarms were still going off, and I didn't know what to do. I knew the jig was up. Suddenly I burst into tears and in doing so, I was admitting my guilt.

The security guard, who still had hold of my arm, marched me to the back office, where he made me go through my school bag. He saw the £18 kit of Sally Hansen French Manicured Nails and said, 'Weren't going to pay for those, were you, lass?' He was *so* smug.

I didn't respond; I didn't need to. I just cried while the security guard and manager of the store filled out some paperwork.

'I'm so, so sorry! I'll never do it again, I've learnt my lesson,' I wailed.

'We take shoplifting extremely seriously in this store.'

'Please, please. I... I... didn't mean to... I promise, I'll never do it again,' I pleaded. But it was useless. They were proud as punch to have caught some teenager red-handed.

The next thing I know, I'm being bundled into the back of a police car, like I was an armed robber about to hold up the whole store. Can you believe it? I thought calling the police was a bit unnecessary, they could see from my reaction that I wasn't a bad kid and the whole experience was enough to put me off thieving for life, but that bald bastard of a security guard was hell-bent on throwing the book at me.

The two coppers had showed up, and told me if I co-operated they wouldn't cuff me. I complied with their wishes, so one of them held me under his arm and paraded me through the shop like they had won a trophy. God, it was humiliating! After driving me back to the police station, they gave me a lecture on how much greedy stealing costs the economy each year. They kept telling me I could be prosecuted and fined up to £500 for my crime. I felt sick, I didn't have that kind of money and neither did my mam.

They kept me locked up in a holding cell so I could reflect on the crime I'd committed and how my selfish actions impact on other people. The way they were going on you'd think I'd been involved in the Great Train Robbery or something. I didn't know how long I was going to be in there. I had visions of me wearing a bright orange boiler suit and scratching tally charts in the wall. And I felt such an idiot. I sat there for three hours before they eventually let me have my one phone call, like they do in the movies.

By this time my dad had moved back to the 'boro', so I called him in floods of tears. He had to come and pick me up from the police station and he was so angry with me. He was absolutely furious. I'd never seen him that mad before in my life: his face was red with rage and he just kept yelling and yelling at me. This public bollocking was worse than anything the policemen had said; although when we got in the car he turned to look at me and started laughing. Of course he was mad, but he told me not to be so stupid. Deep down he knew I wasn't that kind of girl and he believed me when I said it was the only time I'd ever done something that daft. He said he'd take me for some tea because my ordeal had made me hungry.

Over dinner, we decided the less people knew about the ASDA incident the better. It was just going to be our secret. We didn't see any point in upsetting Mam because it wasn't like I was going to do it again. It was just a stupid one-off.

So you can imagine the shock Mam got when later that evening she saw a police van pull up outside our home. Apparently the police weren't satisfied I wasn't a bad lass. They were sure I'd been a prolific thief all over Middlesbrough and they'd come round to my house to search for more stolen goods.

As Mam spotted the high-vis vehicle through the window, her mother's instinct must have kicked in because she said she knew instantly it would be something to do with leaving me in ASDA. (The same ASDA that my mam shops in every day and is only five minutes from our house, by the way.)

The policeman banged on my mam's front door, like they were gearing up for a raid. They then proceeded to tell her about the thieving of the false nails before demanding to search my bedroom. Well, she was mortified, especially if you'd seen the state of my bedroom. My word, it was a total state! I can just imagine those two bobbies wading through the clothes on my floor, sifting through all my make-up and hair extensions, looking under towels covered in fake tan and hair dye, kicking away my high heels and underwear... Oh, the shame!

The policemen left after about five minutes, satisfied I wasn't a hardened criminal, with stashes of swiped beauty products tucked away. They thanked my mam for being so co-operative and told her to give me a firm warning when I got home.

Of course this was all unbeknown to me at the time. I had no clue as to all that had been going on while I was having a laugh with my dad. When he dropped me off back at my mam's, I waltzed in like nothing had happened, dumped my school bag and hotfooted it upstairs, like I usually did.

'Holly, get down here now!' Mam roared.

I could tell by the tone of her voice this was not going to be one of those sweet little 'what have you done today?' chats over a cuppa. Tentatively, I walked back down the stairs, wishing and hoping she didn't know about the false nails fiasco. But how could she? Only Dad and I knew.

'Yes, Mam?' I asked, trying to disguise the guilt in my voice.

'Have you got anything to tell me?' she said, standing ramrod straight and folding her arms.

I hate these types of questions because I can end up admitting to something else she doesn't know about. A little tip, if you're ever in that situation: say nothing, deny everything... unless there's absolute proof. Then plead forgiveness.

I genuinely started to think about all the other shit I'd done. Maybe one of my teachers had phoned up complaining about me, or she'd found the three bottles of vodka I'd hidden in my room, or perhaps it was the time I'd told her I was staying at Laura's but was actually drinking on a street corner until the early hours. I hadn't a clue why she was so cross.

'No, should I?' I said, still feigning confusion.

'I have just had two policemen round, telling me you were shoplifting this afternoon!' she yelled. 'I had to let them in to search your room.'

Fucking hell! Hadn't Tweedledee and Tweedledum got anything better to do? There was me planning the perfect cover-up and all the time, the rozzers had been round to my mam's, snitching on me and rifling through my drawers.

'They went in my room?' I gasped in amazement.

'Yes, and it's an absolute disgrace! I am so embarrassed,' Mam shouted. 'I can't believe you, Holly!'

I couldn't help but find it funny. Turning on my heel, I ran straight back up the stairs.

'Where are you going?' Mam shouted, stunned that I was just walking off in the middle of a scolding.

'To see what a mess they've made in my room.'

'Mess *they've* made?'

My mam followed me up and continued with her telling-off. She kept going on about how she could never show her face in ASDA again and how I was grounded with no phone for the next week. To tell the truth, I wasn't even listening anymore – I was too busy checking out my bedroom to make sure everything was still in its rightful place. Yeah, it might have looked like a bombsite to anyone else, but I knew exactly where everything was. It was carefully organised chaos.

I get why my mam was angry. She's a very proud woman. I had totally embarrassed and ashamed her to the point where she felt like she couldn't even step foot in our local supermarket. Plus, I had the money on me to actually buy the nail kit. That's what she couldn't get her head around.

To this day, I still think it was an absolute waste of police time. They must have had nothing better to do, but I did learn my lesson.

My mam, bless her, tried to dish out a little punishment by taking my phone off me for a week, but it didn't work. I had it back within three days. By her own admission, she's not the punishing type of parent. Luckily for me, she's just a big softy.

Chapter Ten

ALL I WANT FOR PROM IS MY TWO FRONT TEETH

Never mind my GCSEs, the school leaver's ball was the biggest deal in fifth year. If I could have gained a qualification in prom attire and make-up, I would have been given an A*, for sure.

I'd been planning my outfit since November 2008, seven months before the actual night. I know that seems stupidly well in advance, but the dress cost over £200 and my mam was paying it off weekly, so I had to order it early. My dad went halves with her on the money because even though he couldn't be around to see me on my big night, he still wanted to feel like he'd contributed.

The dress I chose was a huge pink ball gown specially made at a shop in Middlesbrough called Bliss, which was popular with the girls in my school. They specialised in made-to-measure dresses that were so ostentatious, they wouldn't have looked out of place on *My Big Fat Gypsy Wedding*. As you know, Katie Price was my idol growing up, so I had an outfit made which was based on the wedding dress she wore to marry Peter Andre.

It was a pale pink corset with an underskirt swaddled in mounds of pink netting. I'd seen something similar in a bridal magazine, so I ripped out the page and took it to the seamstress. My mam wasn't overly keen on the design, but I didn't care; I had my own idea of what I wanted and I was hell-bent on having this satin marshmallow-pink creation.

In the weeks leading up to prom night, I was masterminding my look. I was going on the sunbeds a couple of times a week because although I could have used fake tan, I didn't want any of my cheap Rimmel Sunshimmer staining my dress. Only a natural tan would do, I figured.

I bought all my accessories and jewellery. It was only cheap junk costume jewellery from Claire's Accessories, but I loved it. I got a new blinging diamante bag from a shop in the town centre, and my mam had ordered me an expensive pink flower corsage from the best florist in town.

The only thing left to do was have my nails done, which I paid for out of my own pocket money. I had the long French manicured tips, which were horrendously tacky when I look back now, but at the time they were all the rage.

I had planned everything so perfectly, down to the last detail. I'd practised my hair and make-up time and time again, making sure I could recreate the right look on the night – I was leaving nothing to chance. But isn't it always the way, when you so badly want something to go right, something always goes wrong?

About a week before the big night, my mam woke me up before she went off to work at Specsavers. She didn't want me for anything in particular; it was just to make sure I wasn't going to be festering in bed all day. Unlike most weeks, where I would snooze until midday, I had no time to fester. After all I only had seven days to make sure I looked absolutely perfect for the ball. I brushed my hair and my teeth before inspecting how the natural tan was progressing. Deciding I still wasn't dark enough, I donned my scruffy trackie bottoms, a hoodie and trainers and headed into the shopping centre for a sunbed.

I was feeling the pressure, so I decided to up my tan time from six minutes to twelve minutes and because I had a base tan, I reckoned I'd be able to handle the lengthy sun exposure. Or so I thought…

X X X

'Is this your daughter?' asked the strange man who had hold of my arm, as he dragged me into Specsavers.

'Yes, what's wrong with her?' my mam asked, completely in shock.

'She's drunk. I've just picked her up off the floor,' he said, disgusted.

'What? She can't be!' Mam replied. 'It's only twelve o'clock.'

'She is. She's hammered, she can't even walk. It's a disgrace,' he said as he threw me into the arms of my mam.

Mam's boss looked anxious that this apparently drunk girl was wailing in the middle of his opticians, so she took me into the back of the shop to sit me down.

'Holly, are you drunk?'

81

'No, Mam. My teeth, my teeth...' I kept saying (I was still hazy from the fall). 'I passed out in the sunbed shop and then hit my face.'

The sunbed salon I'd visited was two floors above the Specsavers branch where Mam worked. I'd felt so ill and dizzy when I came out, I needed to see her. The heat had made me black out and I went all woozy. What on earth was I thinking, going on there for twelve minutes? I thought the cool air outside would make me feel better as I walked to my mam's work but as I came down the stairs, my legs gave way, my knees buckled and BANG! I smacked my face straight on the concrete step.

I felt instant pain in my right front tooth, like a sore bruise. I was in absolute shock and then I tasted the blood.

A man behind me who'd seen me fall picked me up and through my sobs, I managed to tell him my mam worked in Specsavers. The next thing I know, I'm being dragged in there by this total stranger, palmed off to my mother and accused of being a drunk.

I opened my mouth and showed my mam.

'Oh, Holly!' she looked at me in complete horror.

I'd smacked my front tooth and broke half of it off. Just my luck, I'd spent so long preparing for the perfect night and now, thanks to my half a tooth, I was going to look a snaggle in my photos.

After that my mam did everything she could. She phoned around the emergency dentists and luckily managed to get one to see me in two days' time. They couldn't fix it properly, but they did the best they could and filled my tooth temporarily so it wouldn't look so unsightly.

The man who brought me in to my mam, claiming I was some drunken teenager, went back to Specsavers the next day, apparently to see if I was OK. I think one of the staff told him I'd fainted because of the sunbed. The guy must have felt horrible, although I couldn't blame him for jumping to conclusions. I looked like a total townie scruff, the kind of girl who would have been pissed in a shopping precinct in the middle of the day. But he did apologise for what he'd said and told the staff to pass the message on to my mam when she was back in work.

When the night of the prom came round, I gave in and lathered a bottle of Rimmel Sunshimmer all over me. Of course I should have just done that from the beginning, but I suppose you only learn these things the hard way. A word of advice: don't bother with sunbeds, they're bad for you! Plus, they give you wrinkles and no one wants premature wrinkles.

I got ready for the prom just as I'd been planning for the past month. I spent an hour on my hair, an hour on my make-up and then I got my mam to help me with getting into my dress. Honestly, I looked like a pink pantomime fairy and I loved it!

The event was held in a place called Hardwick Hall and it had been decorated beautifully, with a big, tented ceiling and balloons everywhere. All the girls had really made an effort with their dresses and the lads looked so smart in their new suits.

I had such an amazing night. It was like a wedding that all your mates had been invited to. I danced around and spoke to everyone, even the people I had never been friendly with. It's funny how you can go through your whole school life not speaking to half the people in your year and then, when it's almost too late, when it's the last time you're ever going to see each other, this is the moment you choose to start making the effort with people.

There were many girls who hung around in different groups to me, but we very rarely spoke so, on that last night, I spoke to everyone and realised I'd missed out on getting to know some fine young people, a diverse set of girls and boys who weren't like me. That's probably what held me back in the first place – they were slightly different – but in being like that I'd probably missed out on many different experiences. It's only now, as I've got older, that I embrace more people and more opportunities, and if I could go back to those days at school, that's definitely something I would change. But then again, you could say that about most things. I wish I knew then what I know now.

Naturally, no fairy dress would be complete without its own fairy tale... But no, I didn't find my prince (although I did have to leave the party bang on midnight).

Both Mam and John were forty that year and so to celebrate, we were flying to Egypt in the early hours of the morning. It was like something out of *Cinderella*, only instead of leaving a glass slipper behind, all I left was a glass Lambrini bottle for the rest of my mates to enjoy at the after-party. My mam literally had to pick me up at 12pm, drag me away and drive to Manchester Airport while I was still in my full prom attire.

She'd brought me a pair of jogging bottoms in the car, but you should have seen me trying to get this big dress off in the back of a BMW, wedged between three suitcases. The people on the motorway had a fright!

It was nice to get away, but I couldn't actually believe school was over for good. I have some wonderful memories of my time there, but it had also been home to some of the most depressing times of my life.

The holiday was fantastic and I quickly made friends with a few lads and lasses in my hotel. I had my own room, which meant a lot more freedom. Late at night, I would tell Mam and John I was off to bed and then I would silently get myself ready for a night on the Sharm el-Sheikh strip.

We would hitch a ride from a local, which I know was such a dangerous thing to do, but we were young and naïve back then. We'd head for this cool white bar in front of a waterfall, where we'd drink cocktails and smoke shisha pipes. Then we'd head to Pacha and dance in there until the early hours. I used to come back at 3am, drunk and reeking of smoke. Mam would knock on my room early in the morning and wake me for breakfast, but I was always dead to the world. I don't think I made it down for food even once. She must have known I was going out and getting mortal, but I never said anything.

While we were away, it was my sixteenth birthday. I had this cute little outfit on and everyone commented on how great I looked. I remember an American girl stopping me as I walked down the street, telling me how sweet my ra-ra skirt was. Just hearing a genuine compliment like that from a complete stranger was lovely. I always like to dress up, and I've always had my own style.

Back in school, no one would ever say anything nice, unless they wanted something. And it made me realise maybe I shouldn't be sad that school was over; the world outside that institution was what mattered now and it was my time to shine. All the popular girls in school weren't popular anymore and I was happy I never had to be near them again.

Chapter Eleven

BOOZE, BONKS
AND BOOBS

When I left school, I hadn't a clue what I wanted to do with my life. What sixteen-year-old does? I wasn't academic in the way that I had ambitions of going to university. University is only good if you have a clear career path, I think, and I didn't. I would have ended up studying something I had little interest in, finding myself in thousands of pounds worth of debt, getting smashed in more ways than one, never turning up for lectures and struggling to get a job at the end of it. For me, it was pointless. I just wanted to earn money so I could enjoy going out and buying stuff.

The only thing I was interested in was boys and my looks but it had been the same all through secondary school. I've never thought I was particularly pretty and because of my insecurities I would literally cake make-up on. All day long I would trowel it onto my face: in classes, at break time, during lunch. There would never be a time when I didn't have a vast supply of make-up stashed in my bag ready to plaster on again.

My friends were the same. Every lunchtime we'd get together for what we called 'a make-up sesh'. During these sessions, we'd stand around in the toilets, swapping all our products and discussing the boys in our year. None of us were flush. We'd only ever have a little bit of pocket money from our mams, so the stuff we used was all really cheap.

We bought it from a shop called Danglers and the brand we preferred was called Laval. I don't know if it's even still going, but it's all we could afford at the time. My face would be so thick with a £3 foundation it felt like it was never dry. If you accidentally brushed your shirt on me it would instantly be covered with orange marks.

School would always go mad. Teachers would try to make us go and wash it off, but we never did. And this orange tar couldn't be washed off with soap and water, let me tell you. Even if they made us take it off, we would just re-apply it in the afternoon. In the end, they just gave up telling us off about it.

I would honestly have written lines for a week rather than let anyone see me without my make-up. I'd be distraught if anyone had caught a glimpse of my bare face and I suppose, all through school, none of them ever saw the real me. My make-up was more integral to my school routine than my homework was. It was like I was putting a mask on every day. I had to, because I thought no one would like me if I didn't coat it on. I was too self-conscious about the way I looked.

The boys would tease us about it. They would get a piece of paper and try and wipe all our foundation off, and tell us we looked disgusting – but it was their cruel comments that only made me cover myself in it even more.

When I left school, I think my make-up and obsession with my looks became even worse. I enrolled in St Marys College and began to study AS levels. I'd done well in my GCSEs, better than I ever expected, which was good enough for me. I ended up leaving school with nine of them! I also got myself a job at the HMRC Tax Office as an administrative officer. The job itself was boring – soul-destroying, actually – but I was on a good wage for a sixteen-year-old. I was earning £800 a month and when you take out the £10-a-week board I was giving my mam, I was still left with a hefty amount to spend on myself.

Literally every penny I earned went on self-improvement. I was buying better brands of make-up now, like MAC and Bobbi Brown, but I would was still applying them like a transsexual. I'd buy new clothes every week and I'd get my nails done to an obscene length, then I would get them covered in tacky nail art. My extensions were nearly touching my bum and I would make sure I had the deepest unnatural tan by getting sprayed once a week. I knew I was overdone, but I thought I looked glamorous and girls who didn't look like me just couldn't be bothered making much effort.

It's only now when I look back at myself that I realise someone should have put me up for an episode of *Snog Marry Avoid?* I looked absolutely dreadful – like a slag, if I'm honest. It's no wonder I got the wrong kind of attention from the lads.

By the time I was sixteen, I'd had my fair share of lads in the sack, which I wish wasn't the case. I wish I hadn't been so easy all my life, but I think it goes back to some deep-rooted confidence issues and the way I lost my virginity.

This is awful to admit, but I used to be proud of how many people I'd slept with. I relished being a slag. I would play up to it, and I loved getting called a slut. I kind of felt if I admitted my flaws upfront then those words wouldn't hurt me. If someone ever said it to me I'd just shrug and say, 'Yeah, so what if I'm a slag? At least I admit it!'

But I knew boys didn't like it, which is why they would take me home, fuck me and fuck me off. They never wanted to be in a relationship with me. If I'm completely honest, it's only in the past year I've been able to get out of that mindset.

I used to think if I slept with a guy he would like me and then maybe want to be with me. I was using sex as a way to lure them and get some one-on-one time. However, I didn't realise putting out on the first night was the wrong way to go about getting a boy to like you.

A good example would be when I met this lad in work. I'd seen him on my first day on the job at the tax office. One of the team managers, he had a gorgeous cheeky face, but with designer stubble and really amazing blue eyes. Then to top it off, he always wore a sexy suit. Who doesn't love a man in a suit?

I blushed red as our paths crossed and I felt my stomach do a little flip. Honestly, he was fucking fit!

The first time we spoke was during our 'ice-breaker' sessions, I remember I had to stand up and tell the room a little about myself.

I said, 'I'm Holly, I'm sixteen and most Saturday nights you'll find me in Arena club.'

'Arena? You're a bit young for there, aren't you?' he said, looking me dead on in the eye. I felt my stomach and knickers pull together, a fanny flutter.

'I've been going for ages, you should try it once,' I replied cockily.

I think he liked my canny attitude. It had made me stand out from the crowd. After that afternoon, I remember saying to one of the girls in work, 'I will have him, just you watch, I know I will.' And from that day on I made it my mission to sleep with him.

We flirted over a number of weeks and he resisted me for a while because he was twenty-three and I was sixteen. He felt it was wrong, I suppose. One night it was his birthday and we all went out in Middlesbrough. I made an extra-special effort, made sure I had my trusty fake ID in my bag, and got absolutely mortal. He'd been eyeing me up all night and then he invited me back to his. I was delighted at the time. I thought he was one of the best-looking guys I'd ever met and he was inviting me back to his.

Although I'd set myself the challenge of sleeping with him, I tried to play it cool. I wanted him to want me. So I didn't actually have sex with him that evening, I just gave him oral. I know it's not much better but I liked this guy and I didn't want him to think I was *too* much of an easy lay!

The week after, I ended up bumping into him on another night and he took me back to his again. This time we did seal the deal, but it wasn't the big, passionate experience I'd been hoping for. After it was over, he just turned his back away from me and went to sleep. I was a little hurt by that move. I craved some attention, an arm around me or a kiss on the lips. But after we had sex, he was so cold and distant.

That 'friends with benefits' arrangement carried on for a while. Two years, in fact. He knew how to play me and I was completely at his beck and call. When I think back now to how stupid I was, I can't believe it. I would wait up until the early hours, with a full face of make-up on, just in case he'd ask me to go round to his house. Even if he texted me at midnight, I would pack a few clothes, jump in a taxi and be round at his within fifteen minutes. I was still living at home at this point and you should have heard the nonsense excuses I came out with to my mam to get out of the house. I would say my friend's boyfriend had dumped her and she needed me immediately, or I'd left something important at work and I had to pick it up from a friend, and all kinds of drivel. I'm sure she knew I was lying, but she never tried to stop me.

He was a typical lad who used me for sex, but I thought I was in love with him, which is why I let him treat me that way. I wanted him to be more affectionate but either he wasn't an affection person, or he just wasn't with me. I wanted him to kiss me passionately, like he had the first time we kissed, to snog me so much that his stubble would scratch and rash my face. And I wanted him to grab me by surprise, push me up against a wall and make it clear that he really wanted me.

The sex with him was amazing. It was different to any other lad because he was older and more experienced. I couldn't get enough of him. But he was never going to want me in the way I wanted him and so I knew it had to stop. I wasn't like I would miss the sex because I was still sleeping with other people and still fancied other people, but I only really wanted to be with him and it's only when he got a girlfriend our liaisons ended.

We still keep in touch. He sends me the odd Facebook message, telling me how well I've done for myself. Sometimes he's apologetic about the way he treated me and says he didn't realise what he could have had with me. But of course it doesn't work out like that. If I'd got with him back then, he would probably have cheated on me and made me feel like shit. I would never have ended up on *Geordie Shore* and I wouldn't be in the position I am today. He says he now realises the error of his ways, but I realise mine, too.

I was stupid, immature and naïve. It wasn't just his fault, I could have said no to him. I don't ever blame him.

When I first started work I found it tough. I was trying to hold down a job and college at the same time as having a busy social life. Everything was going well until I started drinking. I'd be out four or five nights a week with either people from work, or from college.

My average day would be 9–4pm in college. From there I'd go straight to work, working 5pm–9.30pm, and then I'd be out on the razz until at least 1am and have to do it all again the next day. I was absolutely shattered. All areas of my life were suffering and eventually, something had to give.

In the end I chose to give up college because I couldn't afford to lose my income. I was getting used to earning a wage. I suppose in that respect I'm very much like my mam, she has always been a worker and grafted for everything she's got. She wasn't disappointed when I decided to drop out of college. She knew I had my own mind. As long as I had money to do the things I wanted, she was happy. She couldn't afford to keep me in the lifestyle I wanted, so it was up to me.

I'd never had that much income in my life. I felt like I was a millionaire. But with the money came the problems, and it coincided with me going through a weird, wild, uncontrollable stage.

When I was going out I was getting so fucked up, it was dangerous. My outfits were a disgrace. They were the most skimpy, trashy, brash items of clothing you could imagine and I dressed like that because I always wanted attention. I got it, too, but for all the wrong reasons. I wanted guys to notice me, to want me, to use me and have their wicked way with me. And I used my sexuality as a way to get with boys.

Looking back, I didn't know what was going on in my head. I just thought now I was earning my own money, I could do exactly what I wanted. I didn't have to answer to Mam, or Dad, or John. If I wanted to go back and have a one-night stand or stay out all night, I would. No one had a say in my life apart from me.

Sometimes I'd go to work, pack a slutty outfit, make-up and heels and go out without telling my mam. I'd make up a cover story, usually saying I was staying over at a friend's house, but instead I'd be out in Middlesbrough with a gang of undesirables. And because I'd told Mam a pack of lies, I couldn't go traipsing back to her house at 2am. Instead I would find some random party to go back to and go there until I had to be back in work.

One time I did this I ended up back in some boarded-up drug den with five lads and one other girl. I didn't know the group personally, but I knew of them so I thought I would be safe. I don't know whose house it was, but it was disgusting: there was no furniture, the curtains had all been ripped off the windows, the walls were stained yellow with nicotine, and the toilet thick with black sludge. All the lads were drinking cans of Red Stripe and MC-ing to the worst dance music you can imagine. They offered me some of their rolled-up joint, but I declined.

The room quickly filled with foul-smelling smoke from the

weed. Convinced the fumes would make me ill, I was dying to get out of the place. Then the lads started arguing amongst themselves, I can't remember what about. The next thing I know, four of us were being chased out of the house by one of the lads, who was brandishing a kitchen knife and threatening to cut our faces off. I ran down the street at 5am and burst into tears. It was one of the scariest times of my life.

That incident really shook me up. At the time I felt like I was enjoying going out all the time. I didn't fully realise the severity of the situations I was getting myself into.

Other times I would wake up at a random lad's house and wonder how I got there. My mind would be a complete blank and then I'd have the panic of trying to get myself home somehow. Even admitting to all this makes me sick. Remembering all those times I behaved like that is shameful. All I can say is, I was at a horrible stage in my life. I was completely lost and if I could go back and change it, then I would.

I was so young to be hanging round bars and nightclubs. Now, I wish I'd had more of a childhood, that I'd waited to experience the thrills of going out. But no one else in my peer group was doing that and I followed the crowd.

I calmed down slightly when I got together with my boyfriend, Dan. I'm not proud of telling you how we met, but I will anyway. I'd slept with his best friend a few weeks before, but I wasn't interested in him romantically. Through his mate, Dan and me became good pals and started spending loads of time together.

My mam went away for two weeks, so he spent the majority of his time at my house. We weren't having sex at that stage, we were just hanging out. We'd make pancakes, or wander down to McDonald's for some fast food, watch films and chill out.

After a few months we ended up making it official. He didn't care I'd already shagged his best friend and he wasn't worried about my chequered past either. I suppose he didn't have that kind of pride. Either that or he was just deeply in love with me. I have to say Dan genuinely would have done anything for me and when I was with him, it was the happiest time of my life.

We were both really young but he would do little cute things for me, like take me to work every morning and pick me up again when I'd finished. He'd bring me a Maccies in the car, too, which was sweet of him, but it's also the reason I started piling on the weight.

I'd always been a size 10, but during my relationship with Dan I was struggling to fit into a size 14. I would stay round at his all the time and he'd literally feed me up. And it's Sod's law that as my body was getting bigger and bigger, none of this fat was storing in my boobs. All my life I'd been flat-chested, like I'd never properly reached puberty. I thought I looked ridiculous, and I was always uncomfortable, showing myself naked.

I was a small B cup and there was absolutely nothing wrong with my boobs. They looked fine to anyone else, but I hated them and I never wanted to show them to anyone.

One time, the guy from the tax office took off my bra without me realising. He unhooked my arms out of it and, because I didn't want to make a big fuss, I just let my boobs hang free. At the time I remember feeling sick. I was literally shaking with nerves as he looked at my naked chest. I was inexplicably embarrassed.

No one ever knew how big my real boobs were because, when I went out, I'd wear three bras and two pairs of chicken fillets.

But I knew as soon as I turned eighteen, I would go under the knife and get bigger bangers. I wanted huge knockers.

Mam and Dad knew of my plans to enlarge my chest. They were never going to stop me, but they were unwilling to give me a penny towards the procedure. I'd begun enquiries about the cost even before I was old enough to have the surgery, but because I was only eighteen, with no credit history, the company wouldn't give me the finance. I couldn't afford to pay upfront either, so where was I going to get £4,000 cash from?

I called my mam while she was out shopping and asked her if she would be the guarantor for me. To my horror she flatly refused. I spent the whole of my break from work crying my eyes out. I was sobbing because I couldn't have my boobs. For weeks, I begged and begged her. Luckily, she finally gave in, probably just to shut me up. I was paying for them myself, but I needed the money to come out of my mam's account, so we set up an arrangement where I would give her £125 a month.

On the day of the surgery, my mam was in work so I had to go on my own. I didn't mind as I was looking forward to finally having the chest I'd always wanted. I wasn't nervous about the procedure, although I was apprehensive. Having any kind of cosmetic procedure should not be a decision that you take lightly. I had thought about what I'd wanted to do for many years and researched all the possibilities. I knew the possible downsides and the risks involved.

But when I woke up after the surgery, all of a sudden, I had breasts. And they were gigantic, just what I'd wanted. Two big, fake, solid, round breasts! The enlargements had been well done, and the difference was dramatic. I loved them literally from the moment I saw them. The recovery process wasn't too bad either. I think because I opted for the implants in front of the muscle, it didn't hurt that much. I was discharged from hospital the next morning and went shopping for all the new bras I would need.

After the surgery, my body confidence soared and if you think I'd shown off my boobs in skimpy outfits before, well, you should have seen me after the tit job! I'd gone from a small B cup to a fucking fantastic double F. Now I wasn't going to keep those babies hidden, was I?

For me it was £4,000 well spent, but if you can't afford the plastic surgery, my advice would be to enhance your beauty by getting those around you blind drunk!

Chapter Twelve

GEORDIE
SHORE

Have you ever wondered how they cast shows like *Geordie Shore*? How they find these people, the ones who will become unforgettable characters?

I already know thousands of hopefuls will be looking for some hints and tips here. Well, there's no magic formula. I certainly didn't know before I actually got my place on *Geordie Shore*. But here's a piece of advice… if you're not embarrassed by it, then don't even bother saying it.

I was still dating Dan when I applied for the show. In fact it was he who mentioned the possibility of being cast for a new reality show. He told me he'd seen something on Facebook. Everyone was saying it was going to be similar to *Jersey Shore*, one of my favourite reality shows of all time.

All I had to do was add the *Geordie Shore* page to my Facebook account and they would accept you if you looked good enough. I remember having the most awful slutty profile picture on there at the time. The production crew must have had a right old laugh rifling through my photos. There were some horrendous howlers.

I never thought much about the show after that, I certainly never expected anything to come of it. Obviously I wasn't a Geordie, which I thought might go against me in the audition process, but they said it didn't matter and that anyone from the north-east was welcome.

The next thing I know, I got a message sent to me by a researcher. They'd obviously had a nosey through my profile and decided they wanted to know more. They sent me a list of questions and told me to answer them as honestly as possible. I'll give you some examples:

What's your best asset? – Boobs, obviously, they were costing me enough!
What's your most embarrassing moment? – Getting caught for shoplifting a pack of false nails.
What's your most interesting skill? – Blowjobs.

No wonder they called me up the next day.

The producer on the line wanted to do an interview over the phone about my life. I made them laugh, telling them I wore nine pairs of eyelashes – which I did – and regaling them with my unique technique for applying them. I told them I'd buy the big multipacks of lashes off eBay, sent directly from China. I'd use the super-strength glue and lay them on top of one another, making the lashes as thick and full as possible. I'd be left with this huge brush-like curve of false plastic hairs and then I'd stick them onto my eyelids. Honestly, they were so heavy that my eyes were at half-mast the whole time, like Garfield but with the fluttery lash length of Mr Snuffleupagus from *Sesame Street*.

After that, I met the producers for a face-to-face interview. I remember being up all night, trying to decide on the perfect outfit for my meeting. Well, I say perfect, what I really mean was sluttiest. I found this dress with two strips of fabric to cover my nipples and just enough length to cover the crease in bum. My heels were far too high and tacky; my make-up was an inch thick and my hair a mishmash of fake blonde and black highlighted extensions caked in so much hairspray. It looked like it had been brushed with a toffee apple. Argh! I cringe when I think about it now.

The interview was taking pace in the Jurys Inn hotel in Newcastle during the middle of the day. I remember tottering in and there was this huge stag party in the lounge. They all starting cheering when they saw me. They must have thought I was a hooker, off to buck some client in one of the rooms.

Luckily, a lady called Lauren Benson, the casting producer, came down to meet me and hopefully that dispelled the hooker vibe. She took me through to a conference room, where they had set up a camera with two more producers sat behind it. They all looked at me and what I was wearing, before saying, 'Fucking hell, we can see what you had for dinner.' Duh! That was the point. At least they would remember me.

I sat down on a single chair in the middle of the room while everyone's eyes and cameras focussed on me. I couldn't help fixing my boobs, but this was also a carefully thought-out action. They asked me questions about my life – my background, my family, my boyfriend, my hopes and dreams. Though I didn't realise it at the time, I was giving them gold. I didn't hold back on anything. I was just coming out with the most outrageous random stuff. Throughout the whole interview I had them in stitches; I knew they'd lap it up.

My boyfriend knew everything from the start. He knew I was going to all these meetings and was really supportive although, if I'm honest, we weren't in love with each other anymore. Well, *I* wasn't in love with him and the more I thought about the show, the less I thought about being with Dan.

I decided to tell my mam after I'd had a couple of auditions. I was sat in the kitchen, with a mouthful of McDonald's, when I informed her I'd applied for this wild partying show. She didn't really grasp what I was going on about. I told her it was going to be like a British version of *Jersey Shore*, but she had never seen the programme and couldn't relate in the slightest.

It was only when she sat down and watched *Jersey Shore* for the first time that she saw what I was putting myself up for. She saw the American cast getting drunk and arguing, but they never showed any kind of sex so she was fairly happy for me to continue with the application process.

I went to about three more interviews and met with the big bosses at MTV. The further down the process I got, the more likely it was becoming that I was actually going to end up on the show. At this point I lost interest in work and everything became about *Geordie Shore*. It was literally all I could think about.

I would be sneaking out the house more regularly, trying not to arouse suspicion from my mam. A few times, she'd catch me going out in my dressing gown, pull me back indoors and demand to see what I was wearing underneath. I'd be wearing a dress that barely covered my nether regions or my silicone sisters. She would roar at me to get changed, but I'd just scarper before she could even continue with her scolding.

Mam was just scared for me, I know she was. She knew I'd put on weight and she didn't want me going out in a tiny outfit when I wasn't looking my best. And it was true, I wasn't looking the greatest I could have looked. I was going out drinking all the time, eating takeaways, kebabs and any other kind of crap I could get my hands on. My body was just a mess and I was flaunting it in the worst possible way.

Also, she didn't want me portrayed in a bad light. Shows like that were for other people's kids, not hers. And the further down the selection process I got, the more my mam didn't want to know. On the one hand, after all the interviews I'd had for the show, she knew I'd be heartbroken if I didn't get on. But on the other, she didn't want me on the show, making a tit out of myself by getting my tits out.

Why anyone would want to be famous still mystified Mam. As TV had trained her to do, she associated the word 'fame' with bad things like rehab, drugs, booze, sex and being labelled something I wasn't for the rest of my life. She told me if I gained fame, the paparazzi and the media would watch and wait for me to slip, just to shame my name. And why did I want to put myself through any of it?

But all my life I'd been waiting for a break to come my way. Like I said at the start of this book, I always wanted to be famous – I just didn't know how to go about it. Now that someone was dangling the showbiz carrot in front of me, I wanted to bite their hands off.

I wanted to be a reality star. I knew they got a rough time in the press, but they still had adoring fans, tons of money and a career doing something they loved. The lure of celebrity was all too much. I *had* to get on this show. And if I didn't, well... it didn't bear thinking about.

I knew the relationship between Dan and me wouldn't last. He loved me and at one time, I thought I loved him, too. But we were young and I had no idea what a life in the limelight was ever going to do to me. My mam liked him, too, which meant a lot. He was a nice, canny lad and I'll never say a bad word against him.

When I got the call to say I'd been shortlisted, I was absolutely thrilled. I was going on about it in front of Dan and he kind of looked a little upset, like he knew he was losing me. My mam asked him what he would do if I got into *Geordie Shore* and he said he would be happy for me. He was naïve, he thought it was all going to carry on the same and everything would be rosy between us.

Then it got even further down the line and Lauren the casting producer came round to meet my mam and me. I knew literally nothing about the show until Lauren explained it was based around the concept of a group of young people, four girls and four lads living together in shared accommodation, with a long-suffering boss attempting to control them.

Mam was still concerned, as any mother would be. It's such a strange situation to be involved in and quite unlike anything she'd ever had to deal with before. The pair of them spoke at length because she was so worried, but I suppose if she didn't worry like that, then there would have been something wrong.

By this time I'd moved to Santander and was working as a

loan advisor. One day, when I was aimlessly looking at a huge projector displaying graphs and pie charts, utterly bored to death, I got a call from a producer asking me to film a few days later. I'd been learning about mortgages and I just couldn't do it. It was so hard and I didn't want to know any of it. I wasn't destined to be a number cruncher all my life; I was destined to be in the spotlight. I could feel it.

They needed me to film a few snippets for them and even though I hated my job, I'd taken too much time off work and I couldn't just drop everything when MTV wanted me to be there.

'Sorry, I'm in work. I can't take any more time off,' I said, exasperated.

'Well, we need you to film. We need to know that you would be committed to the show,' said the voice on the other end of the line.

'I would be committed if I knew I was on it,' I tutted.

'Well, what if we said you had been selected for the programme?'

'Then that would be a different story.'

There was a long pause, where neither of us said anything and then I heard the words, 'Welcome aboard, you're on *Geordie Shore*.'

Deliriously happy, I screamed with delight – I was going to be famous! For once, something I had wanted so badly had finally gone my way. I was eighteen and old enough to make my own decisions, no one, not Mam, Dad or Dan, was going to stop me and I was going to give this show everything I had. I'd been chosen out of thousands and thousands of people, which was an achievement in itself. I always wanted to be out there, in the public eye, and now it was finally all falling into place.

My manager at Santander knew I'd applied for the show, so I rang and told him the good news. He was made up for me, everyone at work was. It was like I was breaking out of prison. They were all congratulating me on getting out of that dead-end job and doing something with my life.

But I was sensible. I didn't know how *Geordie Shore* was going to pan out, so my boss agreed to keep my job open for me. They gave me six weeks off just in case I wanted to return to humdrum life at the call centre.

I called my mam after that and she kind of brought me back down to earth with a bang. All she said was, 'It doesn't matter if they want you, Holly. Are you sure you want to do this? I mean, *really* sure?'

I suppose I'd been so preoccupied with making sure I got on the show that I didn't actually stop to think if I should do it. But what were my options? Stay at Santander all my life, or throw myself into a new experience and hope for the best? At that point I still had a choice: I could be famous or I could live out the rest of my life in peaceful anonymity. However I knew what I was going to do and, luckily for me, it's worked out well. That's not to say it will for everyone, so if you ever find yourself in a similar position, you have to be 1,000,000 per cent sure it's what you want. I can't stress this enough. BE SURE. Because once the wheels on the fame train start to turn, it's impossible to go back.

Chapter Thirteen

SHE'S NOT ONE
OF US

I was the last one through the door that day. Everyone else had met and subsequently bonded. I spent hours and hours waiting around in a makeshift holding area, which was some rented apartment down the road from the house. I was sat with a few of the crew, making small talk with the people who would now be in control of my life. Time seemed to drag as I waited until a call came through on their walkie-talkies, summoning me to be filmed for the first time.

To say I was nervous would be an understatement. I paced the room, looking my appearance up and down, touching up my heavy black eye make-up and tousling my hair. I couldn't stop fidgeting. I'd spent days trying to choose the perfect outfit for my TV debut. The producers told me to wear something I'd normally wear on a night out, something that showed off my best assets. I chose a low-neck, punky grey T-shirt, a black skirt so tight I'm surprised my circulation wasn't cut off, and a pair of Henry Holland suspender stockings. The look was finished off with some skyscraper ankle boots, mountains of brown hair extensions, including some tacky peroxide blonde highlights, and my nine pairs of eyelashes. Back then, I actually thought I looked great, but now I'm so embarrassed when I see pictures of myself looking like a total dolly bird, plastered in fakery.

I was impatient with all the hanging around but the crew kept appeasing me, saying, 'Don't worry, we've kept the best till last'. Eventually, after a lengthy six hours of chit-chat, a crackly voice was heard coming from the two-way radio. 'We're ready for Holly's arrival,' said the man, and a nervous flush of excitement filled me.

My new lodgings for the next four weeks would be a funky townhouse in Jesmond, which had been rigged up with fifty fixed cameras to record our every move, along with three separate camera crews for the close-ups. I strutted through the door, pulling my heavy suitcase, and made my way through to the back garden, where the rest of the housemates already sounded absolutely mortal. I could hear them all screaming and laughing. 'What the hell am I walking into?' I kept thinking.

All I could see was beaming white lights on me, from all angles. It was only then that it dawned on me this wasn't a house, but a living, breathing TV set. I scoped the garden and felt the eyes of all the other housemates boring into me. Suddenly I became a little self-conscious.

I said a huge hello to the group and made my way over to a drunken girl, fully dressed and submerged in a hot tub.

'Hiya, pet, I'm Sophie,' she slurred.

'Hi, I'm Holly, I brought you all a present,' I said, pulling out a cheap bottle of vodka as a gift, not realising there was an entire fridge full of booze already stocked up.

As I got a better look at them, I noticed the lads were all seriously hunky, like stereotypical Geordies: spiky hair, too-tight T-shirts, super-tanned with big muscles. The girls were all fake tanned, thick-lashed, with the mandatory mounds of flesh on parade.

They all introduced themselves in turn and, as they probably did with me, I made snap judgements and pigeonholed them straight away. Jay was the alpha-male, Gaz was the womaniser, James the muscles, and the sensitive one was Greg. Charlotte was the ditzy girl, Vicky would be the queen bee and Sophie was the crazy one. Me? Well, looking around, I guess I was 'the tits'.

I'd only been in the house a few hours, but I pretty much felt like an outcast from the word go. We were all standing around the island unit in the kitchen and Vicky asked me which part of Newcastle I was from. Without even thinking it would be a problem, I said, 'Actually, I'm from Middlesbrough.'

Well, it was like I'd just slapped them all round the face. The group looked at me in shock. I could feel their stares boring into me and my face instantly reddened; it was like I'd just said I hailed from the depths of hell.

'You're a smoggy?' James asked in disbelief.

'Yeah, but I act like a Geordie in every way,' I replied and took a large gulp of my drink, embarrassed to look them all in the eye.

You see a 'Geordie' is someone born in Newcastle, not Middlesbrough, Sunderland or anywhere else in the north-east.

Thoroughbred Geordies get a bee in their bonnets if you claim to be one of them when you're not. However, I wasn't claiming to be a Geordie. Yes, I'm on a show called *Geordie Shore* but my inclusion was down to the casting directors, not me. They didn't have a problem with my hometown, so why should the housemates?

I couldn't believe the group were so closed-minded. Why did it matter if I was from Middlesbrough? It wasn't like I was from Spain. I was still a north-east lass and that was the only stipulation to be involved with the programme. As far as I was concerned, no one was better than anyone else. We were all in this show together. It became clear that from then on, I would be the outsider of the group. Jay was twenty-five, seven years my senior, and probably the hardest to get on with. He had no time to get to know an eighteen-year-old kid like me. I remember him saying, 'She's from Middlesbrough, she might as well be from Mars. She doesn't look like a Geordie, she doesn't talk like a Geordie – she's not one of us.'

A quick geography lesson just in case you were wondering the distance between where I'm from and where Jay is talking about. Middlesbrough is roughly thirty miles from Newcastle city centre, while Mars is about 139,000,000 miles away. Treating me as if I was some kind of intergalactic alien was just pathetic and they wondered why I felt so alienated from day one.

It was crazy because Geordies are usually famous for their ability to get on with anyone, but it was like this bunch of housemates all had some clear-cut fear of anyone who lived outside of a ten-mile radius. I'll be honest, they intimidated me but all I wanted to do was fit in, so I tried to do so the only way I could... I started drinking quickly and heavily to calm my nerves.

Sophie and Charlotte were already so paralytic they had to be put to bed early, but I was determined to join in with the rest of them. I donned a bikini and a vest top to cover my overweight stomach and then climbed in the hot tub, bottle of cheap champagne in one hand, plastic beaker of vodka coke in the other. And I was knocking them back like it was going out of fashion.

It was here the subject of my boyfriend reared its head for the first time. The lads were astonished when I confessed to having a boyfriend because they would never let their lasses do a show like *Geordie Shore*. Dan probably shouldn't have let me either, but what choice did he have? He loved me and wouldn't stand in the way of me pursing my dreams. If it came to a toss up between him and *Geordie Shore*, he knew he wouldn't win. So, like the decent lad he was, he took a back seat and let me do my own thing, even if he was going to be mugged off in the process.

Fuck, I feel terrible when I think about the way I behaved on that first night. A disgrace was the only way to put it. I was letting the lads drink beer from in between my boobs and then, without any kind of persuasion, I just got them out. I unleashed my big bangers for all the cameras to see! It was like I'd forgotten we were being filmed. I was going for the shock factor and I know it seems stupid now, but I thought it was the only way I'd get the lads in the house to like me. I'd show them I was a good time girl, who didn't give two shits about my boyfriend and would flash them my chest for no apparent reason. What can I say? I was hammered and everything seems a good idea when you're hammered.

Dan had said to me before I went into the house that I wasn't allowed to do anything apart from kiss other people, but that kissing was OK. Obviously it wasn't OK, but he knew me too well. He knew if he didn't have this cool attitude regarding me and other lads, he would lose me forever and that's the last thing he wanted. I don't think he actually thought I would go through with anything, or maybe he did, I don't know. All I knew was, deep down, I didn't have much respect for him. If I did, I wouldn't have been carrying on like I was single.

As the night got colder, we all left the hot tub and gathered in the living room, sitting around and chatting. But the only subject they wanted to talk about was my relationship with Dan. They kept asking me barbed questions. I wouldn't have minded if they were asking me about him with genuine interest, but they began to interrogate me as if they were trying to embarrass me. They'd ask me a question and just laugh when I answered them with complete honesty.

After a while, I realised what they were doing. Making cruel jokes at my expense. I couldn't put up with it. I was so sad. Ever since I'd got in there, I felt like I was under attack: firstly for being from Middlesbrough and now because of my boyfriend. It was Vicky's snide remarks that finally tipped me over the edge. She just kept questioning me over and over again. She couldn't get to grips with my relationship and how my boyfriend was so open-minded, and the way she was talking just made me feel shit. Suddenly I could feel the tears forming in my eyes. Not wanting to let them see me upset, I quickly bolted for the door. I ran into the bathroom, curled up in the shower and just sobbed. I was crying so hard that I could feel the thick, fat salty drops of water rushing down my face.

A few minutes later, a guilt-ridden Vicky came tiptoeing in with the film crew to comfort me – I thought she was being genuine at the time. Five years older than me, I kind of looked up to her. She'd been away to university and was far more worldly-wise. I thought she was a stunner, too. She could handle herself in any situation and I just wished I could have had her confidence.

When she reassured me in the shower, she told me everything was going to be OK. This was a new experience to everyone, we were all in the same boat and we were going to be one big happy family. So you can imagine how upset I was when I watched the footage and heard what she actually thought of me. Vicky had said, 'She's not real, she irritates the hell out of me!'

As if that wasn't enough drama for one night, things were about to get steamier. Sophie and Charlotte had been throwing up in the girls' bedroom for the majority of the evening. I didn't want to sleep in sick stench, so when Gary said I could join him in his bed, I thought it would be a good idea. All night he'd been flirting with me on the sly, allowing me to touch his washboard abs and toned pecs. I'd go so far as to say I fancied him.

When we got into bed together, it wasn't long before his hands and my hands began to wander. We didn't have sex, but let's just say there was some undercover action and we did some rude things, which I'll let you in on later.

That was only my first night in the house and already I'd set the tone for the rest of the series. The producers must have been rubbing their hands with glee at my downright outrageous behaviour, but I honestly didn't care.

Like the north-east's own torrid coastline, *Geordie Shore* promised to be anything but plain sailing. Times ahead were going to be stormy, rough, turbulent, wet and wild. Only the ones with a crazy sense of adventure would be able to hack it. I'd thrown caution to the wind and was up for the journey from the moment I stepped into the house. It was clear to everyone who ran the show: I was the one who would ride the surf and take the boatload of chances that came my way. Already I'd made more waves than anyone on the first night, which was great for the programme. I was delivering gold star footage without even being told what to do.

Only that night, when I was asleep in Gary's bed, I began to wonder if I could actually survive there. I was game for anything but thinking about the unwelcoming reception I'd received from the other housemates made me feel doubtful. I'd been interrogated and chastised, grilled by a gang of guzzling Geordies and then ridiculed. I had this sick feeling in the pit of my stomach. What had I let myself in for?

Already I'd been reduced to tears in a matter of hours and maybe I wasn't so tough after all. Maybe I'd made a bad decision, signing up to live with these people. Perhaps it was a horrendous mistake, getting involved in something out of my control. Maybe I should have listen to my mam when she tried to shield me from this upset. For the first time since I'd applied for the show, I was scared and confused.

I was *Geordie* Un*shore*.

Chapter Fourteen

THE OUTSIDER

I'd like to say those 'outsider' feelings subsided after the first night in the *Geordie Shore* house. And I'd like to tell you that I never cried tears for the rest of the series and we were one big happy family, just as Vicky had said we would be, but fans of the show will know that's not how it worked out.

The cracks began to appear on our first official night out, down at Riverside club. For me the whole evening was awkward, from start to finish. Everyone was chatting and buzzing off each other, but I was always the one left out on the sidelines. All night, I was pretty much ignored by everyone, which made me so upset. By the end of the evening, I was in floods of tears again over the way I'd been snubbed.

I felt slightly guiltily, too. I still hadn't told my boyfriend about the liaison with Gaz. It was irking me, so I called him the next day and decided to confess just to kissing him. I didn't say anything else had happened, because to be honest I wasn't quite sure what went on. When I told Dan, he was, quite rightly, gutted. I'd made him look like a mug and I made myself look like a slag, too. Despite this upset, he managed to keep his cool. He said he still loved me and it hadn't changed anything between us.

On my second night out with the group we headed to Oh So. It was the same shit, different day. They all continued to ignore me and were only interested in pulling. And because I had a boyfriend, I felt like I wasn't included. I'm not proud of it, but I cheated on Dan again. I grabbed the nearest half-decent lad to me, started grinding all over him, cornered the guy and kissed his face off. Yeah, I know it sounds ridiculous, but snogging on with that guy made me feel more like part of the gang, even though I knew it was destroying my relationship.

The producers then decided to shake up the action by inviting Dan and my best friend Christie to come and visit me in the house. I was absolutely thrilled to see them both – it was a tiny piece of familiarity in this strange place. While we were sitting in the garden I admitted to Dan about cheating on him for a second time. It was pretty cruel of me. I just blurted it out, like it was no big deal, while all the other housemates were in the kitchen. I knew he would never cause a scene in front of them, but I'd totally embarrassed him.

If that wasn't bad enough, then poor Dan had to meet Gary face to face, knowing full well this was the guy I'd cheated on him with on the first night. You could tell Dan was humiliated, especially when Gary strode over to him confidently, smiled like a Cheshire cat and shook his hand. It was ruthless.

But I never appreciated how Dan must have felt because I

didn't love him in the way he loved me. I just kept telling him to 'get over it', 'forget about it' and 'don't mention it again' – not fully understanding my behaviour was tearing him apart inside. In hindsight, I think I was deliberately sabotaging the relationship. I didn't need Dan anymore. I was young, wild and having fun on a TV show. I didn't know what the future had in store for me, but whatever it was, in my heart of hearts, I knew it didn't involve Dan. The trouble was I didn't have the guts to tell him it was over. If he'd have turned round to me and said 'You're dumped', I wouldn't have cared.

That evening, Dan came out with the *Geordie Shore* gang. It was a Friday night and we were all in the VIP room of Tup Tup Palace. I'd spent about three hours getting ready. Newcastle is a tiny city and a busy scene; you're always under constant scrutiny so it's always important to look your absolute best. Never mind the fact I was being filmed for a TV show.

I was excited to get out and I wanted to get absolutely mortal so I drank everything I could get my hands on. I necked shot after shot. I sank wine, Jägermeister, vodka, gin, sambuca, rum... everything, until I couldn't physically pick up another drink. I was acting like a complete lunatic. So much so that when I was dancing all over the furniture, I fell backwards and smashed a windowsill of decorative vases.

Vicky saw me do it and, instead of just laughing it off because I was hammered, she scolded me like I was a child in front of the entire VIP room, humiliating me. For Christ's sake, I hadn't meant to do it intentionally! I wouldn't have minded but it's not like Vicky was prim and proper and had never got into a state in her life.

After she yelled at me, the alcohol took hold. I burst into

tears again and stormed out of the club. Dan tried to stop me, but I was hell-bent on leaving. Like a woman possessed, I kept screaming at him. I didn't want to be with these people anymore. I wanted to be as far away from them as I could be. Dan tried to restrain me and calm me down, but I was having none of it. I was leathered and lashing out at him like some kind of crazed animal. I didn't know if I could live with these people any longer. I was nearly at breaking point.

When he left the next day, I was sad to see him go because he was the only person I could speak to and I realised for the first time I was so terribly unhappy. By contrast, everyone else in the house, in their own way, looked happy. Whether they *were* happy or just looked it, I couldn't be sure. All I knew was how I was feeling and I was lonely. Sounds crazy, doesn't it? In a room full of people, I was lonely. It was as if I were the only one there who was not truly part of the scene. But it doesn't matter if you're in the biggest crowd, if you don't feel you can trust or talk to anyone then you really do feel alone.

Everything came to a head when we went out to Bijoux. That morning I'd decided if things didn't change between the group and me then I would leave the show for good. I gave it my best shot that night and tried everything I could to involve myself. I remember trying to dance with the girls but they would deliberately leave me out, turn their backs and start dancing with someone else. And let me tell you, there is no gesture more devastating than a back turning away. I knew this wasn't all in my head; they genuinely didn't like me and they had no time for me. It was pointless putting myself through this stomach-churning agony any longer: I had to go.

Back at the house, I packed my suitcase and wrote Charlotte

a note, saying, 'I'm sorry, I love you. Hol x'. She was the only one who'd ever given me the time of day. The other guys didn't give a fuck when I left... they just saw it as another way to bitch about me behind my back. They never gave me a chance because they weren't interested in getting into my knickers. That bunch of lads, excuse my crudeness, were total fanny rats. For those unfamiliar with the term, a 'fanny rat' is a lad who is after all the fanny (girls) and getting into all the fanny. It's a vile turn of phrase, if you ask me, but I'm only using it here because that's the way they used to describe themselves. I wasn't the type of girl they wanted to get into. If I'd been the house stunner, just imagine how different my time there would have been – they would have been begging me to stay.

I left for three days, relaxed with Mam and my boyfriend, and thought about my future on the show. The producers weren't happy with my departure, but they understood I needed some time away from the housemates.

Going home did me the world of good and it made me realise I didn't want to leave the show. I wasn't going to let these people ruin my opportunity, my dream; whatever it took, I was determined to make it work. I called the producers and told them I wanted to be reinstated in the house, a decision they were delighted with. They would have the full cast back in action, ready to tear up Newcastle once again.

Now, I'd be lying if I said I wasn't nervous about going back into the house. I felt like I'd been a tad irrational in leaving in the first place, but that night after Bijoux, I couldn't take any more of their ignorance. When I returned, I crept in and went to visit each one of the housemates in their bedrooms to tell them I had returned. I don't know what kind of reception I was expecting, not a huge fanfare or anything like that, but I kind of hoped they'd be pleased to see me. But as I spoke to each one of them, they were totally nonplussed. Whether or not I was there had no effect whatsoever. I gave them all the benefit of the doubt because they were all hungover and sleeping, so maybe I couldn't blame them for not being more thrilled.

The first night I was back, we all went out as one big group and it was like they had completely changed. I felt included, I could be myself, no one ignored me and I had one of the best nights ever. I was on a high.

Only, like everything in life, what goes up, must come down.

The night after, when we were discussing the bedroom situation, I realised the change had been short-lived. Since I'd left, Vicky had taken my place in the girls' room and now she didn't want to budge. We discussed a few options between ourselves and it basically became this horrible conversation where everybody said in a roundabout way that they didn't want me in their room. I sat there in silence, feeling incredibly awkward. No one wanted to get lumbered with me, which cemented me as the outsider again. They made me feel like I'd come back and spoilt everything.

And they all kind of sighed, tutted and muttered. They were annoyed that they were going to have to move around bedrooms, but if everyone had just gone back to the way they were, there would have been no stress. The whole group was seething because of a minor upheaval. I couldn't understand why it was such an issue. The reason I couldn't understand was because I didn't realise how much they actually disliked me.

I was feeling low when we went out that evening and no

matter how much I drank, I was just miserable. Everything had reverted back to the way it had been before. Once again I was totally ignored by everyone. I was left out of everything. No one wanted to be in a room with me, or talk to me, or get to know me. It was heartbreaking.

Distressed, glum and hysterical, I was a whirlwind of emotions. All those feelings mixed up with a mass quantity of alcohol proved a recipe for disaster. I hated everyone, hated myself, hated the way I looked, hated the way I felt, and most of all, the way I was treating Dan. He still had no idea what had happened with Gaz on the first night. I'll admit it got to third base with him and the guilt was eating me up inside. In a drunken stupor, I fled back to the house and called him to confess all.

When he answered the phone, he could instantly tell I was in a state, so he just let me talk.

And so I began. 'The first night, I can't remember a fucking thing,' I sniffled, 'and everyone said, including Gary, that I wanked Gary off. I can't remember a fucking thing, Dan.'

There was a long pause.

'You need to finish with me now, just do it,' I added, between sobs.

'I thought you loved me,' he said, devastated.

'I *do* love you!' I howled, 'I can't even remember what happened, but why would Gary lie? He has no reason to.'

Meanwhile Dan was just breathing heavily down the other end of the phone. He was stunned into silence.

'You're fucking well better than I am! You deserve so much better than me,' I kept wailing. 'Don't look like a fucking mug, just finish with me.'

And I was gutless. I should have been the one to finish our relationship because I was clearly not as into him as I should have been. It should have been me that cut him loose, not me begging him to dump me. I realise now that I was being a coward, trying to get him to ditch me so I wouldn't feel so bad about him.

'It's fucking ridiculous how I'm treating you. It's fucking horrible and I hate myself!' I bawled. 'And I wish I could be better… but… I'm not. And I wish… I hadn't done it, but I did…'

All of a sudden the line went dead.

He'd hung up.

I threw the phone down in anger, continued to cry and once again felt completely alone.

Chapter Fifteen

FOOT LOOSE AND FANCY-FREE

The next day, I woke up feeling marginally better, but still empty. Finally, I'd admitted to Dan about the extent of my cheating, but I had no idea where this left our relationship. I called him again and he was still in a complete state of shock. He didn't know what to think, nor did I. I didn't want to be in a relationship, but I didn't want to be on my own either. He kept asking me, 'Do you want me to finish you?' and I didn't know what to say. I was being incredibly selfish. Maybe if I saw him again, I thought, I'd know how to feel, so I invited him to Oh So in Newcastle that evening. Whether he would actually turn up was anyone's guess.

I went out with the cast, as planned, and I was having a really good night. And I was well on my way to mortal when a friend of Gaz's took a shine to me. His name was Billy. He had spiky dark hair, toned muscles and a cheeky way about him. I remember thinking he was totally hot at the time and it made me laugh, the way he was engrossed by my huge boobs – he was fascinated by them, kept staring at them, touching them and feeling me up. I didn't try and stop him either. We danced together and I forgot about the situation with my boyfriend. It felt great to finally take my mind off the whole thing and relax.

Everything was shaping up nicely into a fantastic night. The music was great, I felt happy and I had this gorgeous guy giving me attention. Things were looking up… when all of a sudden Dan strolled in with three of my best friends, Christie, Leah and Tom.

Regardless of me inviting him, I didn't think he would actually come. Yes, I know I'd offered him a night out, but in all honesty it was an empty offer. Now he was there, I didn't want him to be. I wanted my own space, to do my own thing and not to have to worry about someone else.

The atmosphere had changed, too. Now that my boyfriend was in the same place as Gaz, the tension in the room was undeniable, and he knew I'd tossed him off behind his back. Any lad in his right mind should have tried to lamp Gaz and chuck me before you could even say 'Geordie Whore' but he didn't, which aggravated me. Either he didn't care enough, or he was spineless. Whichever it was, it totally put me off. I didn't have much respect for him before and now I had none.

So I continued chatting up Billy, practically in front of Dan. I even invited him back to the house so we could continue our flirt-fest. Jesus, my behaviour was dreadful! I had a lad who worshipped the ground I walked on, who had driven up thirty miles from Middlesbrough to spend some time with his girlfriend and I had completely fucked him off for a disco-dancing gel head only interested in my tits, who couldn't care less about me.

My priorities were all wrong.

Dan took me aside and asked me, 'Holly, do you want to be with me?' For the first time in our relationship, I said, 'I don't know.'

I watched as his face fell. He looked broken-hearted.

Dan must have loved me dearly because why else would he have bothered with me? He should have ended me a long time ago, but he was just clinging on to anything, I suppose. I said goodbye to him outside the club, left him like a wounded puppy, preferring to get in a taxi with his new arch-enemy Gaz and the boob-obsessed Billy. What a total bitch!

The next time I saw Dan was while my cast mate Greg and I were working at a furniture store, handing out flyers in Stockton. He turned up and kept asking, 'Do you want me to finish you? Is that what you want?'

And I was sick of the same conversation. I wanted to say 'yes' but I still didn't have the heart, so I gutlessly said, 'I don't know, Dan!' But I was getting really irritated. Couldn't he read between the lines?

I wanted out of this relationship – I had ever since I knew I was joining the *Geordie Shore* cast. There was no fight in me; I didn't care if I lost him. Eventually he did the right thing and told me it was over. I didn't try to stop him either or even protest. I just let him walk away.

For the first time in ages, I felt like a huge weight had been lifted from my shoulders. I could just concentrate on being myself. I could get more involved with the rest of the group, and I could be selfish without hurting anyone in the process.

Chapter Sixteen

BE CAREFUL WHAT YOU WISH FOR

'I'm not going back there, not ever!' I shrieked. 'I'm not living with fucking fake people. I've never known so many fake people in all my life!'

'What's happened?' my mam shouted, as she flung her arms around me. 'Tell me now, Holly. What's the matter?'

I could hardly get my words out. It was like they were stuck between breaths.

'I won't go back, Mam! I swear this time it's for good!'

I was struggling to make any sense. My face was covered in streams of mascara, there was a white snail trail where the tears had run through my tan and I could hardly stand up because I was so hammered.

It was around 10pm and my mam had been in bed when she heard a car screech up the driveway and a wailing girl outside her house. She wasn't expecting me home for another three days, so you can imagine how alarmed she was to see me home unexpectedly and in such a complete state.

She ran to the door and saw me blubbing and struggling to pull my big suitcase, flanked by two senior producers. I continued to scream over and over again, 'I fucking hate them! I hate that fucking house!'

Mam was flabbergasted. She didn't know what was real and what wasn't. She was trying to get me to calm down so I could explain the situation to her, but I was so drunk, everything was just coming out as one big repetitive sentence.

The producers enlightened her about what had happened and said I'd decided to leave *Geordie Shore* for good – again. She was angry she hadn't been informed of how unhappy I was and swiftly showed the producers the door. Her main concern now was me and my welfare. Calmly, she sat me down at the kitchen table and asked me to tell her exactly why I was so distraught.

X X X

The day had started off brilliantly. It was a Bank Holiday Monday and we were all out in Whitley Bay, having an all-day drinking session. I was really happy and getting on with everyone like a house on fire. It was the first time I actually thought, 'This is for me now.' We were coming to the end of the *Geordie Shore* experience and I was determined to go out on a high. I'd spent enough time being upset. I could have filled the Tyne with the amount of tears I'd cried. Now, it was time to have some guiltless fun before the series was over.

But as soon as we got back to the house, the turbulence hit.

It was pathetic when you think about why this argument broke out, but when you've got eight pissed-up, sleep-deprived Geordies there was bound to be some kind of kick-off.

We had all gathered outside by the hot tub. I wanted to have a cigarette, but Greg told me to 'fuck off down the other end of the garden' because no one else wanted to breathe my smoke, which was fair enough. But the way he said it was totally out of order. He screamed at me and, because I had a few drinks inside me, I screamed back. I was standing up for myself for the first time in four weeks.

'Shut the fuck up, man!' he yelled, more aggressively than was necessary.

'Don't you *dare* speak to me like that!' I screamed.

'What the fuck are you going to do about it?' he said, snarling at me.

'I swear to God...'

'What the fuck are you going to do about it?' he interrupted again.

I felt the temper inside me burst and in a surge of anger, I threw the wine glass I was holding down at the table next to Gaz and stormed off before I could even hear it smash.

This time I knew I'd gone too far. Like a grenade with the pin out, I had exploded into a ferocious rage.

'Greg, you're a fucking idiot!' I thundered. 'All I wanted was a fag and you had to be a fucking dick!' My eyes stung and filled.

'Don't call me a fucking idiot, you've just fucking swilled Gaz. Just fuck off!'

His reaction had been irrational. Greg was the eldest in the house, while I was the youngest and there was no need to threaten me in that way. It was so unnecessary. What hurt the most was no one was trying to calm the situation down. No one backed me up. I always remember someone saying, 'In the end, we will remember not the words of our enemies, but the silence of our friends'. And it was abundantly clear I had no friends here.

I stormed back into the house, dragged my suitcase out and began to gather my things. Now I was the outsider again and I couldn't cope with it. I needed to go. I couldn't handle the housemates anymore. Utter turmoil was what I was feeling. It made me so angry and frustrated that I wanted to smash the house up – I'd never felt rage like this before.

Bags packed, I walked into the kitchen where all the housemates were sitting. I don't think they thought I would actually leave this time, but when they saw me with my luggage in tow, they knew I was serious.

Charlotte and Vicky both tried to get me to change my mind, but I was gone. With every breath, my distress and agitation increased. I was so upset that I couldn't even recognise the faces of the people sat before me.

I was just a naïve eighteen-year-old girl, homesick and sad, reacting to a stupid argument in the only way I knew how.

As I was about to walk out the door, Jay suddenly piped up. I thought, like Vicky, he was going to wade into this argument, sort it all out and ask me to stay. The alpha male of the group, everyone looked up to him, and if anyone could have nipped this in the bud it would have been him.

'Holly, stay there,' he said, looking me straight in the eye.

At last I thought he was going to fight my corner, leap to my defence and make Greg apologise for his behaviour.

But Jay continued, 'Because I'm not a two-faced cunt, I'm going to tell you how it is…'

Above: On my dad Barry's lap, with my half-brother Leon.

Below: I was always destined to get mortal, even in nappies!

Above: This is my nana's partner Alan, just after Middlesborough won the Carling Cup at Wembley. He was a great guy and I miss him dearly.

Below left: My school photo when I was nine. Check out the blue clip-in pieces… I suppose I've always had a thing for changing my hair colour.

Below right: Just look at me here – sweet and innocent. Who knew I would wind up being a ladette on TV?

Above: Doing it in style! My mam got me and my friends a limo for my tenth birthday. I felt like such a diva.

Below: I had such an amazing time swimming with dolphins on the island of Margarita.

Above: With my mam Vicky and sister Darci in Egypt on my 16th birthday.

Below left: Ready for a night out on holiday in Portugal when I was 15.

Below right: THAT prom dress! I loved it at the time.

Above: One of our first ever photoshoots for *Geordie Shore*. It was mint.

©Tony Kyriacou/REX

Below: Maybe it was a bit cold for bikinis, but it was so exciting to be involved in the show!

© WireImage

Above left: With (from left to right) Lizzie Cundy, Amy Childs, and Harry Derbidge at the opening of Amy's salon in Essex. I get on really well with the *TOWIE* cast.

© *Getty Images*

Above right: I've made it! With Perez Hilton at his party in London in 2012.

© *Redferns via Getty Images*

Below: The girls doing what we do best at the MTV Europe Music Awards in Amsterdam.

© *Getty Images for MTV*

Above: Just after I jetted back from Australia, still sporting the purple locks. Here I am with Chidgey from *The Valleys*. ©*REX*

Below: Who would have thought we would end up being invited here? It was such an amazing day. © *Greg Blatchford/REX*

Back to my (nearly) natural hair colour at the *Reveal* awards in 2014.

© James Shaw/REX

I was baffled and confused, I didn't know if he was being sound or snide.

'Before you left the first time,' he started, a finger pointing in my face, 'I thought you were alreet. Now, since you've been back, you've done my head in!'

Talk about kicking me when I was down. It was a low blow. As if I hadn't been through enough, his callous words went through my heart like a knife. I was overcome with pain and I had to get out of there as fast as possible.

Everyone seemed to get along and have this bond, except me. They would make jokes behind my back. It was as if I didn't know what they were talking about. Everyone seemed to be able to relate to each other in some way, yet they treated me like I was a foreigner and I didn't understand the language.

No matter how much I wished for it, no matter how many eyelashes or dandelion seeds I could have blown on, no matter how much of my heart I tore out and slapped on my sleeve, it just wasn't going to happen: I was never going to fit. I'd tried to blend in with them before and couldn't.

For the first time in years, I felt what it was like to be an outcast once again. It was like school all over again. And with tears coming to my eyes, I recalled every time I'd been cruelly teased and bullied for no reason over the past four weeks. None of it was physical, yet somehow the names I'd been called, the comments about my boyfriend and where I was from hurt more than the pain any hand could have inflicted. Not all forms of abuse leave bruises, you know. Right then, I was hurting like I was when I'd been battered round the schoolyard.

X X X

'That's it now, Holly. It's over. You're not going back on that show,' Mam said, as she cuddled me tightly.

'I just don't get why they hate me so much, Mam. What have I done?'

But my mam couldn't answer me. No one could, except for the other housemates. If I knew why I was pissing them off so much then I would obviously have tried to change. I didn't want to leave the show, this was my absolute dream and now it was ruined for reasons I just didn't get.

After that argument, I never wanted to see any of them again. I felt like I'd made the biggest mistake of my life being part of the show. My mam was in bits for weeks, knowing all this drama was going to be shown on TV. In a way, she blamed herself for not putting her foot down more with me, but she was never going to stop me from pursuing my dreams. The whole situation was tough on her, but not once did she say 'I told you so'. She was there to pick up the pieces.

My dad was sad for me, too. He knew how excited I'd been about being picked for the show and he was gutted it hadn't worked out the way I'd wanted. He would tell me to keep my chin up and make the best of a bad situation, but I couldn't see the wood for the trees at that point. Like an empty shell of my former self, I hid myself away and hibernated in my bedroom for what seemed like weeks. My stepdad John was a good support, too. Although he didn't really say anything directly to me, I knew he was there for me instinctively and, if I had wanted any advice from him, I knew I could have asked him. Being around Darci also helped me take my mind off things. She was such an innocent little thing and just playing with her for a few hours would help me forget all that had happened on the show. It was a welcomed break, and one I desperately needed.

It's right what they say – 'Be careful what you wish for, because it might come true'. I'd wished so badly to get on *Geordie Shore*; I never considered the consequences might be bad. I never envisaged being hated by the cast and having such a terrible time that I'd be forced to leave twice in four weeks.

I was in a worse position than ever. No money. No job. No boyfriend. No reason to get out of bed anymore. When I think back, I was quite depressed after filming and I definitely lost my sparkle.

At that point *Geordie Shore* had only been commissioned for one season. I didn't even know if there was going to be another series but if there was, I most certainly didn't want to be a part of it.

Chapter Seventeen

TV FILTH SPARKS ANGER

24 May 2011 was the day my life completely changed. It was the day *Geordie Shore* aired on MTV for the very first time.

For most of the evening I'd been on tenterhooks, pacing up and down the house, counting down the hours until it was nearly onscreen. A part of me couldn't wait to watch it, to see how I looked, how it had been edited and what the other housemates had said about me. Then the other part of me was so nervous my heart would race uncontrollably when I thought about my debauched antics in the house.

It had been roughly three months between when we'd filmed *Geordie Shore* and the launch night. In that time I hadn't spoken to any of the other cast members. I was still upset with them all. As far as I was concerned, we weren't friends and I had no interest in becoming their friends. But that night I was going to have to man up because MTV was throwing a huge launch party at the Grosvenor Casino in Newcastle, where we could watch a preview of the show an hour before it was due to air. It was kind of awkward when I saw the housemates again, but everyone was pleasant, as if nothing had ever happened between us all.

We were allowed to invite our friends to the screening and I was delighted that I could take my friends Laura and Christie. I was glad they were with me, especially because it was just the support I needed. The mams and dads weren't invited, I think because the producers didn't want the backlash from parents, which would probably end up in big screaming matches about how their beloved child had been edited. Plus, if they weren't there, we could all go out later and get mortal.

I couldn't quite believe what they were about to witness, though. Sick with nervous anticipation, I was biting my nails and I couldn't concentrate on anything.

We all sat down ready to view our brand new show, which was about to take the world by storm. I don't think I'm exaggerating when I say we exploded onto the screen like an atomic bomb of six packs, shots, fights, booze, bust-ups and exposed boobs. At various points in the show, the 80-strong room fell silent because of our vulgar exploits. They watched us strip, vomit and saw me cheat on my boyfriend.

Many times, I had my head in my hands. Seeing myself behaving like a complete trollop with my tits and ass hanging out wasn't the best way to start a media career. And I hated the way I looked onscreen, too. I knew I'd put on weight, but at the time of filming it hadn't bothered me. I thought I was only a few pounds over the norm, but when I saw myself in glorious two-dimensional HD, it certainly didn't look that way. I know they say the camera adds ten pounds, but in my case it was more like ten stone. I looked colossal. My chin and legs were humongous!

I didn't come across very well at all but I'm not one of those reality stars who'll say I was edited badly on purpose. They can only show what you, yourself, have done. If they haven't got the footage of you getting your boobs out, obviously they can't show it. I knew they wanted to make the best show they could, so they were going to pick out the juiciest and worst parts of our behaviour. I can't blame anyone for that.

After I'd seen the preview I called my mam just to prepare her for the shock of what she was about to see. I told her straight: I'd bared my chest and ended up in a steamy clinch with Gaz. The topless thing she wasn't overly concerned with, but she was really pissed at me when I confessed to fooling around with Gaz. To hear me say I'd cheated on my boyfriend didn't sit well with her. She knew what people would say about me, and that was why she never wanted me to get involved in the show in the first place.

The morning after the first show aired, John's brother knocked on the door of our house at 7am. My mam answered and he handed her a copy of the *Daily Star* newspaper. I was on the front page with my boobs out under the headline, 'SEX AND BOOZE TV FILTH SPARKS ANGER. MTV SHOW IS INSULT SAY VIEWERS – BAN IT!'

He was stunned and my mam didn't know what to say apart from, 'Thanks, I'll look at that later.' I mean, what could she say? I'd mentally prepared her for what she was about to see, but when she witnessed it for herself she was dumbfounded.

The whole of John's family had been sending him texts. Like the rest of the nation, they were speechless. The young girl they knew, the little bridesmaid at that wedding, had grown up into a beer-swilling loon, parading herself on national TV with her ginormous breasts out. A couple of texts just said, 'We don't know what to say.' And John, bless him, would simply reply, 'Don't say anything at all.'

Like I said, they weren't the only ones who went berserk. The whole country had been disgusted by the show and Newcastle folk more so than anyone else. With their angry comments, they almost sent the social networking sites into meltdown. Within minutes of the programme being aired, they were demanding it should be axed for giving Geordies a bad name. Dozens of Facebook protest pages were set up, including 'Geordie Shore aka Geordie Whore', 'GET Geordie Shore AXED' and 'RIP Geordie Pride'. And because I was the most outrageous character on the show, all the negativity centred on me. I was used as the poster girl for their bashing. The critics hated it, Geordies hated it, my family hated it and in some ways I hated it, too. I'd had a horrible experience on *Geordie Shore* and I would have to endure another five episodes of grief still to come.

Having said that, I still loved the fact that even though the coverage was wholly negative, it was me they were writing about. They weren't featuring any of the other girls or lads, it was just me. So I kind of reasoned in my own head I wasn't going to get anywhere without causing a stir. The way I saw it, if people don't gossip or talk about you, you are not making waves. And I was making huge rip curls on the *Shore*: any press is good press.

I knew that's why the show's producers had picked me in the

first place, because I gave them what they wanted. The least popular housemate, I was also the least popular on Twitter, but I had all the exposure, too. They adored the fact I was so unscrupulous. Even though I had a boyfriend, I was willing to cheat on him. I told them I didn't mind having sex on camera. I would get pissed, get my tits out, shout and scream, and argue if I had to; I wouldn't hold back. Plus, I was young and stupid enough to be manipulated. When they heard my interviews, it must have been music to their ears because everything I was saying was giving them content for the show.

In true professional style, I had under-promised and over-delivered. Without me in the house, the storylines would have been pretty thin on the ground. Yeah, you had the Gary and Charlotte story, plus the Jay and Vicky will-they, won't-they scenario, but it was up to me to provide the rest of the drama.

X X X

I never knew what all the other housemates were saying about me at the time, but one part of that first series really sticks in my mind. It was episode three, during Charlotte's green screen, when she said, 'Holly doesn't realise they all hate her.' I'd been watching the episode round at one of my friends and I kind of felt embarrassed even watching it in front of someone else. When I heard what she'd said I hit rock bottom. I didn't let on to my friend that those words had really affected me, I just plastered on a smile in front of her, but as I walked home that evening, I was incredibly upset. I kept reading my tweets and the majority of them were nasty. That night I went straight into my house and shut myself away in the bedroom. One of the producers called to see if I was OK and, as soon as I got on the phone, I just unloaded. I cried all night. But I didn't want anyone to know how much the show was affecting me, especially not my mam. That was exactly what she'd been trying to shield me from in the first place and I didn't want her to turn round and give me the third degree.

Mam would never have known I was upset had it not been for one of the producers ringing her and asking her to check on me. She was shocked when she heard I'd been crying the night before because she'd seen the way I'd handled the backlash from the press. I'd taken all that in my stride because to me those opinions didn't matter. They weren't people who knew me, or had ever met me so why would their opinions count? What really bothered me was the rest of the house. They had met me, spoken to me, lived with me and still they hated me. I couldn't understand what I'd done to rub them up the wrong way so badly. It was tough hearing the other housemates slag me off but what could I do? That was the whole point of the show: to air your opinions and say what you liked.

Before *Geordie Shore* I thought I was such a confident person, who didn't care what people thought of me. With hindsight, nothing could be further from the truth. I was terribly insecure. I'm not making excuses for it, but I believe the way I'd behaved was an attempt at masking all my insecurities. I was self-conscious, I had low self-esteem, but I would act like I was the most confident girl in the room. Now, I didn't know what I was: confident or shy, bold or timid, secure or insecure, acting or being real? I was head-spinningly confused, a total contradiction in terms.

By the end of the first series, I was a shattered girl. The last episode aired and I was inexplicably disturbed by it. What the viewers saw onscreen, when Greg and I had the big bust-up, was a complete car crash. I was having a breakdown and no one realised just how destructive the whole experience had been. I could barely watch the episode. It was as if I was observing someone else, a different girl in the unfolding scene. My whole body began to tremble and I felt a burning red-hot anguish from deep within my belly. It was horrendous.

If that wasn't bad enough, everyone now had an opinion on me. If I went out, girls would start arguing with me for no reason. Lads would point at me in the street and say, 'There's that slag off *Geordie Shore*'. I don't care who you are, but abusive and threatening language is never OK, and those comments really hurt.

It was terrifying at times, too. Once I was out in a club and I had a drink thrown over me, which was fucking horrible. I was constantly living in fear that next time it was going to be a fist, or a glass or a knife. The whole time I felt like a zoo animal, with people leering at me.

Meanwhile, my Twitter followers were growing daily but so too was the online abuse. I had to read the backstabbing comments from the other housemates and, at the same time, abuse was constantly being tweeted to my phone. I'm not embellishing the facts when I say ninety per cent of the comments I received were despicable.

They were vile, disgusting messages that no one should ever have to endure. I didn't know how to handle it. Yeah, we'd had media training, but nothing could prepare me for being called a 'fat slag who needs to die'. Or grown men telling me I 'deserved to be raped, have my throat slit and be dumped in the Tyne'. I kid you not; they were actual comments I received. None of the other cast got grief like that, which is why they never understood why, at that point, I was at my lowest ebb.

Some of the less sympathetic around me kept saying, 'Well, you knew what you were signing up for', which is fucking ridiculous. I'd signed up for a reality TV show, not physical and mental abuse, arguments, threats and downright cruelty. Just because I was now in the public eye didn't mean every man and his dog had carte blanche to give me hell. It was wrong for a naïve eighteen-year-old to receive death threats from grown men.

Those days were dark, I'm not going to lie. I had no clue what to do with my life and I had to borrow money she didn't have off Mam. I wasn't spending it on going out and getting drunk either, it was just to survive.

At the time I was being represented by Money North, who were in charge of getting me paid media work, but because I was so unpopular no one wanted to know. I didn't even have enough money to pay my £30 phone bill.

The more of the series I watched, the more I hated it and everyone else on it. It had been a disaster from start to finish, but I was still under contract with MTV and so I had to honour it in certain ways. I remember one morning I was booked to go to London with the rest of the cast for three days to do press interviews. That day I woke up and just stared at my train tickets, feeling sick in the pit of my stomach. The thought of spending the next seventy-two hours in the other housemates' company was impossible. I hadn't really slept the night before and when I did eventually manage to nod off, my dreams were filled with feelings of inadequacy, anxiousness and embarrassment. It was really playing on my mind and I didn't want to go.

My mam came in and sat on the edge of my bed. Seeing my distress, she even offered to call the producers to say I was too ill to go down to London. But while I didn't feel any loyalty towards the rest of the cast, I didn't want to let the producers and crew down. During filming I had grown close to them because I felt they were the only ones I could talk to. In the end, I dragged myself out of bed because I was sick of festering.

At that time, *Geordie Shore* was the only thing going on in my life. If I didn't have that, I would have no purpose whatsoever. I had to ignore my feelings and make the best out of a bad situation.

Chapter Eighteen

MAGALUF MADNESS

It was the legendary Coco Chanel who once said, 'A woman who cuts her hair is about to change her life', and she wasn't wrong. I'd not only cut my tresses but dyed them a bright, cherry-red hue, too. Gone was the mass of black and blonde straggly extensions; now I had luscious scarlet locks. It had been an impulse decision at the hairdressers one afternoon, but ever since my mane modification, things had started to look up.

I'd also been on a diet and managed to lose a stone in four weeks, an incredible achievement for a McDonald's addict like me. The diet was nothing special, just smaller healthier meals. Basically if you couldn't kill it, catch it or pick it, I wouldn't eat it. Absolutely nothing processed was passing my lips. It's amazing what you can do with a little determination and self-motivation. And there was nothing more motivating than those two fear-inspiring words: 'bikini season'. With that in mind, I was hell-bent on getting my ass into shape.

I was about to parade myself on TV in a two-piece while partying in Magaluf on the Majorcan isle because *Geordie Shore* had been commissioned for a summer special and they wanted me back in the mix.

At first I didn't want to be part of the show again. For me the first series had been extremely heartbreaking and I wanted nothing more to do with the other housemates, but the producers were determined to persuade me to come back and give the whole thing another go. They explained the summer special could be my chance to turn it all around. I could see what they were saying, but it took me a while before I came to my decision.

For a few days I thought long and hard about it, reflecting on my behaviour and the way I came across onscreen. If I'm totally honest, I realised that maybe I was partly to blame. I hadn't been myself in the first series; I'd been the person that I thought they wanted me to be. Vicky was right – I wasn't being real. I was just trying to fit in, in all the wrong ways.

It was only after I bumped into Greg on a night out in Newcastle that I finally changed my mind. We had a little chat and I explained why I was dubious about going back. Greg had also felt a little left out at the beginning and understood where I was coming from. He actually rang the rest of the lads individually before we filmed in Magaluf and told them to give me a chance. He didn't need to do it, but I'll always be so grateful he did. I never properly thanked him... until now: Greg, thank you – you don't know how much that meant to me.

So there I was, with my hair dyed a marvellous shade of shocking red (the kind that would be popular with Parisian tarts, I should imagine), boarding a flight to Magaluf. Only this time instead of being the last one in the house, I was the first. And my God, what a house it was – it was mint! In all my life I had never set foot in such a beautiful place. A stunning five-bedroom villa, it was out of the way of the party strip, tucked neatly into the Majorcan hills, with a stunning azure-blue pool and beautifully landscaped gardens all round the side. The kitchen and living room had modern décor with all mod cons (not forgetting the requisite *Geordie Shore* fixed cameras). Of course the house was far too sumptuous for a group of lads and lasses like us, and it was only going to be a matter of hours before we desecrated it.

Although I was nervous about the way the housemates would act towards me, we were only filming for six days, so I figured I could stick it out for that long at the very least. One by one as each housemate entered our huge villa, they were all taken aback and over-complimentary about my new look, which made me feel a million dollars.

This series couldn't have started any better and it felt like a fresh beginning. I was in Magaluf, I was single... and more than ready to mingle!

It was on our first night out on the infamous strip that I started to look at James in a whole new light. At first I'd thought he was just like the rest, a typical pumped-up Geordie lad out to pull a worldie. Don't get me wrong, that's what he's like, but over the years I've also seen different sides to him. That particular night we'd been partnered up to play a game demonstrating different sex positions. He gripped me in all kinds of weird and wonderful ways. And when he *really* got going, I was given a glimpse of what he had to offer. My God, the lad had it all – strength, stamina, technique and the ability to give a girl a good pounding! He just went for it. During the first series of *Geordie Shore* I'd often wondered what it would have been like to bang James. I'd had some filthy dreams about him and now I was getting to feel what it would be like for real. Hands down, I can pinpoint my crush back to this very moment.

If that wasn't wild enough, I was about to turn lesbian for five minutes. We were in BCM nightclub and they were calling for girls to be involved in a wet T-shirt competition onstage. Now I'd seen a few of these competitions before on those boozy Brits abroad documentaries and instead of being repulsed by them, I actually thought they were ace. I'd already decided if ever the opportunity arose, I would compete in one.

Here was my chance. I grabbed a white top off the DJ, whipped off my bra and took my place under the shower onstage. The whole crowd was cheering, the music was thumping and I just let go. It was like watching one of those Herbal Essences shampoo adverts, where the girl screams with pleasure as she rubs her fingers through her hair and gyrates under the water. I was thrashing about under the downpour, twisting my hips, shaking my ass and fondling my own boobs in front of a riotous throng of clubbers.

I was completely and utterly soaked by the time I noticed another girl had joined me onstage. Without even thinking, I grabbed her by the petite waist and pulled her towards me. I ground my body against hers sexily, as if we were two women in a porno movie. The crowd loved it and I was determined to give them the show they wanted. In a moment of madness, I looked deep into her eyes, grabbed the girl by the face and began to kiss her passionately in front of everyone. The room erupted with screams and cheers. Tell you the truth, I enjoyed it – I'd never kissed another female before and might never do so again, so I took the chance when I could.

Call me crazy, but I think she enjoyed it, too. It wasn't like she was fighting me off and she kissed me back with more passion than most men I'd encountered. When we finished our eager stage snog, she whispered in my ear, 'I love redheads. It's not the hair colour, it's the crazy. You're so wild!' I laughed and showed her just how crazy I could be by pulling down my top and flashing my tits to a few thousand clubbers.

I loved the way I'd been so uninhibited, although I was still holding back in other ways. Throughout that series I was so scared of causing any controversy and during one major argument I left and went to bed. It had kicked off because Charlotte and me decided not to housesit the villa even though we'd been specifically told we must do so by our Magaluf boss. You see we weren't just in Magaluf to party, we were supposed to be looking after the villa for a week. (Yeah right!) Each night either one or two of us would have to stay in and mind the place. Having met six big burly men from Manchester, we were buzzing to meet up with them again in the evening.

I didn't mind staying in and housesitting too much because I didn't want to piss the lads off, giving them a reason to have a go at me, but Charlotte and the rest of the girls were adamant we were all going out. I was torn between not wanting to let the girls down and not wanting to annoy the lads. In the end, the girls wouldn't take no for an answer and dragged me out.

When the *Geordie Shore* lads came home to find the house empty they were pissed off. Then when we traipsed home with half a dozen Mancunian hunks behind us, they were raging. A huge argument kicked off because of all the noise we were making. Usually, I would have been in the thick of it but now, at the first sign of trouble, I removed myself from any of the drama.

In Magaluf, I had the best time of my life. I felt like I'd gone there a girl and come home a woman, like I'd been through a rite of passage. Most people my age go away to university, where they develop as a person and stand on their own two feet. I felt in some ways that's what I was doing on *Geordie Shore* and the difference in me from series one had been phenomenal. If the first series had been like this, it would have been amazing.

This time around when the summer special aired, I couldn't wait to watch it. The audience loved it, too, and the media work began to pick up. Don't get me wrong, I still hadn't 'made it' – I had very little money but now I had a new agent, Luke Mills from Misfits management, who really took me under his wing and started to fight my corner in terms of media exposure. I had previously been managed by Money North, but for whatever reason I just wasn't getting any work with them. A friend passed me Luke's email address and, out of the blue, I sent him a message. Luckily for me, he took me on. He really believed in me and it's a business relationship that is still going strong today.

Although I was still the least popular girl, Luke was about

to change all of that for me. I continued getting negative comments on Twitter, the majority of them disgusting, but they were peppered with the odd nice tweet about my new hair and the way I looked, which I really appreciated. My family and friends had all noticed a difference. They all commented that they had seen a positive change in myself. Now I was looking forward to every day and enjoying being on this adventure. For the first time in my life, I knew I was onto something good. It didn't know what, but I had a feeling that everything was going to be OK.

Chapter Nineteen

IT STARTED WITH
A TWEET

I was sat at home with my mam when I first saw him. That trademark, dishevelled hair, cheeky grin and trendy image immediately caught my eye. He bounded enthusiastically onto the screen wearing a plain white T-shirt, casual blue jeans and worn-in white trainers. It was effortlessly cool and I guess you could say I fancied him straight away.

It was a little Saturday night ritual Mam and I always had. We'd sit down and watch the *X Factor* together with a takeaway. Even if I was going out with my friends that night, I always made sure I kept that time free for some mother-daughter bonding. She'd commented on him, too. I remember her saying something about him being 'a cheeky chappie' and a boy I'd probably take a shine to. She really does know me well.

Of course the boy I'm talking about was Frankie Cocozza and I was watching his first ever audition on the *X Factor*, back in 2011. Despite his obvious good looks, it was also his confident honesty that attracted me to him. He wasn't afraid to embarrass himself a little, even when he admitted to tattooing seven girls' names on his bum and then showed it to the nation.

By the end of his audition song – the Zutons' 'Valerie' – he had won me over. So I searched for him on Twitter and sent him a harmless message, telling him how much I loved his performance. I never expected a reply or a follow-back and I certainly could never have predicted what would happen in the months that followed such an innocent tweet.

Later that evening, while I was busy applying my third layer of tan and getting ready for a night on the toon, I heard my phone spring to life with an email alert. I dismissed it as being spam and since my hands were covered in a thick layer of dark orange slime, I wasn't in a rush to check it. It was only after I'd fitted my lashes, plastered on the make-up and backcombed my hair into a huge bouffant, I even bothered to look.

I clicked on my emails and I'm not ashamed to admit, but I was instantly giddy when I saw the words 'Frankie Cocozza has sent you a direct message' in my inbox. I remember running downstairs and telling my mam with excitement.

'Mam! That Frankie from the *X Factor* has sent me a message on Twitter!' It sounds stupid saying this now, but I'd never had anyone in the public eye take an interest in me up until that point. To me this was like a proper celeb and he'd sent me a message. I was ecstatic. I was like a hyperactive schoolgirl.

His message simply said, 'As if YOU followed me. ;)'

At this point, I wasn't *that* well known. I had about 67,000 followers on Twitter. We had filmed series one and a Magaluf special of *Geordie Shore*. I was getting recognised more and more, mainly because of the red hair, but I was still largely anonymous outside of Newcastle so I couldn't quite believe he knew who I was. Maybe he'd seen the show? Perhaps he was a fan? I didn't know. All I did know was I was hugely excited, but I still played it cool when I tapped back my reply, 'And why not? I thought you were great on X Factor ;)'

Our messages continued like this for a while, just innocent chit-chat about anything and everything. Things only started to get a little steamier when he asked for my number, which I gave him without question. He was Frankie from the *X Factor* and he was hot, why wouldn't I want to take things further? Afterwards he sent a barrage of naughty texts. I really wished I'd kept them to tell you about because they weren't half imaginative!

As he progressed on the *X Factor* I'd tune in with my mam and watch him take to the stage, singing his heart out. Frankie quickly became a favourite in our house and I'd text him a sweet message after every time I'd seen him perform, at boot camp and then at judges' houses. I remember being so happy for him when he made it to the live shows. I was really proud.

When we did eventually decide to meet up, we'd been exchanging strings of racy texts and the anticipation had been building up for weeks. I was down in London doing some media interviews for *Geordie Shore* and he asked to see me while I was in the capital. Of course I was flattered. I'd been flirting with him for ages and I was looking forward to the day when we could actually meet up in person. I thought he was a cocky bad boy. And what girl doesn't love a thoroughly good bad boy?

I remember feeling nervously excited in the afternoon before we were meeting, but I was stressing over what to wear. I'm sure most girls reading this have been there, trying to find the perfect outfit to impress the boy you like. Trying on a gazillion different outfits until you find the right one.

My hotel room was strewn with piles of clothes. I was in a complete tailspin. It was a cold October so I couldn't wear anything too skimpy, which meant half the clothes I'd brought would be unsuitable. I didn't want to wear anything too colourful either because it would clash with my bright red barnet. I must have tried on about fifteen different outfit combinations before eventually settling on a fail-safe LBD from Topshop and a chic black blazer to add an extra bit of warmth.

I took my time getting ready. I bathed, plucked, shaved and made sure I was as smooth as possible because, well, you never know where the night might take you. Then I washed, blow-dried and added volume to my hair with help from a handful of rollers and a half-hair wig. Layers and layers of tan were applied before I carefully did my make-up and finished off the look with some glam long lashes.

It was midnight before I was able to meet Frankie and I took two girlfriends along with me. He texted me the address of a private party he was throwing at a plush flat in Kensington. He'd been singing on the live shows that evening and said he was unwinding, away from the *X Factor* house.

On the way over there I was incredibly edgy. I had butterflies in my stomach and my palms were sweating. I kept asking my mates, how did I look and if they thought I needed more bronzer, or more lip gloss or to redo my hair. I was flapping so much. When the cab eventually pulled up outside the address, I couldn't believe how gorgeous the place was – a huge Georgian townhouse with pristine manicured gardens all round the outside. It must have easily been worth a few million.

Frankie was waiting at the door with his characteristic cheeky grin, beaming at me. As soon as I strolled over he took me by the hand, pulled me close and kissed me on the cheek.

'It's so good to finally meet you, babe,' he whispered in my ear.

'Good to meet you too, Frankie,' I replied, with a hint of excitement in my voice.

He took us through to the lounge, where the party was already in full swing. There must have been at least twenty people all mingling around, dancing to music and drinking. Some were Frankie's friends, some were his family and others were female groupies he'd picked up outside Fountain Studios, which is where the *X Factor* was being filmed. Some girls might have got jealous about that, but I just found it funny. I'd expect nothing less from the long-haired lothario, although, having said that, Frankie was a gentleman from the outset and, ever since I'd arrived, it was like he only had eyes for me.

He ushered me through to the kitchen, keeping his hand on the small of my back, and asked what I'd like to drink. Every surface in there was scattered with alcohol: vodka, beer, champagne, gin, tequila… You name it, he had it. It was almost like being back in the *Geordie Shore* house. I chose a vodka and coke and watched him as he carefully poured the mixture into a tumbler before handing me the glass.

'Cheers. Here's to a great night. You look gorgeous, by the way,' he said, clinking his glass with mine.

'Cheers,' I beamed, before adding, 'It's so nice to meet you in person.' We locked eyes for the first time.

The night continued in much the same way. Frankie was charming and attentive. He introduced me to all his friends and we had a great time. It wasn't until about 2am that anything romantic began to happen. He was still wearing eyeliner from his performance on the show and I kept ripping him, telling him he looked like Beetlejuice. Then, just as I was still giggling away at my own unfunny joke, he clutched my face gently and began to kiss me in the lounge in full view of everyone. At first I was taken aback but he was a good kisser and he put me at ease.

Immediately after, he led me away to the bedroom so we could be alone. Frankie was passionate and I could tell what he wanted straight away. He took the lead and I let him. Obviously, you can guess what happened next: we had sex and it's fair to say we both enjoyed it. He was a good lover and all in all, I had a great experience with fun-time Frankie.

Now, a lot has been in the press about what happened next, but this is the God's honest truth and how it actually happened.

After we'd slept together, my agent Luke texted me to see how my night had gone. I told him I'd spent the night with Frankie and like any publicist worth his salt, he asked if we could do some set-up pictures with the pair of us. I asked Frankie if he would be up for doing a few pap shots together in return for £1,000 and, without a moment's hesitation, he said yes.

Luke arranged for a pap to meet us at the address in Kensington with his camera. He made us stand outside and kiss while he took the shots he needed. I know lots of celebrities do this kind of thing all the time – they set up photographs and sell them to the newspapers for a good sum of money. This would be good publicity for the both of us and to be honest, I needed the cash. For the first time since I hit the screen, I was taking my career in my own hands.

Luke had scrabbled around his apartment, trying to find enough cash for Frankie. In the end he only managed to get £960 together, which he handed over in lots of crumpled-up notes. He had to write Frankie a cheque for the other £40, although to this day he's never cashed it. In hindsight, we should perhaps have offered him a lot less money because he would probably have done it just for a laugh. That's the type of guy he was; he just didn't care.

We sold the pictures for £10,000, although I didn't receive that amount. Don't get me wrong, I did well out of the photos and that was my first big pay cheque. It gave me the press I needed and it was the first time anything to do with *Geordie Shore* had really been of any interest to the tabloids. I remember buying the paper on the Monday and seeing the photos splashed over the front page of the *Daily Star* under the headline 'FRANKIE SHORE IS NAUGHTY'.

However, the week after was when all the trouble started. Frankie was giving an interview on the *Xtra Factor* to Caroline Flack and Olly Murs. They brought out a board that had the photos of us kissing on the front. Caroline asked him in a playful manner, 'So what's the truth behind the story?' and Frankie replied by saying, 'I met her, I banged her', with a shrug. To which a shocked Olly Murs replied, 'You can't say that!'

I never saw this exchange happen live onscreen because a few days after our liaison I was back in the *Geordie Shore* house filming series two. The first I heard about it was when a senior producer took me aside to tell me my mam had been on the phone in floods of tears about what Frankie had said. She'd been sat there with my little sister Darci and was absolutely devastated when she heard him disrespect me live on TV for millions of viewers to see.

I too was stunned when I saw the footage because I could have told the world I'd slept with him and earned three times as much money from the story, but I didn't; I didn't want to be a kiss and tell girl. I couldn't believe he had let me down like that. Yeah, I can take the abuse, and I wasn't bothered about how he'd made me look, but I was furious with him for upsetting my mam.

The producers took me out of the house for an hour and gave me a right to reply. I wrote a message on Twitter saying something along the lines of 'I would never have said what he said because I didn't want to embarrass his family and my family, despite being offered lots of money.'

I know what you're all probably thinking. Why did Mam get so upset? She'd seen me behave like that on *Geordie Shore*, surely she should be used to it by now? Well, it's never easy for any mother to hear her daughter being spoken of in such a degrading way. Also, you have to take the context of the show into account. The *X Factor* is a wholesome family show watched by millions and millions of people whereas *Geordie Shore* is on late at night on a Sky channel. You might not think that would make a difference, but it does. My little sister was watching and she shouldn't have to see her sister being disrespected by some guy. My mam does her best to shield Darci away from the nasty things that people say about me. Obviously I told my housemates and they were all gunning for Frankie. Yeah, we call each other horrible names at times, like all families do, but if anyone else says anything, you better watch out!

Four weeks later, when I got out of the *Geordie Shore* house, I texted him, telling him how much he'd humiliated me. 'It was a mistake,' he said. But the funny thing was, it felt like the mistake was mine, for trusting him to keep what went on in the bedroom private. How could I have been so naïve? I mean really, what did I expect? I know what lads are like – he was trying to act the big 'I am'.

I got so much abuse at the time, too, from girls telling me to back off Frankie. People were calling me a slag and saying Frankie was theirs, not mine. It was ridiculous. The only good thing to come out of it was I got an extra 9,000 Twitter followers.

I wish I could say my fraternising with Frankie ended there, but it didn't. A few months later, I saw he was doing an appearance in a club called Blue Bamboo in Newcastle. For a laugh, I thought it would be funny to drop in on him and have a drink for old times' sake, bury the hatchet and show there were no hard feelings anymore. I dragged my friend Leah who had been dying to meet him, along for the ride and I knew if anyone could appreciate a wild one like Frankie, it would be her.

We strutted into Blue Bamboo, which was already heaving with clubbers waiting to see the man of the moment. I never expected anyone would even be bothered about seeing me when there was a bona fide *X Factor* star on the bill, but as soon as I walked over to the bar, I had lads and lasses all over me. Grabbing me, pulling me, asking me questions and dragging me this way and that for photos. Stuff like that never really bothers me, but I was conscious there were only two of us out. I was worried all the unwanted attention was bothering Leah, so I decided we should leave. Ten minutes after we walked through the door, we were out of there before Frankie even arrived. Of course I wanted to see him, but not at the detriment of our night out. It would have been no fun for her to be standing round all night while fans chatted to me about the show.

We carried on our evening, hitting a few other clubs, until at 4am it was time to get back to our base for the night, The Royal Station Hotel. Weirdly enough, it was the same hotel Frankie was staying in.

Leah and me were in bed but still wide awake when we heard a light knock at the door. I leapt up from the bed in just my black lace underwear, looked through the spy hole and saw that unmistakable cheeky grin.

'What the hell are you doing here?' I said with a smile as I flung open the door.

'Alright, Holly!' he slurred in his southern accent. 'The desk told me what room you were in. Can we come in?'

Frankie had one of his pals with him and a bottle of vodka in his hand.

I let them both in and poured everyone a drink, using mixers from the minibar.

Frankie apologised again for his stupid comments on the *Xtra Factor* and he was genuine when he said it. I told him to forget about it and we made a toast.

It was clear there was still a huge attraction between us. I was flirting like it was going out of fashion, while Frankie kept getting all touchy-feely with me under the duvet. We both knew what we wanted, but it was kind of difficult because our friends were there, although Frankie didn't seem to care and in one bold swoop, he gently turned my face to his, kissing me full-on.

A few minutes later, we found ourselves in the tiny bathroom and, well, you've guessed it... we had sex over the sink. It was great, to be honest, and I have absolutely no regrets. We both came out of the bathroom beaming. Our friends just giggled, they knew exactly what we'd been doing.

After that I never heard from Frankie, which was fine. I was busy and so was he. Let's be honest, it was never going to be a great love affair, was it? In fact, I totally forgot about him until I picked up the *Daily Star Sunday* a few months later and saw he'd sold a story on me. He said in an exclusive interview with the paper that he got paid £1,000 to sleep with me. Which, as I've explained, wasn't the case: he got £1,000 for pictures of us kissing. When I read the article, I kind of felt like a dirty old man – he made out like I was paying for sex with a prostitute.

I'm not making excuses for him, but I understand why he did it. He obviously needed the money from the story. His fame was wavering on a downward slope, while mine was on the up. We did the photos for the publicity, to get us both some press coverage, nothing else. I laughed when I read the piece because he just made himself out to sound like a gigolo.

But I also think he did that interview out of spite because I once rated his bedroom skills as only being a four out of ten. To be honest I only said it in passing, but the press just jumped on it and made a mountain out of a molehill. If that was the reason then I probably can't blame him, but he shouldn't have lied about the details of our arrangement. I never have.

From start to finish the whole escapade with Frankie made me realise that I never want a famous boyfriend. It's totally put me off the idea of having a fella in the public eye. I have my home life and my work life and I don't want to mix the two.

I knew then that the guy I would end up with would just be someone normal, someone at the other end of the spectrum who had nothing to do with the media, but could handle my life in the limelight. Forget your drop-dead gorgeous actors and trendy pop stars, give me a big burly builder or a hunky lad from the forces any day!

Chapter Twenty

SECOND CHANCE

I'd spent most of the morning chain smoking and applying layer upon layer of make-up. I was so giddy with excitement I had to keep my hands busy; double-checking my eyelashes were on straight, making sure my lip liner was defined enough and shuffling my mahoosive boobies around until they were pushed up as far as possible. I'm renowned for taking an unusually long time to get ready, but today I'd taken even longer to make sure I looked good because I hadn't seen him for months.

The minute I heard the shrill of the doorbell ring, an overjoyed smile crept across my face. Just knowing he was outside the door gave me a little fanny flutter. I leapt up from the kitchen counter and yelled to Mother dearest, 'Mam, he's here! I'll be leaving in a minute.'

I swung open the door and was disarmed by his mischievous smirk. I hadn't lost any of my feelings for him and I still had a proper crush.

As you probably guessed, the guy was James. He was picking me up from my house and driving us to the new *Geordie Shore* digs for another six weeks of madcap madness. Series two was about to start filming and I couldn't have been in a better place.

I'd lost a bit of timber since I'd been working out with a personal trainer and keeping to a fairly strict diet (I limited the amount of kebabs and McDonald's I was scoffing). This time I felt positive, eager and confident. Half a stone lighter, hair even brighter, and now I'd seen James again, I was looking forward to our first overnighter. It was sexy smiles all round.

The pair of us rocked up to the new gaff, which was a converted warehouse on the outskirts of Newcastle. It was a fucking pad and a half! Bigger and better than anything I'd ever seen before.

Series two had also brought with it some cast changes. Greg had now left and even though we'd had our bust-ups, I was sad to see him go. He was the only nice, sensitive guy in the house. During the arguments he would be the voice of reason, which was great for the dynamics in the group but not for the producers who thrived on the disagreements and drama. In his place came two new housemates, Rebecca and Ricci.

Charlotte, James and me were all sharing a room, which really helped cement my friendship with her and my feelings for him. The producers knew what they were doing when they put us three in a room together. They had visions of Charlotte always being with Gary, which would leave James and me alone to flirt.

From the moment he'd collected me from home, I was hot for James. I don't really know what it was, probably the fact that I saw him as a challenge. I'd set my sights on him. I knew what

I wanted and I knew I would get him by any means possible. Resistance was going to be futile. Although that didn't stop me from tashing on with other canny lads. I was determined to get a bang on this series, whether with James, some other fit lad, or both. We had a new shag pad, which we aptly named 'the fuck hut' because it was like a shed in the bottom of the garden. One night I met a lad called Ben, who was actually one of James's best friends. I took him back to the fuck hut, but I was so mortal, we only ended up spooning. And it really was just spooning, no forking.

The filming had started brilliantly, the whole house loving the experience and the majority of the time we were all one big happy dysfunctional family. Except Charlotte was having a tough time. One morning quite unexpectedly she decided to leave the house because she couldn't stand to watch Gaz pull other girls in front of her. I never even got a chance to say goodbye. And I was gutted when I found out she'd left. I felt like I should have been there for her more.

I kind of knew how she must have been feeling because I was starting to get jealous when I saw James with other girls. My feelings were nowhere near as strong as Charlotte's for Gary, but when I saw him pull a girl called Lucy in front of me, it really got to me. I was watching them kiss and laugh together and I wished it could have been me in her place. She was James's type to a tee, skinny, naturally stunning and well, I just couldn't compete with her.

James aside, I'd also grown as a more confident person in this series. A fine example of how I'd changed was when Vicky and me had an argument about Charlotte leaving. We were pissed and she totally got the wrong end of the stick. Vicky blamed Gaz for making Charlotte leave and she thought I was backing him up rather than her, which wasn't the case. We got into a huge slanging match in front of the whole house. Back in the day, I would have probably tried to run off home, but now I was finally starting to stick up for myself. I'll admit Vicky did scare and intimidate me at first, but now I'd turned a corner. I wasn't going to be spoken to like a child anymore so I gave as good as I got and wouldn't be frightened off by her any longer. The feud didn't last long, we both ended up apologising to each other the next day, but it proved to me how far I'd come. Everyone else had seen a change in me, too – they were glad I was fighting my own corner.

Anyway, back to James and my mission to bang him. We were flirting outrageously, everyone could see it, but he still wasn't giving in. One evening when we were all out in town, James had pulled that worldie Lucy again. But I wasn't about to sit around and get upset about it. Two could play at that game and I'd fight fire with fire. I spotted this gorgeous guy called Aaron with funky floral tattoos all over his arms. As soon as I saw him, I grabbed him and necked on with him.

James took Lucy back to the house and not wanting to be left out, I took Aaron back, too... although someone else was using the fuck hut, which meant both James and me were going to be shagging in the same room. That might have put off some girls, but I thought it was hilarious. Determined to make James jealous and put him off his sexual stride, I was going to give Aaron the ride of his life and, at the same time, show James exactly what he was missing.

Aaron was great in bed and when the climaxing moment came, I couldn't help but be noisy with it. It must have been embarrassing for James, hearing us two go at it, but this was *Geordie Shore*, not a nunnery.

Over the next few days James and me carried on with our flirty banter or 'flanter' as we called it. I could tell he liked me and because I was more or less offering it on a plate to him, I couldn't understand why he didn't want a slice. I wasn't used to being turned down (usually lads can't wait to get a grip of the silicone girls), but I think James was worried about what the other housemates would say. I wished he would stop pretending like he didn't want to have his wicked way with me. I was his guilty pleasure and he knew it. It always came down to his freaking pride. However, his resistance only made me want him more. Excuse me for sounding like a predator, but I was just being persistent. If I genuinely thought James wouldn't touch me with a barge pole then I would have backed off, but he loved the attention, no matter what he might say these days. I just had to be craftier with my seduction techniques.

One night after we'd been drinking, I deliberately threw my baby wipes under his bed so I had an excuse to go over to his side of the room. God, it makes me cringe to remember how I was carrying on, but fuck it, fortune favours the brave and all that!

I put my hands under his duvet and slowly started fondling his crotch. He was embarrassed at first and quite confused, but he wasn't exactly fighting me off. I don't think he'd ever had a girl be that forward with him before. It sounds terrible to say I did that to him. Imagine if a boy had done that to a girl, it would be a totally different story. Anyway, despite his confusion, James didn't seem to mind me touching him up, and he was getting more excited by the second. Then he pulled back the covers and let me in for a cuddle.

James greatly overestimated his self-control because within minutes we were having sex – wild, rampant, full-on banging. This is what I'd wanted ever since we did those sex positions in Magaluf. Mission accomplished. Although, when I'd done the deed, I was a little disappointed. I suppose when you build something up so much, it's never as good as you expect. We lasted about fifteen minutes before I rolled off and went back in my own bed.

The morning after, James was annoyed at himself. He was actually ashamed he'd had sex with me. So much so that he made Rebecca swap rooms with him, which really upset me. He made me feel cheap and worthless. He was being so overly dramatic and it didn't have to be such a big deal as the sex hadn't been *that* bad. In fact it can't have been bad at all because it was only a week later that he was limbering up for round two. Only this time, the sex was a-maz-ing! I suppose we got all the nervous first time feelings out the way and now it had been pure, unadulterated lustful bonking.

During that series, we became really close. And soon it became less and less about wanting to have sex with him and more about wanting him to want me. I don't know if I wanted him as a boyfriend, but I certainly didn't want anyone else to have him; I was totally hooked.

You know what it's like when you sleep with someone, especially as a girl. You can't help but get feelings for them. It's a chemical reaction hardwired into us. Emotional attachment was inevitable. Women are emotional beings and the friends-with-benefits scenario very seldom works, but I got the feeling that's all James wanted.

I didn't want to leave the house because I knew I'd miss him.

Waking up to each other every day had been nice. Looking back now, I can see how he led me on, but at the time I was totally blindsided.

It would hurt me when I watched the series back and he'd say how much I annoyed him because at the end of the day, he *did* have sex with me. If he didn't want to, then he shouldn't have. I wasn't forcing him – believe me, when he was in the throes of passion, he was well into it.

Everyone thinks I'm this rough, tough girl who will take shit all day, but I'm not. Like everybody else I have feelings, so you can imagine how I felt when I watched him calling me all sorts on the show. He was a complete asshole about me. I know lads speak like that all the time to each other about girls they've banged, but most of the time the women are blissfully unaware because they don't have to see it all in a public arena. To be honest, it shocked me. I would have expected that sort of comment from Gaz or Jay, but not James. It was so out of character for him, which is why it hurt me more. It's not nice to see what you shouldn't be able to see.

Anyhow, I was happy because we'd finally had sex and in that moment it had felt right, for me anyway. It was the most perfect ending to a perfect experience.

Chapter Twenty-One

SEXICO

The captain asked us all to return to our seats and fasten our seatbelts. As I heard the words 'Crew crosscheck for landing, please' a ripple of excitement crept up my spine. I looked over at Rebecca, who was reading the latest *Heat* magazine, and then at James, who began to stir from his slumber. He stretched his arms, looked around to see me and smiled broadly.

I gazed out of the window and caught my first glimpse of Mexico. Cancun looked like a heavenly paradise from the air. Miles of beautiful white golden sand, clear blue waters and lush greenery were a far cry from the dirty grey skyline in Newcastle I'd just left. It felt like I was in a dream.

The aeroplane door swung open and I was immediately engulfed by the close heat and bright sunshine. And as I breathed in deeply, I was looking forward to taking on my next adventure.

We'd had a bitch of a journey. The three of us met up at Newcastle airport and flew to London, then from London to Canada and then Canada to Mexico. It was such a long-winded way to travel, but we had to go through Canada because some of the cast had had a few run-ins with the law and, as a result, the Americans wouldn't allow us to land there. The rest of the cast would all be arriving at different times.

Ever since Newcastle airport, James and me had been indulging in lots of flanter. He'd been laughing at how excited I was when I saw we had premium economy seats – I've only ever sat in the bog standard cheap sections when I've been away. When I saw we'd been slightly upgraded, I squealed with delight. I told him it was my dream to one day fly first or business class and hopefully I'd be in a position where I could spend that amount of money just to be comfortable on a flight.

The series started with a bang. Cancun was like no place I'd ever been to in all my life – it was unbelievable, everywhere was gorgeous! Our mansion was stunning and for the most part, everyone was having an absolute ball.

The James jealousy had reared its head a few times whenever I saw him chatting up birds but I found solace in the fact that he could never seal the deal. Even if he was dancing with girls and licking vodka shots off their tits, he wouldn't get a bang. He was useless at it. But I was pissed off he would choose to pull in front of me because he had been overtly flirtatious ever since the plane.

I was sure that was how the holiday was going to continue, him aimlessly trying to nail birds and me getting upset about it. That was until James, Gaz and Jay went Mexican wrestling one afternoon. They'd been gone an unusually long time and when they finally returned back to the house, James was hobbling in on crutches with his entire leg in a cast. The silly sod had dislocated his kneecap while they were play-fighting and would now be out of action for the rest of the trip.

I'm not even joking; the first thing that came into my mind was how am I supposed to have sex with him now? What was I supposed to do with this broken boy? I was devastated for the lad and for myself, although in hindsight that dislocated kneecap was my absolute saviour. I couldn't have wished for anything better because now James needed me. For the rest of the trip I slipped into my role as nurse Holly, and I was more than happy to help him out.

I literally did everything for him. I would wrap cling film around his cast before a shower, I would get his crutches, his wheelchair, make sure he had pillows under his leg and keep it elevated. I'd do everything in my power to make sure he didn't want to go home early and miss out on this fantastic Mexico experience.

We would play games, watch films, and have deep and meaningful chats well into the early hours about everything: our lives, our hopes and dreams, our thoughts for the future. We had the kind of conversations that new couples do when they want to know everything about the other person, so excuse me for thinking we had a connection.

The time we spent together was hardly shown on the programme because most of the crew would be out filming with the rest of the cast. Everyone was going out to these amazing nightclubs and having a great time, but I would deliberately stay behind because James couldn't be left on his own. No one picked up on how genuinely close we had become. I could feel myself really falling for him.

One night, there was one camera guy in the house who was there to film us if we got up to anything. Luckily for us, he'd nodded off on the sofa in the lounge while James and I were watching a film. It was a large curved sofa, the cameraman was at one end of the semi-circle and we were at the other, almost like we were facing each other. As soon as we heard him snoring, I leaned over to James and kissed him. The action was reciprocated, too, and soon we were embroiled in a deep passionate kiss, one that made your stomach flip and your heart quicken.

We were silent but we just looked at each other and could tell what we were both thinking. Without saying a word, I hitched up my skirt and climbed on top of James. Seconds later, we were having sex on the sofa while the cameraman slept soundly just a few feet away from us. The fact that he was in the room only added to the excitement. We had to be so quiet so we didn't wake him up. It was one of the most intense experiences of my life. No shouting, screaming, puffing or panting, everything was intensified. We kept our eyes locked on each other throughout. It was almost as if we were in a bubble, completely cut off from the rest of the world.

I know James felt the connection, too, because he told me so. He whispered in my ear how amazing it had been for him. Of course, he could have been lying but something in my gut told me he wasn't. Plus, after that he wanted me more and more. We would wake up earlier than everyone in the house and sneak off somewhere quiet. He would get me up at 6am and I would help him down the stairs and lead him into the kitchen, where there were no fixed cameras. We would open the fridge door because it was so hot and he would have sex with me over the breakfast bar. Most mornings we did this and no one in the house ever knew: it was our little secret.

He can say what he wants now but at that time we were extremely close. And it was the little things that I loved about our time together. We'd spend hours playing this game with a balloon. It had been someone's birthday in the house and there were balloons everywhere so we invented this game where we would bat it back to one another for ages. I know it was stupid, but it was that type of stuff that I knew I would miss so much when we left Cancun. It wasn't really much fun, but James literally couldn't move off the bed at times. What else could we do?

He was affectionate with me, too – he would tickle me and play with my hair. We'd go under the covers and he would kiss me passionately, but no one ever saw those parts of our relationship. I knew he liked me, but no one else would believe it. It was difficult for me because he would never show that side to anyone else and it totally knocked my confidence.

Maybe I read into the situation more than I should, but he used to send me mixed signals. He would blow hot and cold so he can't blame me for gaining feelings for him. I'm not a robot; we had been intimate with each other so it was hard not to feel something for him. I was just too stupid to see what he was doing. Using me for sex.

We'd kept the fact we were having sex to ourselves for a few weeks, but then I told a couple of the girls and the producers overheard me. Obviously, they wanted to show our relationship hotting up again. They were pretty livid we'd kept it from them for such a long time. We're supposed to be upfront with them about everything that goes on in the house so they can make the show the best it can be. Of course I totally get where they're coming from and I know that's what I signed up for, but a part of me just wanted to keep the whole James thing private. I wanted to keep it to myself and just enjoy it on my own for as long as possible. I knew when everyone found out about us, it might put James off wanting to spend time with me, or being intimate with me. I didn't want anyone else passing comment on our relationship because it was none of their business.

Once the cat was out of the bag, the cameramen were much more savvy about catching us in the act. We did have sex a few times on camera and that satisfied the producers. Over time, James gradually began to get better; he was able to move around slightly more and began coming out on nights out with the group. At this point he was still on crutches, but we were all there to make sure he wasn't going to get hurt, and if he'd had enough, he knew I'd be on hand to take him home again.

Even though he was out, the fact he was on crutches meant he still couldn't pull. I was delighted with this. Yes, I know it's probably wildly selfish of me, but I'd been nursing him for weeks so I didn't want some floozy coming up to him and undoing all my hard work. Anyone would have been the same.

I'd effectively sacrificed my own holiday for James. I just hoped he would see how much I thought of him and how genuinely I cared for him. I wasn't doing any of it for the cameras. I just wanted to help the guy out and while I wasn't looking for anything in return, I thought that if he did get the chance to prove how much he appreciated my efforts, he'd take it and show me.

I couldn't have been more wrong.

x x x

Word came through from the boss that James would be flying home business class since the insurance company would be paying for his flight because of his injury. He could take one other person with him to keep him company and enjoy the luxurious flight home. When the phone call came through, everyone immediately looked round at me because I was the one who had been there for him the whole time. You would think he might have given the plane ticket to me as a thank you, right? Wrong.

James looked uncomfortable when he heard the news. Not just like a man who'd been told he had been bumped up to amazing seats, instead he looked pretty sheepish. I could tell he was struggling to make his decision even though it should have been the easiest choice in the world. There was no contest. Who was he closest to in the house? Me. Who had looked after him all holiday? Me. Who had told him about my dream to fly business class one day? Me. And who had he been intimate with nearly every day for the past six weeks? Me. So, who did he choose to keep him company on the flight home? Gaz.

Before I'd heard James make his decision, I went upstairs and told the crew to call me back down when they needed me again for filming. I wasn't going to sit down there and beg James to pick me, so I left and lay down on my bed. I didn't want to know he didn't want me. So I closed my eyes and I remember having a nervous butterfly feeling in my stomach, somewhere between upset and embarrassment. I already knew from his face before that he wasn't going to pick me, but I still had this glimmer of hope that maybe he would. And I didn't want him to pick me because the producers were telling him to do that, but because he wanted to choose me.

They called us downstairs again and we all sat around the kitchen table – the same kitchen table where, for weeks, James and I had swapped bodily fluids in wild moments of passion. I sat there in the same room where he'd first told me how amazing I was and how much he enjoyed my company. Fast forward a few weeks and now he was telling me how he was going to take Gary on the luxury flight home with him. When he said it, he was smirking. I'd like to think it was just nerves that made him want to laugh rather than that he was actually enjoying seeing me upset. Not even James could have been that cruel, surely?

I didn't say a word. I couldn't. I was completely gutted by his decision. I'd looked after him for so long, when no one else gave a shit about him. He could have just repaid my kindness by offering me the plane ticket, but he didn't. It still stuns me to this day and at this point I kind of realise everything he'd ever said to me had been rubbish, complete lies. He cared more about Gaz than me, which is saying something because all James did, the whole time in Mexico, was bitch about Gaz. There was no consideration for my feelings.

Maybe he thought he would be giving me the wrong impression if he'd taken me back on that flight, who knows? All I know is that I was completely devastated.

Immediately after, I went back to my room and lay back down

on the bed. That same sick feeling in the pit of my stomach had intensified and was now threatening to seep out in the form of tears. I wanted to cry so badly, but I didn't want to let anyone know how much he'd upset me. I was so let down, rejected by another guy again. You would think I'd have got used to it by now, but no. It never gets any easier. I had fallen for James – I couldn't help it, he made me fall for him. Trouble was, he had no plans on catching me. Why couldn't I see it?

Looking back, James was just using me, but at the time I thought he genuinely cared. I didn't think he'd abuse my kindness and use it for his own advantage.

They never showed this on TV, but James tried to explain his actions. Just as the mists of tears were forming in my eyes, I heard a light tap on my door.

'Holly, can I come in?'

Wiping the tears away, I swallowed down my emotions. I didn't want him to hear the crack in my voice.

'Yeah, come in, James,' I said, trying to sound as breezy as possible.

'I'm sorry about that,' he said, struggling to close the door with his crutch. 'I just thought you'd probably want to fly back with the girls.'

'It's fine, forget it,' I snapped.

'No, honestly. I thought you'd prefer to go back home with them,' he rambled on, trying to justify his decision.

There was a long, uncomfortable pause.

'Don't be like...'

Before he could finish his sentence, I viciously interrupted.

'What's Gary done for you?'

'Huh?'

'What's Gary done for you this whole time we've been here to deserve going home on that flight with you?'

'Sorry... it's not like...'

'He's done fuck all for you! I've done everything!' I screeched. 'I've sacrificed MY holiday! MY experience! MY fun! Just to make your time here a little bit more comfortable. You're so fucking selfish!'

'Holly, stop...'

'Just get out, you've made your decision!' I said sharply. 'You're obviously too embarrassed to pick me in front of the rest of the boys. You're fucking gutless, James, and I'm not helping you anymore. See if Gary will push you around and get your crutches and wait behind with you while I go and have fun. See if I care anymore!'

'Calm down...'

'Get out!' I screamed.

James didn't say another word. He just left, like a dog with his tail between his legs and an ashamed look on his face.

And it was true: I wasn't going to be a mug anymore. I was annoyed with myself for letting it happen in the first place but sometimes when you want to believe something so badly you allow yourself to be taken advantage of. I wanted to believe that James actually cared about me when it was quite clear he didn't. But I couldn't just switch off my feelings for him and I spent the last few days in Mexico miserable.

It felt like I'd broken up with someone. At first there was the upset, then the anger, then all the hurt and eventually I knew I'd heal when I was back home and surrounded by my family, real friends and people who actually did appreciate me. I was fine before Cancun and I bet I'd be just fine after Cancun.

What disappointed me the most was the fact he'd chosen Gaz over me. It's no big secret that those two lads don't get on and he should have been the last person out of the whole house to go home with him. I get it now – James just wanted to look like a lad in front of everyone and obviously Gaz is the most popular one on the show. It's pathetic and shows a distinct lack of character.

We were in Mexico for another few days after the flight debacle. For the rest of the trip I refused to speak to James, let alone help him out. It was only then when he was struggling to do everything on his own that he truly realised how much I had done for him and no one else, not even Gaz, was going to help him out. He had to muddle through on his own and most of the time he was left behind, with no one waiting for him, while he carried his own wheelchair and crutches.

A part of me felt sorry for him but that's just because I'm a kind-hearted person and I wouldn't like to see anyone having a rough time. It's not in my nature.

James must have felt bad, though, because he came over to me and apologised again.

'Holly, I am really sorry. I should have taken you.'

'It's too late now. It's fine, James, no need to apologise.'

'Then can you snap out of this mood? We've had a great time here, let's not spoil it.'

'I never expected anything back for looking after you, James, but you have just made yourself look so ungrateful and made me look like a fucking idiot. *You* spoilt it.'

'Well, I am sorry, Holly.'

But his apology was pointless now – the damage had been done.

My best friend in Mexico had been him. I was hardly ever with the girls, because I was always with James.

On the last night, we played Twister and we were messing around. I'd softened up towards him again. We ended up in bed together and had sex for the last time in Cancun. It was slow and quite sensual, like he made love to me. I think I knew things would never be the same, so I tried to hold onto that moment. I was still so mad at him, but I cared about him so much I allowed him to treat me that way. It made me upset and, as I rolled over to sleep, I let out a tiny sob. I think James must have heard because he turned me over, put his arm around my shoulder and pulled me tight into him before we both dozed off.

It was on the flight back that a few home truths began to dawn on me. The thing is, and James could never see it, is that the public strived for us to get together. They liked the little relationship we had going on. It didn't matter that I could have been the best girlfriend in the world to James because he never looked at me in that way. I wasn't the perfect worldie and because of that I was only ever good for a shag behind closed doors. That was the harsh reality of the situation. It took me a while to realise it, but when I did it completely shattered my confidence. I know I'm loud, I'm leery, I'm not the size 8 supermodel he wants, but on some level I thought we had a good thing going on. He was embarrassed about me, and all the times he made me keep our relationship a secret wasn't so he could keep it all private, but because he was too ashamed to say he'd slept with me.

Chapter Twenty-Two

FAMILY REACTION

I'm pretty sure that when my mother gave birth to me, cradled me in her arms, looked down into my big brown eyes and wondered what would become of me, the last thing she could have imagined would be a larger-than-life ladette who's been known to have nookie on TV. It's not a career any mother would ever envisage for her daughter. Having said that, she *is* incredibly proud of me.

When the show first aired, she had to endure a few no-marks in the street who would offer their opinion, whether she wanted it or not. 'Is that your Holly on *Geordie Shore*?' they'd ask. 'She's a disgrace, it's disgusting!' they'd say. 'How can you let your daughter behave like that?'

My mam would never go shouting who *she* is from the rooftops or anything, trying to get preferential treatment. She's not that type of lady. Although if anyone asks her about me in passing or at Darci's school gates, she's more than happy to talk about it and defend me to the hilt, if needs be.

I've had hundreds, maybe even a thousand, interviews over the years regarding *Geordie Shore* and it's still the question I get asked the most: 'What *does* your mother say?'

Well, in all honesty, I'm sick of trotting out the same old answer so I'll let her do it for me.

My daughter isn't out there on the streets, doing drugs or on the dole. She has her own job, her own life. She pays her way. Pays her taxes. Treats her friends, her parents and her family. She's living the life she has always wanted to live. She's travelled the world and been to places I could never have afforded to take her. She is living out my dreams.

I settled with Holly's dad when I was young, had a baby by the age of twenty-three and got straight back to work. It's a life I was content with, because I never knew how it could be different. I didn't want that for Holly.

Through Geordie Shore *she has been given an amazing opportunity, to exhaust her youth and build a future for herself. She's not sat at home with two kids watching repeats of* The Jeremy Kyle Show *most days and living on benefits. She's being paid to travel the world, walk down red carpets, meet exciting, interesting people and expand her mind. She's sensible and knows what she wants, making her more stable and secure than most forty-year-olds I know.*

While I realise there's no skill in being a reality TV star, I take comfort in the knowledge you have to be an entertaining and interesting individual to have any longevity on TV, which is a credit to Holly and her vivacious personality. I know her spell in the limelight won't last forever and so does she, that's why I tell her to say 'yes' to the chances that come her way and never to complain about the opportunities she's been given, no matter how tired or fed-up she may be.

If your children had the opportunity to earn very good 'easy' money, doing something they enjoyed doing, why would you stop them? I say the money is easy, like there's no downside to Holly's notoriety, but there is. Constantly being taunted and critiqued by complete strangers is tough for anyone to take, let alone a young, impressionable girl. Lesser women would have crumbled under the pressure, but it's a sink-or-swim scenario and my Holly has fought off everyone and their barbed comments along the way. I used to get into many arguments on Twitter, but now I just ignore the slurs. I understand that she has willingly put her life on TV for all to scrutinise. This is what she signed up for and you have to take the rough with the smooth. I suppose in her line of work, it's better to be talked about, even negatively, than not at all. I've watched my daughter weep because of the nasty online bullying, but I tell her, life is too short to waste any amount of time on wondering what people think about you. If they had better things going on in their lives, they wouldn't have the time to sit around and talk about yours.

Many probably think I'm too accepting and lenient on my daughter, but really, why is anyone else bothered?

I've lost count of how many times I've heard the phrase 'I wouldn't let them do a show like that if it was my child.' Well, she's not your child and you'll probably never have to even comprehend your child being involved in a television programme like Geordie Shore. Until other parents are in the same situation you really can't comment.

I'll defend her in every way I can, but I don't make excuses for her. I'm not happy with her having sex on TV because what mother would be? But it's not porn. You don't see anything other than a few undercover clinches. If it bothers you to watch it, there's a button on the remote – switch it off.

I just want my daughter to be happy and right now she is. She works incredibly hard and she's making a good living while she can. I tell her every single day to remember how lucky she is and I keep her grounded because one day Geordie Shore will be a distant memory and I want her to look back on her time with fond memories. Hopefully by then, when it's all over, she'll have something to show for all her efforts. And when she's sitting in her own house, which she paid for, lounging on her own furniture and reminiscing about her time on the TV, she can ask herself, was it worth it?

I know what she would say.

My dad, on the other hand, doesn't watch the show. I don't think he's ever watched one episode. Likewise my stepdad doesn't watch it either. I suppose it's awkward for them to see me like that, warts and all. My mam and dad did have quite a few rows in the beginning. He would phone her up, like any concerned dad would. He wasn't happy with me slagging myself about on TV, being vulgar and doing rude bits with boys. In a way, I kind of felt like my dad blamed my mam a little bit for me wanting to do this with my life, but she did her best. And it had nothing to do with her.

I never saw my mam going out and getting pissed once. I never saw her bring another bloke home, have a one-night stand or behave in any way inappropriately. It's not like I saw my mam do those things and thought it was acceptable, normal behaviour, it's the way I wanted to behave. Gone are the days when little girls want to learn to cook like their mothers. They want to drink like their fathers. How times have changed.

Chapter Twenty-Three

KEEPING IT REAL

People are always interested in how the show works. They ask me if we use a script, they want to know how much is fudged up in the editing process and if our reality show is really real.

Well, I'll try and answer it all for you now.

Geordie Shore isn't like other reality shows in the UK, where they take a bunch of good-looking wannabes with just enough brain cells to be able to improvise a scene when the producers give them a few pointers. Those shows will have one of their 'storywriters' drum up some juicy conflict loosely based on their lives. In our show we create all the drama. It's for that reason I don't really watch other reality shows. Well, that, and because I don't get much time.

When it's on, I do like *TOWIE*, even though most of it is scripted and set up. It appeals to a different audience.

Something that's interesting in their show just isn't interesting in ours. *Geordie Shore* is such a higher bar of entertainment whereas their show is just like a soap. Don't get me wrong, I'm not slagging the programme off – there's clearly a market for it because it's so hugely successful – but I think our show is much more authentic. If they tell someone to 'shut up', it's like a big deal, whereas in our programme no one would bat an eyelid. I don't feel like you can relate to *TOWIE* as much as us because all the shots are of their amazing cars and massive houses. There aren't many people who watch these shows who have a lifestyle like that. Even I wouldn't rock up to a club, buy a table and pay five times over the odds for a bottle of vodka. Up north we call those people 'Grey Goose wankers'. It's a completely different lifestyle. I suppose you're getting to see how the other half lives, but more than anything I think it just makes people jealous.

I suppose *Made in Chelsea* is the same. I feel like I'm watching *Coronation Street* and I have to bite my tongue when I watch it with my friends because I can now tell a million miles away what has been set up just from the camera angles. The continuity isn't right and it's funny because now I scrutinise these programmes almost without thinking about it. I start looking at it from an editor's perspective and how they've angled everything to portray the story.

The Valleys is probably our closest competitor because it's like a replica format to our show but set in Wales. There's four girls, four boys, living in a house, getting drunk and arguing. Our cast was dubious about the show in the beginning: we wanted to see if they were going to try and be like us, or carve out characters for themselves.

When we first met the cast, one of the girls turned round to Vicky and said 'I'm the new Charlotte' and another said 'I'm the new Holly'. Which we all agreed was a massive mistake because they should just be themselves, not imitations of us. In my opinion, it was never going to be as good as *Geordie Shore* because we had already pushed the boundaries. In the beginning the cast were quite hostile and hard-faced towards the *Geordie Shore* cast. They came out with an attitude, thinking they were going to be better than us. In reality, their show actually made ours more popular as the viewers liked us because we were more real. It did us nothing but favours. They had unfounded bravado in the beginning because no one know if they would be successful.

Don't get me wrong, I do like the cast. They aren't like that in real life. When they're not performing for the cameras they are really cool, genuine people and now we all get on great.

With *Geordie Shore* a lot of people think the show is scripted: it's not. There is a running order that the producers have but it will only contain topics. It might say something like 'Charlotte and Holly are going to go to the gym today. At the gym they will talk about Gaz'. But that's as much guidance as we will ever get. Everything that comes out of our mouths is natural and the producers don't know what we are going to say. We don't have lines, we don't have any pressure to say certain things... we can say what we want. Most of the time we are all fucking mortal. How can you give a script to a bunch of hammered housemates? And what would be the point anyway, when what we get up to without a script is bad enough?

When we are being filmed sometimes there's one crew,

sometimes two, sometimes there's three and then behind each of those crews, you have the sound man, the runner, the logger, the cameraman and the producer. So even though it can look like there's only two people in the room having a chat onscreen, there are usually a few more behind the camera. In some big shots you may even see some of the crew. At times they've had to break up a few arguments.

Other times it might just be one cameraman capturing everything, in addition to the fixed cameras that are placed round the house. One thing our show never does is rehearse or reshoot anything, though. If we did, we would lose the integrity of the show. So if they miss any action for any reason, that's it, they missed it. It's rule number one: keep it real.

From day one, I've loved our crew. They really know what they are doing. Our cameramen are so great and professional. It's like they can sense when the drama is about to happen and straight away they are ready with the right shot. That kind of skill only comes when you are experienced in reality TV. You've got to have the best of the best; they sense the drama. And when there is any drama, there will be a hut outside and someone controlling all the fixed cameras so if anyone has missed anything on the big camera, hopefully they will have got it on the fixed cameras. They are probably some of the best cameramen in the country; they possess that elusive 'third eye' which allows them to get good coverage of whatever they're shooting, while simultaneously monitoring the action that's happening outside the window of the lens. They were always ready to go above and beyond when the action begins.

In our show, we film green screens and it's the most intense part of the whole production. For those not familiar with the term green screen, I'll explain. We sit in front of a large green background and talk directly to the camera about something that's already happened on the show. It's kind of like what a weatherman stands in front of, so a computer graphic can be edited in at a later date. It gives us a chance to have a one-on-one with the audience and explain how we were feeling at that time. People don't realise the green screen interviews make up seventy per cent of the 'forty-two minute hour'. It's the narrative of the show, it tells the story. It's not like other reality shows, where they tell the story throughout the scene. This is our way of explaining what's happened in the house.

Sometimes we film a green screen straight after a big row, and sometimes it can be weeks down the line. It's better in the heat of the moment because the camera can capture the raw emotion. Then there are other times when we won't film a green screen until after the event, which is obviously harder because your emotions have changed. You might have hated another housemate a few days ago, but have kissed and made up since. It can be difficult, especially when you might have to slag off someone. I don't mind filming green screens and we'll only ever redo them if I muddle my words up, or if it's not clear enough, or I can't express myself in the right way, but other than that our show is never scripted.

And we always have to wear the same clothes as we were wearing in the scene – to help the audience – so our clothes can never be lent out or binned if we've worn them before. We never get any help with our wardrobe. No one ever tells us what we can or can't wear which is great because it means we can show off our different personalities through our style. But I can't change my hair until I know they definitely don't need me to film anymore, which is difficult for someone like me, who loves to change my look regularly.

In the beginning *Geordie Shore* was slated beyond belief and it angers people because we are so successful. The older generation can't understand it, but I do. It's car crash TV. Have you ever driven by an accident on the motorway? I dare you not to look. In reality TV, the viewer always gets the close-up of the carnage, too. This is why audiences eat it up, because we're always on the verge of impending disaster.

People don't want heroes onscreen: they want villains, backstabbers and conflict they can sink their teeth into. They want to see people they can relate to, people who say, 'I have a shitty, shameful, disgusting life just like you do'. Or they want to feel superior to us in some ways like, 'Yeah, I sleep around, but I'm not a slag like those girls'.

That's why *Geordie Shore* is so popular. Today's generation don't want to watch actors reciting the same old tired lines, they wanted to see themselves reflected onscreen – rude, raw, entitled. People need to believe that they themselves are only one daring, controversial act away from being up on that screen themselves.

Our job when we first started the show, whether or not MTV told us at the time, was to be hated. It took me a while to realise this, but then the penny dropped, everything made sense. We were hated, so hated by our audience that they couldn't avert their eyes. We provoked a reaction because we were so outrageous. People were stunned or repulsed, but either way we caused them to talk about us. There's a certain crudeness and crassness that has suddenly become accepted behaviour and on our show, it's the norm.

I just wonder where TV can go from here because it's getting more and more outrageous, but that's the wonderful unpredictability of unscripted television.

Chapter Twenty-Four

GOING NUTS

Ever since my early teens I've thumbed through the bosom-heavy pages of lads' mags, not because I'm a closet lesbian or anything, but because I admired the girls in them, who look beautiful and photograph sexy. I'd look at them with their gorgeous curvaceous figures, smouldering make-up, carefree attitude and wish one day I could be like them.

I've never made a secret of my desire to be a glamour model. I used to go on about it all the time, but my school friends would laugh and say I was never pretty enough or didn't have the right body. I'll admit I've never had much confidence when it comes to my looks, probably because I've had so much shit in my life from boys and girls constantly telling me I'm ugly. You probably think it's strange that a girl with virtually zero confidence should want to be a glamour model, right? I agree it's pretty odd, but what I've learned over the last few years is because of all the grief I've to deal with, I crave validation on a huge scale.

That's not easy to admit, by the way, and it's taken me years to realise it, too. It's like I desperately want affirmation of my value or to give me some kind of social approval. I'm not saying it's the right way to be, I'm just being honest about the way I feel and it hopefully explains why I want be like the beautiful lads' mag lovelies.

One day, after we'd filmed our first series of *Geordie Shore*, my dream of being spread across a glossy men's mag in nothing but seductive underwear was about to come true. The magazine *Nuts* (which has now closed) had contacted my agent at the time, Money North, about a potential shoot to promote our newly aired reality show. They wanted all four girls – Vicky, Sophie, Charlotte and me – to be photographed in some racy underwear and suggestive poses.

Let me tell you, I was on cloud nine. Just to be considered for a magazine like *Nuts* was a huge deal for me. They didn't have to ask me twice. I was doing the shoot, no matter what. Vicky, on the other hand, was dubious about it. She's not the type of girl to show off her hot bod in saucy underwear. Plus, we weren't getting any money for the shoot as it was part of the publicity MTV said would be helpful in promoting *Geordie Shore*.

I literally had to beg Vicky to agree to the spread because they wanted all four of us and it was all or nothing. We all had to consent or it wouldn't go ahead. Thankfully, after a little persuasion, she came round to the idea and the shoot was booked for a week later.

At this point I was probably about two and half stone heavier than I am now. I was over twelve stone and when you consider

I'm only five foot three, you can imagine I was fairly chunky. Regardless of whether I was at my biggest size, I was still so confident and excited about our upcoming photos. I considered it to be a once-in-a-lifetime opportunity and I wasn't about to mess it up.

We all travelled to London together and had a great time on the journey down. We'd bought several of the men's mags so we could study the poses the girls used to make themselves look sexy. It was our first proper photoshoot together and we kind of felt excited about our new media careers.

We arrived at Jet Studios in Fulham, which was a huge blank room, rigged up with lights, umbrellas, an area for hair and make-up and rails of high-street underwear we could choose from. You'd think having four rowdy lasses like us, there might be some competitiveness and cattiness, especially over what we were wearing, but there wasn't at all. I chose some French knickers, a black balcony bra (which only just concealed my nipples), and some fancy lace stockings.

When I was in front of the camera I felt alive and it was every bit as exciting and fun as I thought it would be. I shoved my heaving chest towards the lens, made the oh-so-sexy 'come to me' eyes, bit my lip seductively, pulled my knickers slightly down to give a little more hip and made like I was Katie Price, commanding the room with some typically seductive poses. I was in my element.

They had all the shots they wanted, but since the photographer said I had the most body confidence, he asked if I'd be willing to go down to 'implied topless', which basically means being photographed with no top on, but covering the nipples with my hands.

I thought about how raunchy I was willing to go and in the end, I jumped at the chance. This was my dream, and for all I knew I was never going to get this opportunity again, so I agreed wholeheartedly, totally forgetting that I was doing this shoot for free. In hindsight, I should have said no because once you do something for free, no one will ever pay you for it again. The photos are out there in the public arena and the more images out there, the more you decrease your own value. You create value by scarcity, but this is something I've had to learn the hard way. I made a stupid mistake by doing implied for nothing.

A few weeks later we had to go to the MTV offices and view the pictures. I can't tell you how excited I was about seeing the end result. All the girls in *Nuts* looked flawless and I couldn't wait to get copies of the photos, upload them to my Facebook and gloat to all the haters at school who'd said I could never do it.

I sat down in front of the computer screen with a girl from the press office, while she opened the email containing the images. One by one, she started to flick through them.

I took one look at them, the result of that mammoth, five-hour long shoot and, as my eyes focussed on the sight of my curves clad in the skimpy black underwear, tears formed and I began to cry. And these were not tears of joy.

My jaw literally hit the floor. The images before me were disgusting. After all that time of wanting to be in *Nuts*, this was the result. I sat sobbing in front of the computer, flipping between one gross image after another, my dreams well and truly shattered. I looked fucking huge! Yeah, I was a good size 14, but I looked more like an 18.

I'm sure people reading this wouldn't even think that was particularly big, but to me it was massive. The way the light had caught the cellulite on my thighs and stomach, the way the underwear had cut into my figure... Urgh, it was vile! My contorted face, my horrible pouted lips, my slinty eyes, it was all wrong. I scrolled through the pictures in sequence, getting more and more upset. Suddenly, I was so self-conscious that I found fault with each pose: they were either too raunchy, too suggestive or I just looked fucking gigantic. I was furious.

Why had I even wanted to do this? Who was I kidding? I was never going to be a glamour model. I felt let down and betrayed by the photographer, who kept telling me I looked gorgeous, when I clearly didn't. I looked more like Shamu during a Moulin Rouge performance.

Immediately, I got into a strop with the girl from the press office and told her to erase every single image. I never wanted to see them again, never mind see them in print. The incinerator was too good for them.

The poor press office girl had the job of calming me down and soothing my upset. Of course, the images I had viewed hadn't been airbrushed and she assured me they wouldn't print anything that made me look less than gorgeous. She made me choose five photographs which I would be happy with them publishing but at that moment in time, I felt horrible. I couldn't look at them again, so I told the press office girl to choose the best of a terrible bunch.

When I finally saw the end result in the mag, I was happy even if I did have to be majorly digitally enhanced. The magazine did some mega airbrushing, but at least I looked semi-slim and semi-gorgeous. So, let that be a lesson to every girl reading this: never compare yourself to a girl in a magazine because you are comparing yourself to a figure that even she has not achieved. Also, I had to look on the bright side – at least I'd accomplished my life-long ambition of being in a lads' mag so, whatever happened next, I could still tick that off the bucket list.

It was only when I started to change my look, lose some weight and get my body confidence back that I decided I'd like to give the lads' mags another shot. A year on, I was much slimmer, I felt sexier and I had a good following of about 250,000 people on Twitter.

By this time I'd switched agents from Money North to Misfits Management and when I told my new representative Luke about wanting to shoot for *Nuts* again, he said he would try his best to organise it. Luke had his reservations, though, because I don't look like your typical *Nuts* cover girl.

Nuts preferred the 'girl next door' kind of gal. They liked curvy, natural and beautiful girls – the kind of women that would grace their covers were Lucy Pinder, Keeley Hazell and Rhian Sugden – so I was as far removed from their ideal lass as you could get. I had unnatural dyed bright red hair, tattoos, piercings, massive fake boobs and a bigger bum than all of them put together. Luke knew trying to get me a cover for *Nuts* was going to be difficult, though not impossible. The magazine would have to take a big risk featuring me in any big way, as it would go against their entire ideology.

At the time Billie Faiers from *TOWIE* was the *Nuts* magazine golden girl who, luckily, was also looked after by my agent, Luke. She was getting regular shoots for the magazine and, every time, Luke would always bring me up in conversation with the editors. They were always kind about me, but never actually gave a specific reason as to why they wouldn't shoot me again. All they would say was 'She's just not right for us' or 'It's not a never, just not right now'.

This backwards and forwards conversation went on for about five months and I was kind of disheartened. I knew Luke was doing all he could to persuade them but I could totally see where they were coming from. They liked to play it safe and go with what sells for them. Using a girl like me on the cover would be a massive gamble. It could alienate their buyers and harm their position in the marketplace.

Still, I was determined. All I wanted was a chance to prove to them I could be a cover girl. In the end, I took matters into my own hands. I went down to watch Billie Faiers do a shoot so I could meet the assistant editor in an attempt to win him over – I knew if I showed up there it would be hard to say no to me in person. It was a pretty cheeky ploy, but you don't get anywhere in this life by sitting around doing nothing. If you want something bad enough, you have to go out and grab it with your two hands.

On the shoot, I met the assistant editor, Sam Riley, and he took one look at me and was pleasantly surprised. He called a meeting with the other heads of departments at the magazine and, luckily for me, they agreed to give me a cover.

When I heard the news, it was like I'd found the Holy Grail. I was ecstatic with a capital E and I couldn't stop screaming. This was even better than when I'd found out I'd been selected for *Geordie Shore*! The magazine made it clear from the outset this was a one-off trial shoot. They wanted to see how I would impact on the sales because they were publishing photos outside their comfort zone. They kept saying to me that it might not work, but I was still willing to give it my all. I'd been waiting for an opportunity like this for too long.

Only there was one stipulation: because I'd done implied nude with the magazine before, they wanted me to go a step further. I had to be completely topless. It's a big decision being topless in a magazine because, once you've unveiled yourself, you can never do it again. I discussed the idea at length with my mam and dad, and they both made it clear it was my decision. They said they wouldn't be angry with me if I went ahead with the shoot and, as long as I was happy, they would support me.

It felt good having my parents' backing and, because of their blessing, I agreed to go topless for a decent amount of money. It was, and still is, my biggest pay cheque to date. Which is the way it should be, if you ask me.

On the day of the shoot I woke up so early it was still dark outside. I couldn't sleep, it was honestly like this was the biggest day of my life. Like I was about to get married or something. The night before, I fake tanned myself everywhere about five times so I was ultra-brown. Probably too brown, but I reasoned no self-respecting north-east girl would be seen dead looking pasty white.

I strutted into the studio wearing just a onesie, my hair in a scruffy bun and a bare face. The first thing the photographer, Zoe McConnell, said to me was, 'Wow, you're so dark.' My tan had still been developing all the way to London and now, rather than a healthy glow, it looked like I'd vaulted headfirst into a bath of Ronseal!

The make-up artist Johanna Dalemo, who's Swedish and totally bonkers, had the task of matching my foundation to my impressive fence-paint tan. But if anyone could pull it off, it would be her, because Johanna is, hands down, the best make-up artist to ever touch my face. She made me look so perfect. I could have been a doll. And I'm sure any girl can relate: when your hair and make-up is right, it makes you feel like a million dollars.

Tell you what, though, it's not as easy as it looks, modelling for one of those lads' mags. The positions they get you in are tough to hold. The photographer, Zoe, was an ex-glamour model herself and helped with all my positions. She quickly put me at ease, but it was still pretty hard work. I just had to trust her and believe that, when I saw the photos, they would be amazing.

I felt on top of the world after the shoot and, even though the team offered me a peek at the pictures, I declined because I didn't want a repeat of last time where I got upset, nitpicking at every unsightly roll or view of my muffin top. The first time I would ever see them would be when I bought a copy of the magazine at the newsagents.

My battle for the front cover didn't end there, though. I was over in Tenerife filming the advert for the Cancun series in June 2012 when Luke called me with some terrible news. He told me that MTV wouldn't give me permission for the front cover or the spread because I was topless. Can you believe it? Five months I'd been painstakingly persuading the magazine to let me be on the cover and now MTV were blocking it.

I was furious. What a liberty! The team at MTV kept fobbing me off with some excuse about how they weren't happy and refused to give me permission. I felt so let down. It was double standards, too. In the very first episode of *Geordie Shore* they had shown footage of me getting my boobs out in the hot tub. They didn't care then, so why did they care now, two years down the line?

Luke had three days of rows with the team at MTV. He didn't want to tell me unless he actually had to because he knew I would be devastated if they wouldn't give permission. Even after arguing my case, they weren't giving in. They told me there would be serious consequences for my contract if I chose to allow the pictures to be published.

In sheer desperation, I went to see Mandy, the head of PR at MTV, to personally beg her to change their minds. We had a meeting in a local coffee shop and I'd never been so defiant in all my life. If they could show my boobs on TV, why not in a magazine? It made no sense. It was so hypocritical. She couldn't really give me a reason, she just kept saying the decision had come from above and there was nothing they could do.

I was beyond frustrated. This was my dream and they were shattering it before my very eyes.

'It's your decision, Holly. We can't tell you what to do, but if you do it we can't guarantee an outcome,' she said nonchalantly, like she wasn't bothered if I were part of the show or not.

'Will I be sacked from *Geordie Shore* if these pictures are printed?' I asked with venom. I wanted to be clear about what they were saying to me.

'We can't promise you anything if you go ahead,' she said, not really committing to an answer.

Those words cut through me like a knife. Now I had to choose between my job on *Geordie Shore* or my dream of being a cover girl. I could lose everything I had worked so hard for in the past two years. You should have seen my mood – I was livid! I just got up and walked out before I started throwing things in anger.

Bereft, disappointed and hollow, I couldn't believe how unfairly I was being treated. I took a long walk down by the river and tried to gather my thoughts. Was I going to call Luke and tell him to go ahead with the shoot? Or call Mandy and tell her I was going to spike it? I was risking everything but what was the point of being on the show if I couldn't earn any money from it?

For a long time, I laboured over the decision. (Actually, it wasn't *that* long; I've probably taken longer to toast bread!) In the end I decided I didn't want regrets – you always regret not doing the things you could have done, rather than toeing the line all the time. Fuck them, I thought. I'd rather be sacked from *Geordie Shore* for doing something that means the world to me than back down and kill the magazine feature. As far as I was concerned they didn't have a leg to stand on and MTV could go to hell. I'd take whatever punishment came my way. I dialled Luke's number, told him to go ahead with the publishing, ended the call and prepared myself to be sacked from the show.

Chapter Twenty-Five

COVER GIRL

I woke up extra early. Tell you the truth, I didn't feel like I'd been to sleep all night. I kept having these awful anxious dreams about what the cover would look like. In my vision I saw the magazine for the first time and the girl in the photos looked like the worst possible version of myself: wrinkly, overweight and haggard with orange skin and bright green hair. I woke up in a sweat, having palpitations – I didn't know if it was because of the lucid dream or because I now knew my decision meant I was facing the sack from my beloved *Geordie Shore*.

Because I hadn't told any of the MTV bosses I'd decided to go ahead with the magazine feature. I didn't want to think about what I was going to have to do when I was called in for a meeting to be told I wouldn't be returning onscreen. I could prolong hearing the bad news for another day. Right now I had to focus on what my naked chest looked like in a glossy lads' mag. With that in mind I got up and marched to the newsagents.

Most of you will probably know what it feels like to have that nervous anticipation in your stomach. Just imagine it's the morning of results day. You've got the envelope in your hand with your exam scores and you're too scared to open them, knowing the outcome could determine your whole life. Well, that's how I felt when I walked into the newsagents. That shoot could make or break me as a glamour model. Like I said before, *Nuts* were taking a huge risk putting a girl like me on the front cover. This was either going to be a smart move by the editor in branching out into new territory, or a complete disaster that would probably make him the subject of ridicule amongst his bosses and their competitors.

I scanned the top shelf where all the luscious ladies were looking out at me, posing seductively, just like I'd been told to do. Then I spotted my bright red hair and my own vacant expression I sometimes pull when I'm attempting to be sexy. I hadn't got a clue which photos they had chosen out of the hundreds they took, but now I was about to see my results for the first time.

First of all I studied the cover. I was standing up against a white background, eyes looking straight and my long, marvel-comic red hair dominated the image. I had just a pair of black sheer knickers and stockings on, with my hands covering those all-important nipples. To the left of the image were the words 'GEORDIE SHORE'S HOLLY TOPLESS! FOR THE FIRST TIME!'

I couldn't help but smile. Thank goodness my nightmare hadn't been a premonition. So I stood there looking at myself on the sexy front cover and was overcome by a sense of relief. I loved the photo on the front and as I flicked to the inside feature I was overjoyed. The photos, if I do say so myself, were incredible. I looked so much better than I ever imagined I could. The make-up was phenomenal, my body had curves in all the right places, my tits could have rivalled any highly paid glamour girl and my posing was as playful as could be. Honestly, it was perfect, almost cartoon-like. Jessica Rabbit, eat your heart out!

I know you probably think I sound bigheaded but these were the best photos I'd ever seen of myself. You'd be bigheaded, too! I should have realised the magazine wouldn't make me look anything less than gorgeous, but it's only normal to have a few nerves. When the newsagent saw my delighted reaction in the shop, he put two and two together and realised it was me gracing the cover of the magazine. I remember him saying, 'It's nice to see you. I didn't expect to be seeing quite *so* much of you though.' You had to laugh!

Part of the deal was to post a few messages on Twitter encouraging people to go out and buy the magazine. As soon as I'd seen the results, I tapped out my first message urging my followers to grab themselves a copy, take a photo of them holding it and in return I would follow them.

All through that day and for the rest of the week, I had men and women all over the country telling me they'd bought themselves the mag and, as promised, I followed every single one back. The response I got was amazing. Everyone was so complimentary about the images and I couldn't have been happier.

Still, the success of the shoot ultimately hinged on sales and I didn't find out about what impact my cover would have until a week later. More than anything I wanted for it to have been a triumph, but the situation was out of my hands and now all I could do was wait.

During that week I had a bit of a spat with the feminist pressure group UK Feminista, who were in the thick of a campaign to banish lads' mags. They had already managed, successfully, to get supermarket giant Co-op to cover the magazines in modesty bags and were urging others to follow suit.

Now for the record I am a huge feminist who believes in equality for men and women. And the whole issue of lads' mags objectifying women as sexual objects is a subject too widespread and difficult to debate here. It's quite clear from my choice, and it *is* my choice, of career that I see nothing wrong with women wanting to pose provocatively. I think there's nothing more empowering than having the confidence to stand there looking striking. The female form is beautiful and should be celebrated in a positive way. I actually penned an open letter to the feminist group and invited them to come down to a shoot with me, but to this day they haven't replied.

To me what's more alarming and offensive is the female celebrity magazines that target celebrities for looking overweight, covered in cellulite or just plain fat. These magazines savage celebrity bodies, pinpointing the smallest imperfection.

As someone who constantly struggles with her weight, I find those images send out a worse body image than the evenly proportioned, curvy, healthy women on the cover of men's magazines. In my opinion they are more harmful to female self-esteem. I've been targeted in the past – a photo of myself accompanied by cruel comments about how much weight I'd piled on. Some of my cast members have been equally criticised for how much weight they've lost, their stretch marks, how much cellulite they have, or just because of a few fine lines and wrinkles. If you ask me, that's more demeaning to women. These publications don't show women in a good light at all and most of them are run by women – I mean, where's the sisterhood?

Shooting for a men's magazine is not the seedy experience some might think it could be. I'm always picked up by an E-Class Mercedes and chauffeur-driven to the shoot, like a movie star. Then I'm met at the plush modern studio, where there's a team of lovely people and lunch prepared by an acclaimed chef. I get my hair and make-up done by the best in the business and then I'm given a selection of the newest, most luxurious underwear to choose from and told to pose in it before I'm chauffeur-driven home again. Believe me, as far as glamour modelling goes, it's the least seedy set-up I've ever heard of. We're so looked after by the magazine.

I know that's not always the case for some aspiring young girls who often have bad experiences with rogue photographers, but you get a few bad apples in any industry. The only advice I can give is to make sure you check out credentials and always be safe. Don't hand over any money upfront to an agency: if they want you, you won't need to pay them. Keep clear and accurate records of who you have modelled for and where the photos will be used. Make sure you know who owns the copyright of the images beforehand. If it's your first glamour shoot, take someone with you for moral support as it can be quite nerve wracking. And lastly, always know what you are agreeing to before entering into a contract.

The level of trust I had with *Nuts* was really good. I knew they would never make me look bad, so it made me more confident. I would strut around in heels and knickers, knowing I could be confident about my curves and they weren't going to circle the odd roll of fat and point it out to their readers.

I remember during the shoot, they'd had the nicest lunch prepared, but I didn't want to eat a scrap because I was worried about looking bloated in the photos. The producer laughed and told me not to be so stupid. They'd specially prepared all the food for me and I could eat as much as I liked. Knowing they loved my body shape the way it was made me feel so reassured. They never made me feel big, unlike some of the fashion models, who are screamed at for not being a size zero.

And the day finally arrived when I found out how many magazines were sold. I was crossing all my fingers and toes. My whole future with *Nuts* hinged on these sales, so you can imagine how nervous I was.

My agent Luke called me and I'm glad to say it was great news. The shoot had been a massive success, and the magazine had a huge increase on sales from the week before. A twenty per cent uplift from the previous edition, if you must know.

If that wasn't enough good news, *Geordie Shore* also decided to let me continue with the show, and the head of art relations, Roberta, rang to tell me how beautiful the shots were. At first I thought she was calling to fire me, but she was so positive and congratulatory. It was a huge relief.

But the absolute best news of all came at the end of December 2012 when I found out my cover had been the highest-selling cover of the entire year! When I heard that I literally cried with happiness.

Nuts were so pleased they wanted to book another shoot straight away and to sign me exclusively to their magazine. I was signed up to do six shoots a year and I got paid a good income to do it, too. I was deliriously happy; it was something I'd always wanted to do.

As soon as the ink was dry on my contract, I put it all over Facebook – I couldn't wait to tell everyone. On there I have people who used to laugh at me, take the piss and bully me for having these dreams. Now I could turn around and stick two fingers up to them.

Those were the girls who would constantly pick on me and call me fat, but look what I was doing with my life – I was living out a dream I never thought I could, I was on top of the world. Now, I walked with my head high and shoulders squared. I'm better than them, no matter what whispers and taunts anyone throws out there. Fuck them! I was doing what I loved and whether it all ended tomorrow no one could take that away from me.

Chapter Twenty-Six

CRAZY FANS

A guy on Twitter once offered me £900 for a pair of my scruffy worn trainers. Can you believe it? I couldn't stop laughing when I saw the message and I was seriously tempted. I kept thinking what would be the best way for him to pay me. He could have just transferred the money into my bank account maybe, or a friend's bank account, or a banker's draft, or perhaps a donation in my name for charity? Then I had some weird feeling that this guy would probably be at home cracking one off over my trainers and it really grossed me out. I had to block him after that.

Being on a no-holds-barred show like *Geordie Shore* is good because people can often relate to you onscreen. We don't hide our emotions, we don't come from mega-rich backgrounds – we're just normal people thrown together in a huge house, really. But because we don't keep our lives private sometimes I find people can be quite invasive.

When I first started on *Geordie Shore* I wasn't very popular and never got asked to do nightclub appearances, but as my status grew, so did the offers of work. Doing personal appearances and meeting the fans is your bread and butter as a reality star. It's a good way to earn income while you're in between one series and the next. I genuinely love meeting all the people who enjoy the show and the large majority of them are always so lovely, but I have had a few bad experiences, especially when I first started out.

If it's anything to do with work then I am extremely professional, even if it is just turning up to a nightclub. When I'm on PAs people expect me to behave like I do on the show, getting mortal and acting like I'm completely crazy, but in reality, because I'm working, I make sure I'm focussed on the job in hand.

In the past I've have lads grabbing me, trying to cop a feel of my boobs and my bum. At first I used to take it, and politely tell them to stop because I didn't really know better. I should have kicked up a huge fuss, but I was so naïve and stupid. In any other job, if someone grabbed you inappropriately, they'd never be allowed to get away with it – it's sexual harassment. Why should I have to put up with it? But I'm subjected to it on a daily basis and, if I speak up for myself, they tell me I'm moaning, or to shut up. Honestly, sometimes I've left nightclubs in tears.

Now, I've been doing personal appearances for a while longer and I'm much wiser. If anybody lays a finger on me, I refuse them a photo and have them thrown out of the club. I'm so much more of a stronger person these days and I wish I'd known back then in the first series of *Geordie Shore* what I know now. I suppose hindsight is a wonderful thing and you have to go through the shit before you can learn from it. So, listen up lads: it's not OK and it's *never* OK to do that to a woman.

There was one particular time that really stood out for me. I'd gone to this nightclub in Leeds with my friend Tom. Tom and I have been friends for years – my mam calls him her adoptive son. He's a big lad, but he's also gay and hilariously camp, definitely not some big burly bruiser. I doubt he could fight his way out of a paper bag.

Tom and I arrived at the club and it was quite clear no one knew what they were doing. The promoters who were running the night were occupying the table they'd given me to sit at, and when I looked around at the guys, they were all completely off their faces.

The next thing you know, I was being offered drugs left, right and centre. I kept saying no, but the group of guys persisted the whole time. I'm not the kind of girl who touches drugs and, the more they offered, the more forceful I would have to be in response. I was made to feel like I was letting them down by not having any. Truth be told, I didn't even want to drink, but they were forcing that down my neck, too. And there were hordes of pissed-up clubbers trying to grab me but no security to stop them. Poor Tom was trying his best, but he couldn't keep everyone at bay. It was such a scary situation. The crowd was turning hostile and I could hear a fight breaking out on the dance floor almost beside us. It was absolutely awful and I demanded to leave before things turned ugly. Only, the person who was driving me back to the hotel was off his face, too. He was driving like a lunatic and swerving all over the road. It was terrifying and so irresponsible. No amount of money was worth being in a potential car crash.

On the way back to the hotel I was fuming. To think I'd passed up tickets to see Jessie J for this. She'd personally invited me to her gig and I stupidly said no because I had this PA booked and I didn't want to let anyone down last minute. It was so poorly run anyway, no one even knew I was in there – they hadn't advertised anything.

Other times promoters have ended up trying it on with me and I've actually had to kick them in the balls. Honestly, the cheek of some of them is ridiculous. People think they can do anything to me, try and force themselves on me, or come back to my room, just because I've been on a show like *Geordie Shore*. I think back to when I was eighteen and doing PAs alone, getting drunk and finding myself in scary positions. It makes me angry now to think about how much I've been taken advantage of in the past.

Usually I have my PAs booked months in advance and I try not to let anyone down. I hate it when celebrities don't turn up when they say they are, especially if they haven't got a genuine excuse.

Sometimes I might have travelled twelve hours just to get to the club. I'm knackered and the last thing I want is to have a drink. Obviously I can't be like that, I have to be on form. People have turned up to the club expecting to see the good-time girl Holly from *Geordie Shore* so I have to put a smile on my face. There have been times when I have felt really low and like I can't turn on the charm, but the fans don't care about that. I remember once getting some really bad news about a friend and then a swarm of people came up to me, asking for a photo. I wasn't in the mood to smile, I was actually on the brink of tears, but I couldn't refuse them a photo because I'd just get abuse.

The only time I mind being bothered is when I'm sitting having a meal or out with my family and at those times it's really inappropriate. Other than that I will never refuse people a photo. So, if you see me, say hi (I don't bite).

Back when I worked in the call centre, I used to dream about the day when people would ask me for a photo. Now, I can't even get on a train or walk to the corner shop anymore without it being mentioned on Twitter but I'll never complain because, without the fans of the show, I couldn't be living out my dreams.

I still find Twitter bizarre. People will ask me to tweet them and tell me it will make their day. Young kids have my name in their Twitter handle and that astonishes me. I never expected anyone to be looking up to me at all – I'm just a normal northern girl from Middlesbrough who happens to be on a TV show and I never wanted to be a role model. Tell you the truth, it makes me uncomfortable. Honestly, I sometimes think these young girls should find someone better to idolise than me. But I don't say all this ungratefully, because, believe me, I am so grateful for all of my fans. I don't mind if they think I'm funny or want to copy my style, but it's a bit crazy that these girls want to be like me.

Why not have Olympians or doctors, or powerful business-women as role models, not celebrities? I have parents who tweet me and tell me that their kids want to grow up to be like me, and be famous. Then I kind of have to stop myself from replying something that may sound like I'm being a bit harsh. I know when I was younger I wanted to be famous because of

Katie Price and luckily I've made it, but for every one of me there are thousands who will never make it in the industry, and it's worrying to think they will spend their whole lives trying to do it, to achieve something that's not possible. I'm happier now than when I was working in that call centre and, even though I wanted to be famous, I was never actively trying to get famous. *Geordie Shore* was the only TV show I've ever applied for. I wasn't fame-hungry enough to pursue every reality TV show out there until I was discovered.

Chapter Twenty-Seven

THE WANTED MAN

You might think that because I'm on TV, my life is just one big endless list of showbiz parties, champagne receptions and popping flashbulbs. In actual fact, it's relatively normal for a reality star... so much so that when I do get invited to celeb parties, I feel like I don't belong.

The first time I attended a real proper red carpet event, I didn't know what to expect. It was July 2012 and American blogger Perez Hilton was hosting a bash called 'Perez: One night in London'. He'd invited a whole host of UK celebrities to his annual event and luckily I was one of them. It was a massive coup to be invited. It meant I was finally becoming a celebrity in my own right, away from the other cast and away from the show.

The party had been hyped up for ages. Joe McElderry, Paloma Faith and Cher Lloyd were performing back when they were racking up top ten hits and there promised to be a huge celebrity guest list. I'd be lying if I said I didn't feel the pressure to look my absolute best although, like usual, I'd left everything to the last minute. Sure, I'd known I was going to the event for weeks in advance, but in usual Holly style, I left it to the actual day to organise an outfit.

I looked through the piles of clothes in my bedroom, which get sent to me on a regular basis, but nothing seemed right. That's one of the great perks of being on *Geordie Shore*: every brand wants you to wear their clothes, either on TV or to an event. I get sent hundreds of items of clothing every week on the basis that I will take a photo and post it to my one million Twitter followers. It's great advertising for the brand and it only costs them the price of the dress and a bit of postage so it's a win-win situation.

But that day, I couldn't find anything suitable. Everything I tried on was too big, too small, too short, too formal or too skimpy. Nothing was working for me despite having more clothes at my disposal than the stock room at Topshop. I was just standing there, in typical girl fashion, looking at three wardrobes full of the latest clobber, sighing and moaning.

Pissed off and panicking, I realised I had no time to be messing around. The party was being held in Electric Brixton, in London, and my train was leaving in an hour, so I shoved a purple dress in my case and headed off to the station.

On my way down to London my problem-outfit prayers were answered by two stylish blonde angels, namely Sam and Billie Faiers from *TOWIE*. Those two glamazons always look red-carpet ready and they kindly offered to help me choose an outfit for the evening from their boutique, Minnies, in Essex. I spent hours in there, trying on their huge range of clothes until

I eventually picked a classic figure-hugging black pencil dress (they had told me to go for something sleek and subtle so that my outfit didn't distract from my uber-bright red hair). I teamed my dress up with some nude peep toes and kept my jewellery to a minimum so my fingers wouldn't seem overpowered by my bright orange nails and mountains of bling.

My date for the night was my agent Luke, who was kindly driving me around London and then to my PA in Epsom, later that evening.

When I sauntered down the red carpet a few hours later, I felt a little shy and nervous. I've always admired the likes of Victoria Beckham, who can just stand there, bold as brass, straight-faced, exuding confidence in front of the media, but I was nowhere near that poised.

Huge swarms of paparazzi were taking my photo and calling out my name. Fans lined the barriers and asked to have pictures taken with me. I can't ever remember feeling so important before. It was a nice feeling, but I couldn't help but pull these big cheesy grins to hide my shyness.

As I was posing, holding my stomach in, thrusting out my chest and flicking my hair over my shoulders, I heard a huge commotion from the end of the carpet. The man of the moment, Perez, had just arrived to rapturous applause from the crowd.

I'll admit I was a little anxious when I saw him in the flesh. Fuck, I felt like a fraud next to this larger-than-life Queen of the Media, straight from the glamorous Hollywood Hills. In contrast, I was little Holly Hagan from the unglamorous Grove Hill. Yeah, I might have slimmed down in recent years, my clothes are more stylish, my make-up is better and my mane of hair now a real talking point, but not far beneath my polished surface still lurks the under-confident, shy have-not from Middlesbrough. It was a total fish-out-of-water moment.

The bitchy blogger exited the huge blacked-out limo wearing a zany grey suit, three-quarter trousers and some loud pink trainers. An outfit only he could pull off, it was absolutely crazy. Even crazier still, was when party-boy Perez looked me straight in the eye and made his way over.

And I didn't know where to look. I went all giggly and fidgety and looked behind me to see if I'd mistaken his advances for someone else. Maybe he actually wanted to get the attention of someone more important behind me? But when I turned round there was no one there.

All of a sudden he was next to me. I was tongue-tied with stomach knots.

'Hey, you're Holleeey, right?' he said in his nasal American twang.

'Erm, yeah,' I nodded, as every word in the English language seemed to escape me.

'I thought that was you, I'm in love with the colour of your hair!' he declared as he touched my ruby red tresses.

'Thank you, I tweeted you today. Thanks so much for inviting me to the party,' I replied sheepishly, trying desperately not to look too timid.

'Oh my Gawd, it's my pleasure, honey. This party is gonna rock!' he said, with such infectious enthusiasm, before meandering off to the waiting paparazzi.

His close circle of super A-list friends are testament to his likability. It's just impossible not to be charmed by this guy straight from the off.

The party was absolutely rocking and, even though I'd been

invited, I didn't have a VIP area wristband, so I never got the chance to speak to Perez again after our red-carpet convo. I hadn't cracked my way into the inner circle quite yet, but just being in a room full of these people was good enough for me.

Absolutely buzzing inside, I walked into the party with an added spring in my step. I was giddy, like a hyperactive schoolgirl. Honestly, I couldn't contain my excitement. I strolled over to the bar and saw a few famous faces there, while Luke disappeared off to the toilet, like he always does. I swear that guy has a bladder the size of a garden pea!

I kind of scoped the room, not looking at anything in particular, just minding my own business and trying not to make eye contact with any of the bona fide celebs in my vicinity. I must have looked a little bewildered because two young trendy guys came over to me, probably out of sympathy. They were both good-looking, with super-fit physiques. The taller one of the two tapped me gently on the arm to grab my attention.

'Excuse me, are you Holly from *Geordie Shore*?' he said with a beaming smile (we'll call him Boy A).

'Erm, yeah, I am,' I replied, secretly glad they weren't just there to ask me where the toilets were, or where to hang their coats.

'I knew it was her,' said Boy A to Boy B. 'Do you mind if we get a photo with you? We love *Geordie Shore*.'

'Of course you can.'

Boy B pulled out his phone while Boy A stood next to me with his arm around my shoulder and we posed up for our candid snap.

'Thanks, are you here on your own? You look a little lost,' he asked.

I knew I looked like a loser on my lonesome. Nice one, Luke.

'No, my friend has just gone to the toilet, he'll be back in a bit.'

'So, what's it like being on *Geordie Shore*? It looks absolutely mental!' said Boy A.

'It's every bit as crazy as it looks,' I told him.

'I don't know how you do it. I couldn't cope with the hangovers.'

'It is tough, but we get used to it. It's like second nature now.'

'It's one of my favourite programmes. You girls are just wild, it's amazing.'

I just giggled and our conversation carried on like this for a little while longer, just chatting about the show and the party. The boys must have been huge fans because they invited me to go clubbing with them later that evening.

'We're going to Whisky Mist later, you should come,' said Boy A.

'Ah, I'd love to, lads, but I'm going on a PA later. Sorry.'

'Never mind,' Boy A looked forlorn, 'maybe next time. Have a nice evening, great to meet you.'

'Great to meet you, too.'

Just as they were walking off into the VIP area, Luke returned with a glass of champagne and a grin broader than the Angel of the North's rusty wings.

'Holly, have you *any* idea who they were?' he said, with emphasis.

'I don't know, they were just two lads asking for my picture,' I said, confused.

Luke slapped his hand on his forehead like he was in some kind of slapstick comedy show.

'That was Jay from The Wanted!'

'What? The Wanted – the boyband? Really?'

'Yes!' he said, not quite believing that I could be so out of touch with today's pop stars. 'What were they saying?'

'They just asked me for my picture. I just thought they were two fans, to be honest, Luke. You know I don't know any celebrities.'

And it was true. I rarely have a clue who anyone is. I'm totally oblivious, unlike Luke who can spot someone from the TV a million miles away.

When I stopped to think about it, I was so flattered. Someone from The Wanted asked me for my photo. What the hell! I know it's not much of a life achievement but imagine if a guy from one of the hottest boybands in the world asked for your picture, you'd be buzzing, too.

It was a shame I had to dash off to my PA because the party was just getting into full swing. But work comes first, and about an hour later I was out the door and on my way to a club in Surrey.

On the drive over to Epsom, I was idly checking through my tweets and lo and behold… I had a tweet from Jay.

He said: 'Can anybody locate Holly from *Geordie Shore*. We want to party with her!'

I couldn't believe it. Someone of his calibre was tweeting about me. And to think at first I didn't even know who he was. I liked that he was so normal and down-to-earth. I mean, he'd asked me for a photo! Me, little Holly Hagan from Grove Hill! I always see people like that as big-time celebrities, too busy being important to be nice, but The Wanted lad wasn't like that, he was just a normal guy. I had to ask Luke who was the other lad he was with just in case it was another big time celeb I'd failed to recognise but apparently it was just the Wanted boy's friend.

Jay tweeted the photo of us together to his 900,000 followers and I had all kinds of grief from his female fans. It was so ridiculous. The papers got hold of the snap, too, and by the next week's edition of *Heat Magazine* we were apparently the hottest couple on the scene. I didn't know how I would end up being associated with such a big celebrity. Still, you have to laugh.

Oh, and Jay, if you ever read this, I apologise for not knowing who you were, but let's get that party started soon!

Chapter Twenty-Eight

UNREQUITED LOVE

When we finish a series, we all need some time away from each other to recover after such an intense time of drinking and partying. Everyone thinks *Geordie Shore* is the easiest job in the world, but it doesn't half take its toll on your body: all the booze, sleepless nights and fast food isn't good for your physical health, while the rows and huge personality clashes aren't great for our mental health either.

It had been about a month since I'd seen James in Mexico. We'd both been booked to attend a PA together at a club in Leeds. I'd missed him, I couldn't deny it, and I was looking forward to spending some time together again.

We were staying in the same hotel and travelling down to the club together. I got dressed and made an extra-special effort for him. Then I knocked on his room and he was in there, half-ready, with just a towel wrapped round his waist. He looked

233

great, but then again James always did. He was always in good shape, with a freshly veeted chest and perfectly groomed hair.

As I walked into his room he kissed me on the cheek. He smelt amazing. His aftershave was fresh, powerful and alluring – it was the same familiar masculine scent I remembered from Cancun and smelling it again brought back all those intense feelings.

James poured me a drink and we toasted each other. I'll admit I'd already had a few drinks in my room, so I was well on my way to mortal by the time I knocked on his door. Dutch courage and all that. Although I don't know why I was nervous. Maybe it was just the excitement of the situation, I couldn't tell. I can't remember if he made the first move, or I did, but soon enough he had me pinned up against the wall in the hotel room and his hands were wandering up my dress. He moved me over to the bed and we started having sex, only this time there were no cameras in the room and we didn't have to be quiet in case we woke anyone up. It was just us two and it was amazing.

I didn't know if James had a girlfriend or if he was seeing anyone at this time. He never told me and because he had sex with me, I assumed he didn't. If he did have a girlfriend, I would never have slept with him, despite my obvious feelings. I'm not one of those lasses that would crack on with another girl's man.

When series four began, I still had strong feelings for James. I remember him walking in the house and I had butterflies. My heart flipped. I think I loved him. And it wasn't about sex anymore; we had a really good relationship as mates, but deep down, I wanted to be more.

There had been another shake-up of the *Geordie Shore* cast.

Rebecca and Jay had left and the two new housemates were Scott and Dan.

I was sad to see Rebecca leave. When she first came in, it was a massive shock. She was put in the house to stir things up and clash with Vicky, which she did. I felt sorry for her, though – I saw how she was struggling to fit in with the group and how she was being left out. It was how I'd been treated in the first series. She was just a kid, so I took it upon myself to look after her. We had a really good relationship and she was a lovely girl. We didn't want to argue or fight, we just wanted to get along. In the end, I think that's why she ended up leaving: because she wasn't creating the drama she was put in to cause.

Even when Vicky tried to set me up with a gorgeous-looking personal trainer called Dan I wasn't really interested. You could have thrown Ryan Gosling in front of me and I wouldn't have batted an eyelid. At that time, I was only bothered about James. It's always the way, isn't it? You want what you can't have.

When James finally told me he had a girlfriend, it completely floored me. I knew it would probably happen at some point, but now that it had, I was miserable. There's no worse feeling in the world than knowing the boy you want doesn't want you.

My behaviour towards him changed, too. I didn't know how to act around him. Out of respect for his relationship, I chilled out with the raw and crude language. I never brought up our history and I wouldn't flirt with him the way I used to because now it was clear we were just friends.

When the day finally came to meet his girlfriend Kate for the first time there had been a huge build-up. Everyone thought it was going to be awkward and I'd kick off or act like a total jealous bitch. In reality, nothing could have been further from the truth. What had Kate done to me? Nothing. She was just a girl who fell for a guy and now they were going out; she hadn't done anything wrong. I thought she was going to hate me. Actually, I think I was more nervous about meeting her – I felt sick.

James knew she was going to be joining us in the club that evening and all night you could see him on edge while he waited for her to arrive. When she eventually did turn up, he was so happy, happier than I had ever seen him. His face just lit up. Tell you the truth, I was happy for him, too. I know I never had that effect on the guy and isn't that what we're all looking for, someone who just lights you up when they enter the room? He'd found that and I wasn't going to be the one to stand in the way of them or cause a scene.

I was bowled over by how naturally stunning she was. Tanned, brunette, curvaceous, with a mega-watt smile that would put Simon Cowell to shame. She was the kind of girl any man would be proud to bring home to meet his mother. Hats off to James, he wasn't wrong when he said she was a worldie. Next to her I felt like a fat ugly oompa loompa.

I think everyone was expecting me to hate her, but honestly I kind of felt for her because she had a boyfriend in the public eye. He is part of this crazy TV show that's all about partying and shagging. She had just met all his wild cast mates and had to be filmed for the first time. Add in the fact I had slept with him and, as any girl knows, it's never nice meeting someone your boyfriend has slept with. The poor lass must have been terrified, but she handled herself with dignity and grace.

So I made a point of being overly nice to her, to make sure that she wouldn't feel left out or intimidated by the situation. I was nothing but lovely and attentive, making sure she was all right and her drink was topped up. I'd take her to the toilet so we could do our make-up together and I just wanted her to know, without actually coming right out and saying it, everything was cool. I was glad she and James were happy and she had nothing to worry about.

At the end of the night she told me she appreciated all the effort I'd gone to and that she liked me the best out of everyone, which meant a lot. But I was still hurt, not by her, just at being rejected by someone I had really strong feelings for. I had to get smashed to take my mind off the situation, it was the only way I knew how: to self-destruct. Getting drunk kind of numbed the pain of seeing James bring Kate back to the house because that used to me in bed with him. Regardless, I had nothing against her. She was such a lovely, charming girl.

James will say he didn't care about me, but as soon as Scott came into the show and I began paying him a little bit of attention, he got jealous. We went camping one day and I was sitting in between Scott and James. I was flirting with Scott when James pulled me aside for a chat. I remember him saying, 'Moved on from me, have you?' and I was like, 'What you on about?' and he said, 'No, no, you go off with Scott – it's fine.'

I knew then he was jealous. He must have been to say something like that. At that stage I don't think he wanted me anymore because he had Kate but he wanted to know he could still have me. I think he was disappointed I wasn't going to be at his beck and call anymore, fawning all over him.

When I eventually had sex with Scott it was just a friends-with-benefits scenario. In a way, I wanted to get one over on

James by getting under Scott. I wanted him to know I was no longer available as his go-to-girl for attention. That ship had sailed.

I wasn't too sure when James and Kate had officially got together and I wondered if they were together when he had slept with me. If she'd been seeing him, while he was having sex with me, then I didn't know about it. I would never have forgiven myself if that had been the case but I didn't want her to feel like I was out to steal her boyfriend.

Like I said, Kate and I got on great at first. The trouble only started when she saw series four onscreen. She thought James and I had been quite flirty in the house, but we weren't really and, if we were, it's because that's all we knew how to be. We were playful and we were still quite close, like best friends, but there was never anything inappropriate going on.

There was a time when I got so mortal and James had to put me to bed. He was only being a good friend, but it looked worse than it was. That's the trouble with TV and Twitter. Everything James and me did was commented on. Even if we were just talking, or going for a walk, it was made into such a big deal.

I can put myself in Kate's shoes and I can't blame her for getting annoyed. When she saw us onscreen together, she obviously became jealous: totally understandable. She picked up on every little thing because when you watch it onscreen it was totally taken out of context and things can appear to be a much bigger deal than they ever were in reality.

Let me just make it clear, my intention was never to piss the girl off. I really didn't know how to behave around James at the time. We'd always been slightly more than friends, so it was hard for me to look at him and feel nothing. I can see everything from Kate's point of view and, if that was my boyfriend, I wouldn't have been happy either. I just wish she could have seen it from mine for just a split second and realised I wasn't trying to be a bitch or break the girl code.

Meeting Kate meant I would finally have to get over James. For months now, I felt like a heavy weight had been sitting on me. I'd shed a lot of tears over him, lost a lot of sleep, eaten a lot of McDonald's and now it was time to move on. My life would have been torture if I didn't shake loose from the grip he had over me. I most definitely didn't want to keep feeling this way. He'd got his girl and it wasn't me.

At times I wondered if I was destined to forever fall for people I couldn't have because it seemed to be the story of my life. 'We're cool,' I told everyone who asked about James and me, even though I felt something else. I felt sad, like I'd lost something I never quite had.

Chapter Twenty-Nine

GEORDIE TOURS

So here we went again. Another series… more booze… more bucking… more blazing rows… and more fucking drama with James. It was like déjà vu. In this series, we were told we would be filming it all in Europe representing Geordie Tours, helping hen and stag dos party abroad. We visited Amsterdam, Prague and Barcelona and then I tried skiing for the first time in the French Alps. They are places I've always dreamed of travelling to, and through *Geordie Shore* I get to holiday in these unbelievable cities, all expenses paid, in the most beautiful houses with my best friends.

It's funny how everything's changed isn't it? Like now I use the term best friends when talking about my *Geordie Shore* gang, but, back in series one, they were almost like my worst enemies. I suppose over time we've all just grown to love each other. Don't get me wrong, this didn't happen overnight. It's not like someone suddenly flicked a switch and said 'Ah you'll all get along just fine now'. We still all fall out, but deep down we'll always be a family. I think what made us bond together the most was seeing the public reaction after the first series. Everyone hated our show and we became protective over it. We had this 'kick one, kick us all' mentality. It was the *Geordie Shore* cast vs. the World, if you will, and you'd be surprised how much a shared interest will bring you close to people. We all became more tolerant of each other and got used to each other's personalities. I used to get a hard time in the beginning because I was young, but as time went on, the rest of the cast remembered I was naïve and often silly and instead of having a go at me, they would take that into account. All the girls bonded together, often, over our arguments with the boys and because we started spending quality time with each other outside of the show. Now we are like sisters and I'm so glad I never left the show after the first season because I would have missed out on the most amazing experience. Honestly, sometimes I really do have to pinch myself that my life is not just a dream.

I didn't really know until series five just how much James's girlfriend Kate disliked me. She said in the first episode 'my inappropriate actions' towards James bothered her, so not to run the risk of upsetting her, James unequivocally said he wasn't going to speak to me the whole time we were filming.

I was over James now. It had sunk in that I wasn't going to get with him, but I didn't think that would stop us from being friends, or at the very least being civil towards each other.

When I walked into the house for the first time, James didn't speak a word to me, which I thought so odd at the time. He wouldn't even say hello. For me, that was horrible. After I'd gone out of my way to make so much effort with Kate, I didn't think anything I'd done warranted being ignored. The guy had once been my best friend and now it was like I didn't exist. I know he didn't want to upset his girlfriend, but at the same time his ignorance was so hurtful.

Our first city was Amsterdam and we were living on a houseboat in close proximity. Can you imagine how awkward that was when James was deliberately not speaking to me? I didn't know how to act around him anymore.

As the trip went on, it only got worse. It was a turning point for James, too, and things started spiralling downwards for him. Because he wouldn't speak to me, for a ridiculous reason, it made everyone else's opinions change. I think they lost a little respect for him and the way he was behaving: he'd put his relationship with Kate over his friendship with me.

The only thing more awkward than James's ignorance was having Gaz and Charlotte buck next to me while I was asleep. I thought I was in a nightmare at first but no, it was real life and those noises will be forever etched on my brain.

After Amsterdam, we returned to Newcastle. James made a call to Kate and she reiterated again that he wasn't to speak one word to me. Honestly, I just didn't get it. The girl is a grade A, stone-cold stunner, anyone can see that, so why was she threatened by me? Kate, you won: he picked you. I didn't understand what she had to be jealous of.

In my opinion, she is everything I'm not and that's obviously what James was looking for. It's tough knowing the guy you like doesn't like you. But then to have his new girlfriend be quite mean about it, after I'd made so much effort with her, really wasn't necessary. Everyone knew she was prettier than me. She knows she's better-looking and skinnier than me, so what was she so afraid of? To this day I don't get it.

All I knew was I'd lost my best friend. I couldn't walk around James or be near him. I was scared to even make eye contact. It had an awful impact on the rest of the group, too.

One night Kate came out to meet James and the rest of the *Geordie Shore* gang. Out of respect, I kept my distance. I couldn't be nice to her while James was being cruel to me. To see them all over each other didn't bother me, but I felt like they were laughing at me and it made me upset. All the girls were on my side and the boys just didn't know what to think.

Over the next few weeks, James started staying in all the time and ostracised himself from the rest of the group. He was so boring. He didn't want to communicate with any of us, never mind me. It was like he didn't care about anyone and he didn't want to be there.

It makes me mad to think about how lucky James is to be in the *Geordie Shore* house and how many people would kill to be in there. Yet, it was like he didn't want to be there anymore. I know things change when you get a girlfriend and the appeal of getting pissed and shagging obviously isn't high on your agenda but still, our shelf lives on this show aren't forever and you'll never get that time back. So I always say to myself, get the most out of this experience, because if I don't then one day, I'll wish I had.

I wish I could have sat James down and made him see this, but I couldn't. I had to stay well away from him and let him work it all out on his own. What angered me more was when we did try and have a chat, and I confessed to how he had made me feel, he just fobbed me off. It was like he couldn't be bothered to listen. He belittled me by telling me I wouldn't know what it's like to be in a serious relationship, and I'd never been in a situation where I cared about anyone enough to understand what sacrifices must be made. Fuck you, James! How the fuck would you know? He was wrong because I had cared about him so much I sacrificed my time in Mexico for him. We were supposed to being sorting everything out, but it was useless. The tension was still at an all-time high. I couldn't believe I used to be bucking his brains out, and now we had to pretend like the other didn't exist.

I realised the guy I used to like no longer existed. We were never going to be friends again, not in any real way, anyway. It upset me, too, that James was coming across like an idiot on camera. I knew he wasn't like that deep down, but the audience wouldn't, and I didn't want him to get any grief for the way he was treating me. God, sometimes I wish I didn't care about people as much, but I don't see it as a bad trait. I'd certainly rather be like me than someone who doesn't care at all. I know it might sound like I'm being harsh on the lad, but until you're in that position it's hard to fully understand. The whole group wanted the James we knew and loved to come back out and be himself, but he was gone – it was like he'd had the personality henpecked out of him.

To be fair to Kate, we did eventually clear the air. After we had a face-to-face chat on camera and got everything off our chests we both apologised and felt there didn't need to be any awkwardness. Continuing to live with James for the rest of series was tough, though, as I knew we could never be friends again, which was sad, because apart from the lads I've grown up with, he was the closest guy to me. But he wasn't the same person.

I turned my attention to another boy in the house, Scott. We had ended up in bed a few times and got it on with each other but we both made it clear from the outset that it was a complete friends-with-benefits scenario. I never wanted anything more and neither did he. The last thing I wanted was another James situation.

But you know what the worst part of the whole series was? Never mind the way James was being so cold and distant, it was having to see my best friend Charlotte confess to Gary about being in love with him. I've always felt overly protective towards her and I've felt like we've had the closest bond ever since series one. She's the only one who has never judged me. We are similar in age and we have the same sense of humour. We could be funny, or drunk, or silly together and it didn't matter. We're on the same level, it's like we're almost telepathic – we can just give each other a look and we both know what we are thinking. When I left the house in series one, she was the only one I wrote a note to. I felt like she was the only one who would care. She'll be my friend for life because the girl hasn't got a bad bone in her body. And watching the way Gaz has treated her over the past few years, after everything they've been through, it all came to a climax in Barcelona.

I've always had a weird relationship with Gaz. Obviously we had that clinch on the very first night of *Geordie Shore* which just feels so strange to think about because I now look on him like a big brother. But sometimes you don't know what's real with him. You don't know if he actually wants to be friendly to you because it looks good on camera, or if he's being genuine. He's so hard to read.

It's really difficult for me to see how he treats Charlotte, too. I don't know if he genuinely cares about her. He's a very lonely person and he'll be the first to admit it. Sometimes he's said to us that he often brings girls back because he just wants a cuddle and some affection. I feel like there's some bigger issues going on in Gary's head. You can't be happy going around shagging a different lass every night. He must be feeling some kind of loss because he feels the need to fill that void all the time: he can't go to bed alone. It's quite sad, really.

But it broke my heart when Charlotte finally built up the courage to tell him how she felt about him and he obviously didn't feel the same way. To see her so devastated was, hands down, one of the worst moments in my *Geordie Shore* history.

Chapter Thirty

RITA ORA

Rita Ora called me a whore but that wasn't the first time I'd been mistaken for a hooker. That was in Amsterdam when we were filming series five of *Geordie Shore* and some lads stopped me in the street and asked me how much for a quick ride. Of course I politely declined, although I wasn't too offended. Have you seen the brasses in Amsterdam? Some of them are worldies!

But I was offended when foul-mouthed Rita called me a whore – she was actually implying I was some sort of prostitute, which is obviously not true. Slag, possibly, but whore? Never. I've never been paid for sex and anyone I've banged I've always wanted to, despite some of them being less than desirable.

It was back in February 2013 when this fiery exchange occurred. Now, I don't know if any of this is true or not but I'm just telling you about the spat, the way it happened. I was in bed one night and I'd seen on Twitter that Rita Ora had apparently slept with Jay-Z. It was a bit of gossip and I just wanted to know if there was any truth in the rumour. I tweeted saying 'I've been told to say that Rita Ora has been ALLEGEDLY buckin Jay Z! I repeat ALLEGEDLY'.

My Twitter went through the roof, with favourites, retweets and replies from hundreds of people. I ignored the drama I'd caused, but about ten minutes later, red-faced Rita waded into the messages and it turned into a full-blown virtual argument.

'I stayed silent on one bulls**t rumour but this one I have to speak,' Rita wrote.

'Neva eva will any1 includin a red head dum z listin attention seekin whore try talk s**t about me& my family holly wateva da f*k ur name is,' she rebuked.

I later hit back, taking pride in my 'z-list' status: 'You are all thick if u think just because someone's absolutely stunning they won't get cheated on... Cheryl Cole? No relationship is perfect.'

I continued: 'Oooopsy getting told off don't shoot the messenger! Of course I'm only a Z-list why would anyone care what I say ;)'

Obviously she wasn't very happy, but come on, Rita love! If you're going to have a go at me, why not do it in the Queen's English? The way she spelled her replies was ridiculous – she should at least act more professional than the Z-lister she was arguing with. I *am* a total Z-lister but I don't give a fuck. She should speak like she's an A-lister.

I couldn't believe she reacted to it, to be honest. You would have thought such a playground Twitter row would have been beneath her. I genuinely didn't want to start a row with her. I'm not the type of person who would get into an argument with someone for the sake of it. I just didn't realise the impact that me tweeting would have. But I learned a lesson and now I'm a lot more mindful of what I tweet. And I suppose every cloud has a silver lining because I won Twitter Spat of the Year award from *Heat Magazine*, voted for by the public.

It now has pride of place on my bedside table. I'm not a massive fan of Rita Ora anyway, so it's not like there's any love lost. If I ever bumped into her, I'd probably say hi and apologise. I'd hope she'd see the funny side but in actuality she'd probably be a bitch. She thinks she's a top A-lister because she's friends with Rihanna and Jay-Z, but she shouldn't think she's any better than anyone else. She shouldn't think she's any better than I am. Anyway, I'm sure she's lovely when you get to know her…

Chapter Thirty-One

AUSTRALIA

Ever since I grew up watching the *Neighbours'* escapades on Ramsay Street or the Summer Bay shenanigans on *Home And Away*, I've always wanted to go to Australia. So it was a dream come true when we found out we were flying halfway around the world to the beautiful cosmopolitan city of Sydney.

We were now on our sixth series of *Geordie Shore* and with it came two more cast changes. Vicky and Ricci had split and subsequently Ricci had left the show. I was sad to see him go because he was a lovely lad although I wasn't that close to him. I just saw him as Vicky's boyfriend, but I never had any ill feelings towards him. At times I'd felt for him because it must have been so hard being in a relationship in the house, especially when Ricci and Vicky's relationship was extremely volatile. All the girls stuck up for each other so whenever they fought, the girls would always pick Vicky's side, and I think for that reason he didn't see me as a proper friend. I do think the show brought out the worst in him.

Dan also left the series. Although he was a great lad, he didn't really fit in. He didn't mean any harm to anyone. I just don't think he found his own way – he was trying to be like Gary and Scott too much, whereas he should have just been himself. He was like the little brother of the group and he added comedy value. I enjoyed watching him and I'm sure others did, too, but he detracted from the drama because he never tried to cause any himself and *Geordie Shore* thrives off drama.

After seeing the previous series on TV I made the decision not to have anything to do with James. As far as I was concerned that was the best outcome for all parties. I was still angry with him and when I'd seen everything again onscreen, it reminded me of just how much of a heartless knobhead he'd been to me.

The house we had been given to live in was utterly amazing. A sleek, cool, modern mansion with quirky furniture, the kind you'd find in a boutique hotel. It always baffles me why they want to lend these incredible houses to a bunch of reprobates like us, but I'm not complaining.

The tension was high when we landed in Australia. We were tired from all the travelling. Add in lots of pent-up emotions and alcohol and you have the ingredients for a fiery cocktail. The producers knew something was brewing and they were just waiting for one of us to explode onscreen.

Even worse, James had told everyone he was single. I don't know why he did this, but he told the whole house and crew that he and Kate were over. The girls and me didn't believe it. We had a look on her Twitter and, sure enough, there were pictures and tons of messages about how much she was going to miss James while he was away.

James obviously hadn't told her he was planning on lying to his housemates about their relationship, because she would never go along with it. And why should she? What kind of guy would deny his own girlfriend? It was pathetic.

The first night into the trip, James came over to me and apologised for the way he'd behaved in the previous series. I knew he felt bad for the way he had treated me. He wanted to clear the air, but I couldn't let it go. (A bit of background here to bring you up to speed. Kate and I got into a little spat over Twitter when the last series aired on TV and in one of the messages she called me a slag and a whale.)

'Ya alright?' he said.

I sipped my drink and nodded to signal that I was willing to listen to him.

'I am sorry for everything. Can we just be friends and forget everything?'

I looked at him, dead on in the eye, trying not to let my body sway too much from the alcohol. And I told him straight: 'No.'

'What?'

'No,' I repeated. 'You can't just apologise and we're all happy families again. I mean, I accept your apology but I just think, after what your girlfriend said about me, I'm not ready to be your friend again.'

He kind of sighed and tutted in my direction, like I was supposed to be bowled over by his act of remorse.

'Don't you dare be like that with me. I'm not ready to be your friend again, James.'

'Why are you being so difficult? You slagged Kate off, too.'

'No, I never,' I said defensively. 'I never once said anything about her. She called me a fucking whale!'

'I just want to have a good time with everyone.'

'I'm not going to argue with ya,' I said. 'So stay out of my way.'

'You're being ridiculous.'

'At the end of the day, I don't want to be your friend. I accept your apology but we are not friends.'

'Now you're makin' it awkward,' he moaned.

'No, I'm not.'

'You are.'

'Well, sorry,' I shrugged. 'That's the way it's got to be.'

This was never shown on TV, but later that night I questioned him about why he was falsely claiming to be single.

'Why would you say you are single when you're not? We've seen Kate's Twitter and you are still together.'

James didn't know how to respond, he just spluttered and looked flustered, trying to come up with a decent lie to explain his actions.

'Oh, forget it!' he shouted and left me to slurp my drink in peace.

We all ended up leaving shortly after. James got a taxi back with Vicky and was crying as he told her about our row. I'm not happy he had been reduced to tears because of my actions, but it made a change from me crying over him. He felt lost and left out. He'd been rumbled on the first night lying about his relationship and now I'd refused to accept his apology.

But things were about to erupt even further.

X X X

The next day, we were all out in Pacha, one of the most exclusive nightclubs in Sydney. We'd already been drinking at the house and, by the time I got to the club, I was well on my way to being absolutely mortal. The jet lag was still killing me so I decided to get smashed so I wouldn't notice how tired I was. The whole group was out and everyone was having a great time, apart from James.

He was standing on his own, looking miserable. Fuck, I couldn't help but feel sorry for the guy. It must go back to the days when I was at school and I'd be left out. It's a horrible feeling and I wouldn't want anyone to go through that, especially if I could do something about it. I supposed I'd been a bit of a bitch to him the previous night, which is out of character for me. I felt guilty about the way I'd behaved, but I felt like he needed some comeuppance for his actions. I couldn't just let him get away with treating me so callously.

There were only four of us out that evening, Gaz, James, Sophie and me, which was difficult because James and I weren't speaking, so I went over, put an arm on his shoulder and leaned into his ear.

'I'm not saying that we're never gonna be friends, I'm just saying right now, it's difficult,' I said with genuine meaning.

'Well, I just want to be friends, OK?'

I should have just agreed and let that be an end to it, but when I have a drink in me, it's almost like I crave drama.

'But your girlfriend called me a whale on Twitter. How the fuck am I supposed to react to that, James?' I demanded.

'Holly, you slagged her, too.'

'All I said was she wears white a lot!'

'So what? She's tanned! I wear white...'

I kept repeating it over and over to him.

'Your girlfriend called me a fucking whale. A fucking whale, James!' I shouted, my voice getting louder and louder. 'Who does she think she is, commenting on my weight? A fucking whale!'

Over and over again, I said it. I was like a broken record. And the more I said it, the more wound up I was getting and then James tipped me over the edge.

'Shhhhhhhh!' he laughed and placed a finger on his lips.

Well, that was the last straw. How fucking dare he try and shush me while we were having a heated conversation.

'Don't fucking tell me to shush!' I screeched, pushing him away from me.

The next part was never shown on TV and I'm glad because I'm ashamed of my actions. Violence is never the answer, but at that moment a boiling surge of anger coursed through me. I reeled back my hand, closed it tightly into a fist and *SMACK*! I punched him square in the jaw.

He was absolutely stunned. Everyone turned round to look at the commotion.

'How fucking dare you try and tell me to shut up! After everything you've done to me!' I screamed.

James was holding his freshly punched face with one hand and with the other he grabbed his drink and swilled it all over me. The action unfolded in a flash of whip-pan action. I screamed with the shock of being suddenly soaking wet. Gary, who was standing on my right, tried to get in between us. It was useless, though. I was hell-bent on getting up in his face. I broke away from Gary and ran over to James again.

As I lunged forwards at James my footing slipped and I almost fell over the side of the balcony. Thank goodness someone pulled me back, or who knows what could have happened. It was like I was possessed. I can't ever remember being in such a state. I knew I'd gone too far. I shouldn't have lashed out, but I couldn't bear to look at his shiny smug face laughing at me like that.

Everything after that is kind of blurry. All I remember is being dragged away from the VIP by some bulky security guard and escorted out of the fire exit. I was in Sydney's best nightclub, the world-renowned Pacha, and I'd been ejected for brawling after twenty minutes. If that wasn't bad enough, I had also been removed from the *Geordie Shore* house. Fantastic behaviour, not!

I woke up in a strange hotel room with a member of the crew babysitting me. She had let me sleep off the worst of my hangover before telling me I'd been removed from the house until further notice. Three days I spent secluded from the rest of the cast, which I thought unnecessarily harsh. I was completely alone with no phone, no friends, no familiar faces and all because of what? Because I was finally sticking up for myself. I know I shouldn't have punched him but sometimes you just can't control your limbs.

The only good thing to come out of those tedious three days of solitude was a new hair colour. I had nothing else to occupy my time, so I went to a hairdresser and told them to turn my red hair to purple. I hoped that by changing my look again it would help me turn a corner. I wanted to start afresh. Forget all the upset, drama, the heartache, the bitching that had gone on with James and the red locks.

New hair, new Holly.

When I was allowed back to the house I pulled James aside for a quiet word, just to apologise, because I should never have tried to hit him.

'I'm sorry for punching you,' I said, and I meant it genuinely.

'Is that it?'

'Yeah, I don't know what you expect me to do because everything that did happen...'

'Sympathy vote again,' he said as he walked away from me.

'It's not a sympathy vote.' I was seething because he'd walked off on me. 'You're a stupid little prick!'

'Well, I think raising your hand to somebody is far worse than anything I have done to you,' said James cockily, and folded his arms like it was a chore for him to hear my apology.

'Oh, fuck off! You weren't even bothered. Stop pretending you give a shit! What you did to me was heartbreaking. What I did to you was just physical.'

If James wasn't careful, I was about to lose it again.

'How can you not see that it's wrong?'

'I hit you and you know what? You fucking deserved it!'

'Whatever,' he shrugged.

'You need to realise you have no friends in this house anymore.'

'What do you mean?' he looked confused.

'No one likes you, James.'

I looked around and didn't see any one else in the house disagreeing with my comments. At that point it was true no one liked him. He had lied to all of us about splitting up with his girlfriend. He'd treated me like a mug, which meant the girls weren't happy. Scott and Gary were too into themselves and pulling birds to care about him. He didn't have anyone left.

'That's not a very nice thing to say. Remember how you were treated in series one?'

'Yeah? Well you know what this is? Fucking karma!'

He looked at the floor and never said another word. I sat down with the rest of the group, tossed my new purple locks over my shoulders and vowed that would be the last time I ever, ever had any emotional feelings towards James.

XXX

Later in the series, through another *Geordie Shore* row (this time with Gaz), James and I did make up. We weren't back to being friends, but we were beginning to be civil. All of us girls had stuck up for James during a row with Gary and it had reunited him with us. Well, let's face it, he had no one else. It was the girls or go home.

I wish I had resolved things sooner with him. And I know he just wanted to keep his girlfriend happy because she is the most important person in his world. I get that now and I'm glad to say it's all water under the bridge. After everything that had been said and done I just hoped we could rebuild some sort of friendship.

Australia was our biggest series to date and with it came bigger demands on our time. We only have so long to film a show and to capture the footage we need, so we can't just go to bed when we want to, otherwise how boring would the show be? We can't just have a night off and chill with a DVD when we want, we have to drag ourselves out and make the most of the time.

The producers aren't too hard on us, but if we have to be at a certain night to get the footage then we have no option, no matter how we might be feeling. There was one night when Charlotte was begging to stay in the house. She was exhausted and needed a night off. The producers needed her to get ready and plaster on her party face, despite how much she was protesting. They kept telling her that she couldn't stay in and needed to start getting ready.

Well, you know how crazy Charlotte can get. She grabbed a bottle of vodka and started necking it straight. Her thinking was that if she got so legless before she was supposed to be out, she would be incapable of leaving the house. It didn't take her long to get absolutely steaming and in a fit of frustration she started smashing the house up. Eventually, after seeing her completely flip out, they allowed her to stay in.

I know we get paid lots of money to be part of the show and that's what the producers tell us when we feel low and want some time off. They remind us how grateful we should be to be given such fantastic opportunities, which I totally get and I am forever grateful to be part of such an exhilarating show, but sometimes they forget three lots of crew are filming us. Crew one will start filming, then when their shift is over, crew two will take over and, when they've finished, crew three start and so on. They get time off, while we have to power on through. There's not three sets of housemates but sometimes I wish there was.

Sometimes it feels like they have no idea what we are going through. Yeah, I know we have an amazing opportunity, which is why we've grabbed it with both hands, but don't be fooled… everything comes at a price. Even my parents laugh at me when I tell them how hard it is. They think it's like working a twelve-hour shift and then we get to go to bed. I wish! We don't have shifts. We can be up until 4am and then rudely awoken by the crew at 9am.

I remember once just walking around the house like a zombie, trying to find a place to crash. My head was in another dimension. I think I was delusional.

The only place I could go was the shag pad and as soon as my head hit the pillow, I was out like a light, in a blissful deep slumber I'd been craving for weeks. That was until Scott and some random girl decided to come in and try and turf me out. He was dying to shag her and apparently had nowhere else to go. Well, he could fuck off. Neither did I. I kind of remember getting into a huge argument with him in front of this poor girl. I was screeching like a banshee. It was all so blurry because I was so tired and I only remembered about it a few days later.

I think half of the anger came because it was Scott. Ever since he joined the cast, him and I had been sleeping together or getting down and dirty. We did have an understanding that it was just no-strings attached, but can anything really ever be without feelings? Sex without commitment; it might work in the real world but not in the *Geordie Shore* house.

By the end of the series I was getting annoyed with Scott when he would pull girls in front of me. I wear my heart on my sleeve and I couldn't help it. I'm like an open book when I'm in a jealous mood and I couldn't hide it from him or the rest of the group. I thought Scott and I had bonded when we were sent into the outback for three days. The powers that be, our Australian boss Steve aka Sheep-Shagging Steve sent us on a mission to retrieve something from the Aussie outback. We had no idea what, all we knew is that we were driving to a bed and breakfast six hours away, in the middle of nowhere.

We figured it was his crafty way of trying to make something happen between us, because when we actually reached our destination, we didn't retrieve anything. We just got sent home again after spending a few nights cuddled up in the same double bed. During our time away from the rest of the group Scott and I had grown quite close and we ended up doing rude things, but when we returned to the house, he was only interested in pulling other girls. I know it's stupid and I was an idiot for getting attached. Now, I'm completely cool with him.

It's hard to stay mad at Scott for anything because he can just do this little cheeky smile and you instantly forgive him. You can see why the girls find him so attractive.

Chapter Thirty-Two

BODY BATTLES

I always think it's an airborne virus, this hatred of women and their bodies. It's like there's no way to control it. Every woman I know has some kind of hang-up about the way she looks, like there's not even a choice. Ever since the whole skirt debacle when I was ten years old, I have been critical of my appearance. My obsession with my body has only got worse as the media exposure has grown, too.

It all came to a head after we filmed in Australia. My self-confidence hit rock bottom. I'd been away a total of seven weeks and in that time I'd managed to pile on two stone. When I returned home, I was disgusted with myself. Honestly, I went through a stage where I hated my body so much I wouldn't even wear shorts and a bra in my bedroom in case I passed a mirror and caught a glimpse of my unsightly frame.

I'd gone into the series having trained and dieted for months beforehand. I wanted to make sure I looked my absolute best on Bondi Beach. Then within two days of being in Oz, I began to feel the strain. The massive amount of calorie-laden alcohol we consumed made me feel rough. And, as anyone who knows anything about hangovers understands, the next day all you want is to eat shite. Literally, all I stuffed my face with was carbs, carbs, carbs. We were so busy when we filmed that we'd often just eat on the go, grabbing a takeaway when we could. Within a week, all the weight I'd lost in the previous months quickly started to creep back on.

Sure, we could have said no to the booze. There were nights when we decided not to drink, but the content of what we filmed on those nights was, quite frankly, boring. We'd all be sitting around like miseries, not delivering anything that could be used for the show, and we all want to make *Geordie Shore* the best it can be for our fans.

Don't get me wrong, sometimes we are so physically drained that it's impossible to continue partying. I often get messages on Twitter from girls who say I look like a state when I go out because I'm wearing flat shoes and I've got my hair in a bun. What they don't realise is we've probably only been given thirty minutes to get ourselves ready, we're still hungover from the past two weeks of drinking and all you crave is your bed. I remember one night we were allowed an hour's sleep in the afternoon and the crew woke us up after ten minutes. I was literally sobbing, I was so tired – it felt like torture. Sleep is so important and everyone knows how grumpy you can be when it's deprived. Even when we are in bed, we can be woken periodically during the night by noise from other people. My body takes a battering.

We have no choice but to get back on it and by the end of the series our heads are completely fucked. We've had no sleep, the alcohol makes us moody, our emotions are running high from all the drama – is it any wonder we kick off at times? Even someone with the patience of a saint would find that tough. Everyone thinks *Geordie Shore* is the easiest job in the world and yes, we get many, many perks, but people forget the physical and mental aspects of the show.

So when I returned from Australia, I was looking the nastiest I'd looked in years. And what made it even worse was I had countless PAs booked, which meant I'd be out in nightclubs for weeks on end, so more late nights and alcohol. All my PAs were up and down the country, so I couldn't even organise a daily gym routine or to meet back up with a personal trainer. I was frustrated but I needed to shift the timber quickly.

I'm not proud of it, but around this time I developed a problem with food. I wouldn't call it an eating disorder because it never ruled my life, but I was obsessing about everything I ate.

I do know the healthy ways to lose weight. It's not rocket science: eat well, drink lots of water, exercise and get plenty of rest. All well and good when your life doesn't revolve around binge drinking. Not that I'm making excuses for myself, but I thought the only way I could get the weight off me in a short space of time was to throw it all up.

The only other time in my life when I felt this strongly about losing a dramatic amount of weight was when I was going through that period of self-harming. I used to search the Internet for pro-anorexia websites and get tips on how to be anorexic. It sounds absolutely crazy, doesn't it? But I was willing to do anything. I would read the advice on how you could eat toilet roll to fill your stomach instead of eating. To chug on glasses of water, or suck on ice to trick your body into thinking it's eating when it's not.

But I felt the girls who did that to themselves were stronger than me, they had more willpower. They could control their eating and I couldn't. I would try everything for a few weeks, but I could never sustain it, even if I was looking like I was losing weight. It never took hold of me.

All through my life people have always commented on my body shape. Every summer holiday I would aim to get fit and then come back to school two stone lighter. I would envisage me turning back up to class and people saying how skinny I was and it made me happy. I'd had enough of people calling me fat for so long. It had happened for other girls in my year, so why not me?

When I first went into *Geordie Shore* my size was commented on all the time. It was the first thing the Internet trolls would throw at me. I was always the 'fat minger' of the group and it made me so upset. I know I have to take some responsibility because I put myself out there on TV to be commented on, so I have to take the rough with the smooth. Believe me, if you have any insecurity your audience will find it and run with it.

I remember the first time I made myself sick. I'd been booked on a PA in Nottingham and I caught the train early without eating anything before I left the house. Train food is never the best, but while I was on the platform I bought myself a massive Subway sandwich, crisps, coke and sweets because I couldn't find anything else. After I ate it, I was satisfied for a few minutes but then the guilt crept in. The fullness in my belly made me feel revolting and suddenly all I could feel on myself was extra blubber.

I left the train, rolled my suitcase along the platform and I felt my stomach and fat ass shaking. When I got in the taxi and headed to the hotel I was almost on the verge of tears.

After I'd checked into my room, I did the only thing I could think of to make me feel better: I knelt down on the cold hard tiles and shoved two fingers so far down my throat that I began to wretch violently. I did this a few times until eventually I threw up. I flushed the toilet and felt a weird sense of achievement. If I could do this all the time, then I would be skinny, I thought. I believed it was the answer to all my troubles.

Now I'm not going to exaggerate by saying I did this religiously because I didn't. It was just on the odd occasion when I was out on the road and worried about the food I was eating when I would just make myself sick. In fact, I started eating way too much – I would glut myself for dinner and serve myself vomit as a dessert.

It didn't feel like an eating disorder because in my eyes I was still big. Eating disorders were only for those girls who were stick thin and I wasn't even close. I knew what I was doing was wrong but still I didn't see any harm in doing it, because I had weight to lose. I wasn't in the danger zone.

I was feeling the pressure of everyone's comments, the way they spoke about me, the shit on Twitter, it all adds up and weighs down on you. People must have noticed I had ballooned too because I kept getting invited to boot camps, which is all well and good, but it was like they were whispering to me, 'You're not good enough. You're unacceptable and you need to be fixed.'

I just kept thinking how life would be so much better if I was thin. I could have an amazing fit boyfriend, I could be a better glamour model, I could have my own clothing range because people would be envious and want to look like me and I could be hugely successful. Girls are rewarded again and again for their extreme thinness. It's like self-deprivation is the secret of success.

I never became addicted to that feeling of throwing up, but sometimes I did feel amazing after it. I loved the sense of relief it gave. If I was just a normal girl with a normal job, I wouldn't care if I was this size and neither would anyone else, but because I'm on TV, people expect you to be this size 6 stunner. It's just impossible sometimes. The whole world comments on my weight.

The worst part of it was when I was making myself sick and losing weight rapidly, people would tell me how great I looked and congratulate me on working off the pounds so quickly. I craved those comments more. Being part of the media, it's easy to see why people develop disorders because I've experienced first hand what it's like and how it can get hold of you, if you let it. Luckily, I didn't. I suppose it's the same with surgery. You can become completely obsessed with changing your body until there's nothing left to change and you're still unhappy. The media will comment on your looks and weight regardless, so you might just as well learn to love the skin you're in.

It dawned on me one night that what I was doing was ridiculous. You know you've got problems when your head is hanging over the toilet, puking up your dinner, and what you're thinking of is that boy you like and how he thinks you're not pretty. Or the idiot tweeters who constantly call you fat.

For far too long I had fallen for what the culture said about beauty, youth, features, heights and weights. But I did the smart thing from then on: I called my personal trainer, cut out the booze and got back to eating healthy and fresh. Within a week, I had more energy and my complexion began to brighten up again. I was lucky I never did any long-term damage to my body, and now I berate myself for being so stupid. There really are no quick fixes, just hard work and determination.

Chapter Thirty-Three

NOT SO SEVENTH HEAVEN

Fighting fit and raring to go, I was ready to get back into the mad house. Series seven was about to start shooting. It still amazes me when I think that a few drunken, bed-hopping crazies have managed to be commissioned for seven seasons, but the ratings are getting better and better. Now we are pulling in over a million viewers and the *Geordie Shore* juggernaut shows no signs of slowing down.

I picked Vicky up and drove us both to the house in my brand new car: a black and orange Citroën DS3. I feel like a girl racer in it. I even treated myself to a private registration plate, which resembles the word Holly Dolly. It's the first car I've ever had where I haven't been refused finance and had to ask one of my parents to get it in their name. That's a big deal for me!

Vicky and I were the first ones through the door. We immediately ran up to the bedrooms and counted how many beds they'd furnished us with, thinking more beds meant new housemates. On our hunt I remember finding a massage oil tube that apparently sent you into 'raptures'. I asked Vicky what raptures meant because I'd not heard the word before and she kindly explained it to me. That's one thing people don't give her enough credit for, her intelligence. Vicky's a very clever girl and my vocabulary has improved so much since I met her. She has a way of explaining words and things to me, it's like she's the big sister I never had. We aren't supposed to take books into the house, but Vicky always sneaks a couple in and she lets me borrow the ones she thinks I'd like. Which just goes to show how far Vicky and me have come.

In the beginning we didn't get along at all. We clashed over the smallest of things and I think I irritated her. She's a gutsy, confident girl who knows exactly what she wants. Vicky is not the type of person to go running off crying, like I would at first. She'll stand up for herself and argue her point. And I was really looking forward to having her back to her old self, single in Newcastle.

The next housemates to arrive were Scott and Gary. I looked at Scott, and was still unsure of how I felt about him. I'd be lying if I said I didn't like him. We did get quite close in Australia, and although it was supposed to be no-strings-attached sex, I did have a few feelings for him. I saw him as my banker. He was my go-to guy if I hadn't pulled and needed some attention. My mam liked him, too, and on the first night back in the house, I told him he gave me fizzy knickers.

James, Sophie and Charlotte arrived to complete the bunch and the whole madcap dysfunctional family was back and ready to rip up Newcastle. Everyone was having an absolute ball, drinking and getting smashed and then, like a miserable dawn chorus, a new housemate walked in, threatening to rain on the parade.

My jaw hit the floor when I saw her: long brunette hair, stunning smile, slim petite frame and lovely olive skin. She was gorgeous. She was also Sophie's little cousin, Marnie. I was instantly jealous of her and within minutes of walking through the door she was vying for Scott's attention. I just couldn't put up with it, I couldn't compete with her and it made me resentful. It was like she'd walked in and handed me an inferiority complex. Just a few hours ago I was looking forward to getting back in the house and now I was pissed off, to say the least.

Scott was smitten with her, too, which only added to my fucking foul mood. I thought he and me were good mates with a bit of history, I didn't think he'd want to rub me up the wrong way by flirting with the new girl as soon as she tottered through the door and metaphorically stepped on my toes. I rolled my eyes: when did she become so fucking important, anyway?

I had to tell him how I felt so I pulled him into the bedroom. Basically, I told him he could do what he wanted with Marnie, but I would be jealous if he went there. I had to tell him before anything happened and I hoped that he would respect my feelings.

Even Marnie came over to me, asking what the crack was with Scott. I told her the same as I told him: I'd be jealous. You can't blame me, it's a girl thing. She smiled at me and took everything I said on board and then half an hour later, like the snake she is, she was kissing him in the bedroom. Fucking pair of traitors! Maybe I didn't have any right to voice my opinion, but I would never have forgiven myself if I hadn't.

Marnie had pissed everyone in the house off on the first night. I felt like she'd gone about mixing with the group in totally the wrong way. She was more interested in pulling the lads than making mates with the girls. And Scott was meant to be my banker this series, not hers. Well, I wasn't going to moan about it anymore. She was welcome to my sloppy seconds as far as I was concerned.

Anyway, I had bigger things to worry about. The most momentous birthday of my life was coming up in the house: my twenty-first. Unfortunately Sophie had to leave the series and left me a note saying she didn't know if she was going to be back. I was gutted. It was my birthday and she wasn't going to be there to celebrate it. Sophie is one of my best friends, we speak every day; she's like the mother of the house, she looks after everyone. She's the best at cooking, cleaning and doing laundry. If you need a hug or advice, she's always got her arms and ears wide open. I was devastated she wasn't going to be there and it was a real blow to the group dynamic.

Then, if that wasn't bad enough, it was announced Vicky wouldn't be returning to the house either. Now it was just Charlotte, Marnie and me. And just to make my nightmare even worse, James wanted to invite his girlfriend Kate to my twenty-first birthday party.

Was he for real? His girlfriend hated me, she'd slagged me off on Twitter and now she wanted to come to the house for my momentous birthday? Well, what could I say? Begrudgingly I said she could come, but I told him I wasn't happy about it. I don't even know why Kate would want to come – she had some nerve. In the end my attitude made James uncomfortable and he didn't even bother coming.

With or without him I was determined to have a good night. The theme for the party was the nineties because, duh, that's when I was born. I'd gone to the fancy dress shop and bought a boob-busting denim top, some bright neon tights and a ra-ra skirt. Everyone who came to party had really made the effort and I was touched. I even got over my cock fright and bucked a beautiful lad at the end of the night. It was fucking mint!

I thought this series was going well despite being two housemates down, but I should have known that whenever the waters seem calm there's always a storm brewing on the horizon. Hurricane Marnie was about to erupt and ruin everything.

Scott was hooked on Marnie, but she only had eyes for Gaz. Charlotte and I had seen Gaz and Marnie flirting, snogging and doing sex positions with each other. When we confronted them about it, Marnie got defensive and flew into a rage. I'd never been in a fight since the one in the schoolyard, but now it was about to happen again. All hell broke loose with the girls. Marnie was screaming in Charlotte's face and, like the good friend I am, I tried to defend her. Then all of a sudden mental Marnie turned on me.

We grappled with each other in the middle of Tup Tup Palace like a pair of screaming hyenas. She was viciously pulling at my hair and trying to drag me to the ground. I could hear Charlotte screaming while being held back by James. Eventually the bouncers waded in and split us up, but I was stunned and shocked about what had happened.

In that moment I fucking hated Marnie. She had come into our house and ruined it. All the family had been torn apart and I didn't know if it could ever be the same again. When she eventually did waltz back into the house, she got all the lads back on her side and pretended like nothing had happened. It was a fucking joke and all I kept thinking about was Vicky and Sophie: if they had been there, this wouldn't have been happening. I was so angry, I was shaking. All the lads did was think with their cocks. They should have had our backs, but they were too interested in getting Marnie to fuck them.

I was so upset. I felt betrayed and I remembered all the other times I'd been fucked over in this house. It had happened too much: James, Scott and now Marnie. It was difficult living under the same roof as her because I had so much hate towards her. Honestly, I hadn't felt like this about anyone for years. But one night when we were all out, I couldn't watch her being left out. She really didn't have anyone and she was dancing on her own. She looked intimidated and, because I'd been in that position in series one, it was heartbreaking to see. I was the bigger person and so I decided to call a truce. Much as I didn't want to speak to her, I had to. And in the end I was glad we cleared the air.

The worst part was when I had a row with Charlotte. It was about the way her boyfriend Mitch was speaking to her – I couldn't stand around while he was disrespecting her the way he was. I know he was mortal, and arguments happen when you're pissed, but it did give the group a bad first impression of him.

In the end, Charlotte decided she couldn't be in the house, knowing we didn't like the lad she was in love with. She left one evening and left us a note. I got back to the house and there it was, her scribbled confession telling me she was leaving. Immediately I broke down. No one could understand how inconsolable I was. She is my best friend and I felt partly responsible for her leaving. Now I felt so alone, I was completely heartbroken. *Geordie Shore* just wasn't the same without her.

X X X

At the time of writing this book I'm now preparing myself for series eight. And I'd be lying if I said I was looking forward to it as much as the others. Don't get me wrong, it's not that I'm ungrateful because I love being part of the *Shore*, but I'm just anxious about what it's going to be like and what the producers have in store for us. I ended the last series on a low, not knowing if Sophie, Vicky or Charlotte would ever come back to the house. If I'm honest, I still don't know if they ever will and I don't want to imagine a series without them. They are my best friends, my sisters and the missing pieces of my jigsaw: my soul mates.

The 2014 hardback edition of Not Quite A Geordie concluded with the following epilogue:

So there you go, that's me in a nutshell – the story of my life so far. I hope you've enjoyed getting to know me a little better and maybe it goes some way to explain why I am the way I am.

Sometimes I can't believe I'm the same person as the girl who used to dream of being in the Spice Girls and perform in front of anyone who would listen, but deep down, I always knew I'd be in the limelight. I was never going to get there by being Daddy's little angel. And people call me shallow, but I've made a living from diving off the deep end.

I'm making a good income doing what I love and I'm lucky to have been given opportunities I never thought possible. To date I have put my name to my own hair extension range, my own clothing line and I have a variety of onesies on sale. Add in my contract with MTV and my former contract from *Nuts* magazine and I'd say I'm pretty successful for a girl of my age. My mam has always instilled a good work ethic in me and I'm not the type to rest on my laurels. Every day is different and I find it so exciting.

With the money I earn, I'm saving to buy a house and I like to treat my family. I've paid for a holiday for my mam and John next year. I also helped pay for their new bathroom. It was only fair, since all my red hair dye had completely ruined the grout and turned it pink! I try to be very generous and it gives me genuine pleasure to see them happy with the new gift I got them. They were always there for me when I had nothing and I like that I can repay them.

Right now I'm happy and even though I've been through lots of bullshit with boys, I'm cool with being on my own. The only good thing is, because I've been sharing a house with four pumped-up lads, it's given me a unique perspective on the opposite sex. Besides watching them pluck, preen, pump, squat, lift, shave, shower, tan and tone, I also get to listen to the guys using their best techniques when it comes to pulling women. I've seen more boys trying to tash on with lasses in nightclubs around the world than I've had hot dinners.

You'd think that would make me a seasoned pro when it comes to dating dos and don'ts, right? Wrong! I still haven't a clue when it comes to men. I've not had a boyfriend since series one and, while it would be nice to have someone who really cared for me, right now I want to focus on myself. I've seen first hand what *Geordie Shore* can do to relationships. It's incredibly tough. Eventually you'll end up leaving or splitting because of it. That's why I'm not looking for Mr Right, just Mr Right Now. Although having said that, I haven't had sex in eight months. I've lost count of how many times I've been called a slag for my antics on TV, but I'm giving slags a bad name. You can't be celibate for eight months and still carry the title of a slag, can you? I'll leave that for you to decide.

I get called famous everywhere I turn, but I don't actually believe it. I don't live a glamorous life at all. Usually I'm parked up on an industrial estate, late at night, in a trackie, a pair of Air Max and chain smoking like a trooper. My mates haven't got loads of money, so we prefer just to hang out and chat like that rather than be in some swanky club. Sure, I could live that lifestyle – walking round in skyscraper heels and a big expensive handbag, clamouring to be featured on the *Mail Online* everyday – but it's just not me. I'll always remember where I came from: UTB (Up the 'boro).

From day one, *Geordie Shore* has been a rollercoaster and, if it ends tomorrow, I ask myself, would I miss it? The boozy nights, the blazing rows, the heartache, the filming, the cast, the crew, the highs, the lows, the fame, the parties, the pop of flash bulbs? Then there's the lovers, the haters, the champagne and Jägers. All of it, some or none of it? The simple answer is yes, I would miss it.

I would feel like a part of my life had died but, as every reality TV show character should remember, every single one of us is replaceable. Most TV stars are egomaniacs, so that's a possibility some of them can't fathom but I keep myself grounded. I tell myself every day could be my last day in this mad circus of a lifestyle. To appreciate it for what it is and jump on every opportunity that comes my way. Because one day all this will be over and I'll be a nobody, sidelined for another younger, better model. Holly who?

I've seen it happen to so many people. Look at those nineties pop bands who thought their career was going to last forever. The next thing you know, they are entering the *Big Brother* house or desperately trying to revive their outdated career on *The Big Reunion* just to be able to afford their tax bills. That won't happen to me: I've seen what's happened to the people who have left *Geordie Shore*, so believe me when I say I'm well aware of my shelf life.

At least I'm fulfilling my dreams. Like I said in the beginning, I craved the extraordinary. I was greedy for an exciting life. And if what I'm doing now isn't exciting, I don't know what it is.

Chapter Thirty-Four

GUESS WHO'S BACK

If you're reading this, lucky you. You have the fully updated version of my book, complete with the latest goings on from the *Geordie Shore* house and beyond.

Like most of my other chapters in the book, I don't want to go through an intense rehash of what happened on the show. If you want a running commentary, go and watch it for yourself. All the footage is available online for everyone to enjoy time and time again.

Since my book was published, I've read a lot of reviews and I do notice what people say. Most of my reviewers are pleased that the central theme revolves around *Geordie Shore* – after all, that's why you all know me. But in this book I get to tell you about what you don't see on screen and how some of the other housemates and their actions really affect me.

This is my chance to put forward my side of the story without any TV crews directing, producers editing or anyone else interfering with what I want to tell you all. So with all that said, let's get started on why series eight was one of the most pivotal periods of my life.

I've confessed already that I was anxious about returning to *Geordie Shore* because I had no idea where the cast stood. At the end of the last series, I didn't know if Vicky, Sophie or Charlotte would be returning for various reasons. It was all left up in the air. Add in the fact that we also had the longest break ever in between filming – eight months to be exact – and you can understand why my excitement was tinged with nerves.

I decided to drive myself to the house because I'd just picked up a brand-new blue Mercedes A Class AMG Sport, which I bloody love and wanted to show off. It had always been a dream of mine to own a Merc and now I could say, at the tender age of twenty-one, I managed to achieve my dream. I could probably have an even better car but, hey, I'm a saver, not a spender.

When I waltzed through the infamous house door, I realised just how much I'd missed the place and my dysfunctional *Geordie Shore* family. Sure, they piss me off most of the time but, when they are not around and getting on my double F's, I do pine for them.

I was the first person in the house, which gave me a little time to wander around and see how the producers had changed the place. The most notable difference was the waterbed in the shag pad, which I found hysterical. I'd never been on a waterbed before, never mind had sex on one. Maybe, if I was lucky enough, I might get a go!

Soon after I was joined by Marnie, Scott and James and, after the requisite kisses and hugs, we all started discussing a rumour we'd heard. There was going to be a new cast mate joining us on the show. I'd heard it was going to be a boy, which I was pleased about, but, when Gaz arrived with his heavily tattooed mate Aaron, I couldn't help but put my head in my hands. The reason? Aaron and I already had history and I've already spoken about him in this book.

I think the producers were hoping that Aaron and I might rekindle some kind of romance and, for the first few episodes, Aaron was definitely trying to win my affection but I think he was only doing that because he thought the producers would like it. I thought he was a nice lad but, if I'm honest, I didn't really see a future with him, so I saw no point in sleeping with him again, despite him constantly trying his luck. Plus, this season Holly had turned sassy.

Aaron is a good-looking guy and, yes, I've probably been with many worse but, honestly, we were just friends and neither of us wanted it to go any further than that. I could tell the way he looked at Marnie was different to the way he looked at me and it was clear to everyone that he fancied her but was too afraid of pissing Gaz off and breaking the 'lad code' to do anything about it.

And there was another reason I wasn't interested in Aaron. Outside of the house, I had started to see a really nice lad called Liam. Before I went back into filming, I had to sit him down and tell him that I was single and I would need to 'do what I had to do' to get on with making a great show. If that meant forming relationships in the house, that's what would happen. Liam was obviously disappointed but he appreciated my honesty and agreed to keep it casual between us.

I had known Liam for years. He was good-looking with a

wicked smile, a six-pack and a really friendly personality. We had met through mutual friends and kept in touch via social media. One night I desperately needed a lift from the train station back to my house and Liam agreed to pick me up. After that, we began spending more and more time together but, because I was going back into the house, I hadn't wanted to get myself into anything serious, despite how much I felt for him.

It took a while in this series for all the *Geordie Shore* family to be reunited but, eventually, the other girls arrived. Vicky came a few days after me, while Charlotte missed the first ten days of filming because of other commitments. It was a relief to see them come back. I had missed them both incredibly and I didn't want to go through anymore of the experience without them. Unfortunately, it had been announced that Sophie wouldn't be returning, which still guts me to this day.

For the time being I was delighted to have everyone in the house, where they belonged. Yet in the back of my mind, even though I was having fun on the show – especially since the girls had returned – I was still thinking about Liam. We always have many hours to kill when we are filming and, when I was daydreaming, my mind would wander. I missed him, I suppose. It's hard being away from someone when you spend every day together and then suddenly have no contact with them for a month. As you know, we aren't allowed mobiles, so it's not like I could just drop him a text to see if he was OK. And more than just idle thoughts, I genuinely couldn't wait to see him when I left the house.

I'd felt that way all through the series until, one day, about two weeks after we'd begun filming, someone else turned up and changed everything.

For me, the arrival of our new housemate wasn't just one of the most momentous occasions of the series; it was one of the most momentous occasions in the whole of my entire *Geordie Shore* journey. I know that's a big statement to make, so I'll tell you why everything changed when Kyle Christie walked in.

All the lads – Gaz, James, Scott and Aaron – had gone out for the evening, while all the girls – Vicky, Charlotte, Marnie and myself – were scheduled to stay in and have a pamper. We all thought it was unusual for the producers to let us have a night off but none of us were expecting what happened next.

All of a sudden, we heard a guy shout 'OI OI!'. At first we thought one of the lads had left their keys, which is a private joke between us because the front door is never locked and no one owns keys.

We heard another shout of 'OI OI!' coming from downstairs and, when we peered over the balcony, we saw *Geordie Shore*'s best-kept secret: another new member of the group – Kyle.

We are usually so on the ball when a new housemate is arriving. Even though we aren't supposed to know, we always find out everything because people in Newcastle can't keep their mouths shut. So when there's a new lad or lass, we will already have more than an inkling. But with Kyle, no one knew.

Kyle knew most of the group from outside the show. He had dated Charlotte when he was eighteen for three months; he had kissed Vicky a few times; and he was good friends with Marnie. The only girl he didn't know was me but, when Kyle walked in, I fancied him. I mean, who wouldn't? He's the best-looking lad in the *Geordie Shore* house by a mile. He's 6ft 4in, tanned, has a body to die for and a smile that could make any lass's fanny flutter. But although I knew I fancied him, I still had feelings for Liam, so I wasn't immediately going to act on my desires.

I also knew that, because of Vicky's history with Kyle, they were most likely going to get it on and if there's one thing I've learned over the years it's this: Vicky always gets the guy.

Everyone knows what it's like going up against Vicky. You'll never win. She's so good at flirting; truly masterful. There's no point in entering into the competition with her. So, like I said, even though I fancied Kyle initially, I was never going to act on it because it looked like Vicky would get her acrylic talons into him first.

The first thing I said to him always makes me laugh though. Because he'd arrived, we decided to sack off our pamper night and hit the Toon instead, so he could be properly welcomed into the house. I was wearing a pair of white high-waist jeans, a little net top and some chunky heels. He was sat on the sofa, quite cocky, and he didn't look nervous at all. In fact, he looked like he fit in right from the word go. Until, that is, I decided to whip up my top so the soundman could hook up my microphone. Kyle looked completely dumbfounded at the sight of me and my enormous breasts bulging out of my bra and I remember turning round and saying, 'Don't worry, Kyle. You'll get used to this.'

Everyone welcomed Kyle into the group, although I could tell Gary felt threatened. And why wouldn't he? Here was this tall, blond Adonis, who could probably snap Gary's jaw if he had wanted to, so it was obvious that Gary would be feeling a little intimidated. He was competition.

On the first night out, Kyle ended up kissing Vicky, which definitely put a stop to anything I might have been feeling, but then two nights later, when we were in Bijoux, Kyle and I were flirting outrageously. To be honest, it kind of caught me off guard but I was still really flattered by the attention he was lavishing on me and I began to think, 'Maybe Kyle wants a crack at me.' Stranger things have happened.

Back at the house, we ended up in the kitchen alone and, again, he was being overly flirty: touching my arm, feeling my hair, laughing at all my jokes – I knew I couldn't be misreading the signals. He was being very attentive and, because I fancied him so much, I couldn't contain myself. It was there that we shared our first kiss. I was giddy with excitement after it had happened, so much so that I ran upstairs to the girls and shouted, 'I JUST KISSED THE NEW BOY!' The girls all laughed and Vicky looked at me with complete surprise. I don't know if she was gutted or not. She never said she was but, then again, she never would; she has too much pride and instead told me to crack on with him.

The chemistry between Kyle and me was undeniable. We were flirting at every opportunity and, only a few days later we ended up in bed for the first time. We didn't have sex; we just had a fumble. This was sassy Holly, remember. I think that, because I liked him, I didn't want to have sex with him straight away, which sounds bonkers because I've had one night stands with people I never want to see ever again but it wasn't like that with Kyle. I wanted him to respect me.

I'd love to tell you that it was 'no strings attached' fumbling but I'm a woman: it's just not that simple for us ladies to avoid getting feelings. In fact, I'm pretty sure that it must have been an emotionally inept guy who invented the term 'no strings attached' because, for us women, it doesn't exist.

So the next night, when I saw Kyle kissing other girls, it did wound my ego a little. The cheeky bastard thought he could go round kissing other girls all night and then come back to me when it suited. Well he had another thing coming.

I decided then that I would play it cool. The last thing I wanted to do was get feelings for another lad in the house and then for it all to backfire like it had with James. I wasn't up for being hurt again, so I did my best not to fall into that trap.

It wasn't easy though, having to watch Kyle flirt with other people. Mainly it was just kissing but a couple of times he did actually do the deed and, although I had no right to get upset, it still pissed me off if I'm honest. Like, *really* pissed me off. The only way I got through it was to remember that I still had a great lad on the outside who worshipped the ground I walked on. That gave me a crumb of comfort. Yeah, I fancied Kyle outrageously but he was more likely to fuck me over, whereas I knew Liam never would.

Later in the series, it was decided that we were going to fly to Iceland and it was there that things progressed a little more with Kyle. On our last night out, he was all over me, so I responded by being all over him. I couldn't deny that I was beginning to like him more and I was so flattered that he seemed to like me too. We ended up in bed but, again, we didn't have sex. Not full-on sex anyway – we did do rude bits. The main thing I remember about that night was that it felt so nice to be tucked up next to him and I knew then that I was done for.

I was falling for Kyle and I didn't know how to stop it. He is everything I find attractive in a guy and, because of the way I felt, I didn't want to hold off any longer. When we got back to Newcastle, we finally slept together for the first time. We had been out in town and, as soon as we got home, we sneaked off into the shag pad.

And, my God, it had been worth the wait!

That night of passion was incredible. I don't mind bigging him up by saying he is hands-down unreal between the sheets: heart-pounding, make-up-melting, screaming-his-name kind of unreal.

But I was scared because I was developing deep feelings for Kyle. I wasn't sure how he felt, so I knew I had to squash those feelings and, like I've said before, I didn't think I could handle the rejection if he just wanted sex and then was free to pull other girls. I wasn't up for that. I liked him way more than a friends-with-benefits scenario. I did my best to keep a lid on my affection for him but it was only towards the end of the series that I realised the full extent of my jealousy.

We had a Hawaiian party at the house and Kyle got with a girl in front of me, which really upset me. We had already slept together at this point and I had thought he wouldn't have wanted to rub my nose in it like he did. To this day, I never let him live it down because the girl was a complete munter, with the worst hair extensions imaginable. Why he even bothered to go there was beyond me. If he had tried his luck, maybe he could have had me again.

I felt rejected. Was I bitter? Absolutely. Did it hurt me? You can bet your arse it did. Show me any girl that doesn't feel a piece of their heart break just a little at any rejection.

I confessed to Vicky and Charlotte the next day that his actions had saddened me so much. They were completely spot-on when they said I needed to detach myself from him before I got hurt again. I knew they were right but I was disappointed.

I was angry with myself for feeling this way. But then again, every boy I'd liked over the past four years had rubbed my face in it in some way, so I suppose I should have been used to it, shouldn't I? I'd dealt with this before; I could deal with it again.

Having said that, I know better than anyone that is easier said than done and you just can't switch off your feelings for someone, which is why, at the end of the series, I was pretty gutted to be leaving Kyle. I'd spent two weeks with him in close quarters, getting to know him, chilling, hanging out and sleeping with him. I knew I was really going to miss him.

Most people imagine that the whole *Geordie Shore* cast hang out outside of the house but, in actual fact, we rarely see each other. The only person I really see on the outside is Charlotte, so it is genuine when we all say goodbye because we know it's going to be for a pretty long time.

After I had waved everyone off and was walking away from the house, Kyle shouted over to me.

'Holly, are you wearing a microphone?' he yelled.

'No. Why?'

'Because when we get out of this house, I'm going to fuck you all over,' he said, grinning from ear to ear.

'Oh yeah, right. Whatever.' I said, completely dismissing his comment as banter and walking off to get my car.

I immediately put Kyle out of my mind because I was heading home and I wanted to see Liam – and see if I still had feelings for him. And when we met up, I did. It was so easy and comfortable. We took off right where we left off. Kyle was the reality show but Liam was my reality. At least, that's how I compartmentalised them in my head, despite me having a great deal of feelings for both lads.

Kyle, to his credit, did keep in touch with me. Most of the time it was just friendly, rather than flirty, but it was nice to know he cared enough to drop a text every now and then. None of the other lads from the show have ever done that, so it made me think of him in a different way. Was he really a ruthless shagger like Gary? Or was that all an act he put on in the house? I couldn't tell at the time. But I didn't let it bother me either because I was too occupied with Liam. And after a few weeks of being out of the house, Liam and I became official. I was really confident in my feelings for him and, when he asked me to be his girlfriend, I immediately – and really happily – said yes.

In the back of my mind, I knew I would have to go back into the *Geordie Shore* house and be back living with Kyle but, for the time being, I was content. I put all thoughts of him out of my head and decided I would cross that bridge when it came to it.

Chapter *Thirty-Five*

HEARTBREAK AND PROMISE

I t was July 2014 and life was great.

My personal brand was booming. The offers of work were pouring in, the audience figures for the show were staggering and everything with Liam had been going really, really brilliantly.

Most days I felt like I had to pinch myself because I never imagined I could ever be so lucky, getting to do the job I loved and doing it with my best friends around me. It's like a dream come true.

There was only one niggle in my life that was making me a little anxious. It was the run-up to series nine and I would now have to cross that bridge I talked about. I would have to strike the balance between going wild on *Geordie Shore* and being good to my boyfriend while I was away. Seems easy enough, doesn't it? Well, it would have been if there wasn't someone in the house I kinda liked.

Like with every series, we had meetings with producers, who

asked what had been happening in our lives while we'd been off from filming. A few of them knew I had a boyfriend but it was decided in our discussion that I wouldn't bring him up on the show. My reasons? I didn't want to drag Liam into the *Geordie Shore* circus. I had done that in series one with a guy and it had all gone horribly wrong. I wasn't about to put Liam through the same fate. I would just get on with it, leaving the rest of the cast to do the tashing and bucking.

If I'm being completely honest, I didn't know how I felt about Kyle. I knew I had really strong feelings for Liam but, when I saw Kyle again, would I still be able to keep away from temptation? I wasn't sure. But I never relayed my concerns to anyone at the time. I tried to put it all out of my mind.

On the morning of our new filming schedule, Charlotte arrived at my place to pick me up before we drove round to Scott's and then on to the house. One by one, all the housemates began arriving and, when I saw Kyle again, he was even better looking than I remembered. 'Fucking hell!' I thought to myself. 'This is going to be difficult. How on earth am I going to be able to keep away from him for five weeks straight?'

It should have been easy, shouldn't it? If I cared about my boyfriend Liam so much, why would I even think about jeopardising what we had for a fling in the house?

I couldn't believe I was already beginning to doubt myself on the first day. I dismissed my feelings immediately and put my emotions down to the fact that it was just a sexual attraction to someone I had previously been with. I just had to be strong and NOT forget about my feelings for my boyfriend. I certainly wouldn't be making a play for Kyle any time soon.

However, Kyle had a different idea.

On our first night out, the producers kept encouraging Kyle to try to get with me. He cornered me and tried to neck on with me. I told him politely it wasn't going to happen and I confessed to him off camera that I had a boyfriend and that I was really happy with him. Kyle hadn't realised and instantly felt bad. He turned round to me and said, 'If you're happy with Liam, I will leave you alone, Holly. I don't want to break up a happy couple.' After he'd said that, I found a whole new respect for him. He didn't just want to use me for sex – like some of the other housemates would – he was genuinely respectful of my relationship. But, as far as the audience at home was concerned, they would all just think I'd pied him off.

Even though I *really* wanted to succumb to temptation, I didn't because, in the back of my mind, I knew I had a really good guy on the outside who I wasn't going to screw over. The problem was that I really fucking liked Kyle from day one. He gave me more fluttering feelings than Liam did. Every time I saw Kyle's name pop up on my phone, I would get a rush of adrenalin. But Liam had qualities I hadn't yet seen in Kyle.

For instance, Liam was quite simply lovely. A lad your mum would be over the moon to see you settle with. Someone who wouldn't mess me around and make me feel insecure. Did Kyle make me insecure? Yes, he did. Big time. I still thought of him as a player and I knew deep down that there was far more potential for him to really seriously hurt me.

My thoughts and feelings about him weren't baseless either because, while we were filming, he was still picking up birds and taking them back to the house. It was that kind of behaviour that made me wary of Kyle and made me appreciate Liam all the more.

But viewers never got to see that side of Kyle during series nine. Kyle getting with three girls in front of me and bringing them back to the house never made it to the final edit – which is why I'm glad I've been given this opportunity to tell everyone the real reason behind why I was so scared of getting with him. He has admitted he slept with one of them but not the other two and he's got no reason to lie to me, so I believe him. I've got to say that I was pretty upset when I saw the way Kyle had been edited to make him look like a proper gentleman, not getting with any girls, when, in actual fact, that wasn't the case. It made me look like a bunny boiler and that I was worrying over nothing.

Series nine was really bittersweet for me because, like I said at the beginning, I was so happy that everything in my life had been going well. My dreams were literally coming true but the entire time I was plagued by this emotional rollercoaster I was on involving these two lads I liked.

As time went on, I started having second thoughts about being with Liam while I was on *Geordie Shore* but I was increasingly wary of Kyle's intentions in case he hurt me. Most days I was wishing that I hadn't ever met either bloke because I couldn't deal with the emotions of it all. It was much easier when I was footloose and fancy-free.

My head was completely messed up and I had no idea what would be the best thing to do. Imagine if I finished with my boyfriend and got it on with Kyle and it didn't work out with him. I would have fucked over a lad who I genuinely liked and could have maybe had a future with. On the other hand, I had more chemistry with Kyle and, no matter what you say, nothing in the world can make chemistry happen. It's either there or it's not. And if it's not, what's the point?

It's worth mentioning here that Charlotte was also going through a hard time with her long-term boyfriend Mitch. So when we travelled to the world's most romantic city – Paris – both Charlotte and I began to crave romance. It must be something in the air over there. Everywhere we looked there were loved-up couples, kissing, cuddling and giving each other puppy eyes.

It made me really evaluate my situation and, as I stood under the iconic Eiffel Tower, I looked over at Kyle and smiled. I don't know if it was the romantic movie-set setting or what but I became completely caught up in the moment. It was then that I knew, when I felt the butterflies inside me, that I really wanted him. I couldn't fight it any longer and, after that night, both Char and I began flirting with our old flames, Gary and Kyle.

I know I have said in the past that I hated the way Gary treated Charlotte and, ordinarily, I wouldn't want her going anywhere near him, never mind flirting with him. But Charlotte was having a terrible time with Mitch and Gary was giving her the attention she needed so, for the time being, I was happy to let them crack on.

When we got back from Paris, all the feelings I had been denying I had for Kyle came rushing towards me. It was like I'd been hit by a train. In my own head, I was completely torn to pieces. I had this really sweet guy outside of the house but I also had so many strong feelings for Kyle. My head was saying one thing and my heart another.

The last thing I wanted to do was cheat on Liam but, even without me touching Kyle, I felt like I was cheating already. I shouldn't be feeling like this if I was already happy with someone else, should I?

I remember I was in the kitchen one day and I was trying to explain to Kyle how I felt. I said, 'My head is completely fucked. I don't know what to do.'

Kyle replied, 'Your head is fucked? My head's fucked. How do you think I feel? You're the one with the boyfriend.'

When he said that, I was a little taken aback. It was the first time Kyle had ever let me know he was bothered about me. I thought he just wanted to have sex with me; I didn't actually know he had real feelings for me!

He continued, 'I do really like you and I'm scared because it's the first time in my life I don't want to go out and pull but the thing is you have a boyfriend, Holly. I don't want to get deep feelings for you because you are with someone else. I am still one of the lads, I'm new to the show and it's kind of expected that I get with other girls but I honestly don't want to do that, especially when I could have you.'

I understood completely where he was coming from. He didn't want to look like a pussy in front of the other lads for liking me. He sees the way Gary and Scott treat girls and he hates it. Genuinely, he doesn't like to treat girls that way: that's not him. When he first went on the show, he felt like he had to behave the way they do. But he does have respect for women and I think it stems from the fact that he has such a good relationship with his mam.

After we had that conversation, I said to Kyle, 'Prove yourself to me.' I couldn't do anything about my current situation. I couldn't call Liam and say I'd been having second thoughts about him because we weren't allowed any contact with anyone on the outside. I would have to wait until filming was completely over until I could sort my head out.

At this point me, Kyle, Charlotte and Gary were having a lot of double dates. It was so much fun and, what's more, Kyle hadn't been pulling anyone. He had really taken what I said to heart and was doing everything he could to prove himself to be worthy. Maybe he did really like me. I had to hope he did and wasn't just trying to do this for a storyline on the show. As a result, we were becoming extremely close, sleeping in the same bed and kissing, although it hadn't gone much further than that. All the time, I knew what I was doing was wrong. I was being a complete bitch to Liam and I felt fucking horrible about it.

Near the end of the show, I knew all the storylines would have to be wrapped up. The producers sat me down many times and asked me how I was feeling. They were really pro-Kyle and kept saying, 'What more can he do, Holly? He has proven himself to you. He hasn't been interested in anyone but you. It's like he can't see past you.'

Alarm bells began to ring. Were the producers the ones behind Kyle's feelings, forcing him to like me? Or was he being genuine? I couldn't decide at first but that day was a real turning point. I began to gauge everything in my head and I thought that I would finally have to make a choice: Liam or Kyle.

I knew I had Liam, who was amazing, did everything for me and would never do anything to hurt me. But then I had Kyle, who was meant to be a top shagger like Gary, Scott and Aaron but wasn't behaving like them – and who makes me excited and frightened in equal measure.

It was a very tough decision but, in the end, I took some advice from that quirky movie star Johnny Depp. I always remembered him saying once, 'If you love two people at the same time, choose the second one because, if you really loved the first, you wouldn't have fallen for the second.' So after that I took a chance on Kyle because he evoked so many feelings in me. Feelings that I couldn't ignore, no matter how hard I tried. He gave me butterflies in places I never knew I had. And on the last night, I callously slept with him before I had ended things with Liam. I know it was wrong but, like I've said many, many times before, I'm not a role model. I'm just telling you how it was.

Afterwards I was happy because I felt that the sex between Kyle and I had brought us closer, even though I could have made the biggest mistake of my life by fucking over a genuinely nice lad in the process. But that's a decision I would now have to live by. I didn't know when we left the show if Kyle was ever going to speak to me again on the outside. Kyle tried to reassure me all the time by saying he did want to continue seeing me but you'll forgive me for being cautious because I had heard this all before.

Feeling dejected because another season was over, I couldn't face going home. Charlotte's parents were away, so I decided to go and stay with her for a week. I think I just needed an adjustment period after coming out of the show and I knew that, if I went home, I would have to deal with Liam, which I was trying to put off as long as possible.

Obviously, Liam got in touch as soon as he knew I was out, expecting everything to be fine with us and to carry on where we left off. And before I tell you what happened, I'll hold my hands up right now and say that I handled the whole situation with Liam terribly.

I know what I should have done but I was too wrapped up in my own stuff to be mature about this situation so, instead of just manning up and meeting him, I called him from Charlotte's kitchen and abruptly told him we were over. He sounded devastated, disappointed and distraught. He was so upset but, the more he questioned me, the more irritated I got with him, which was completely the wrong way to be and so unfair to him. I had just shattered this guy and then couldn't even be bothered to go into the reasons why, just because my attention was elsewhere now – with Kyle. It's so much easier being the dumper instead of the dumpee, especially if you have someone else to keep your mind occupied.

I know I should have met him face to face but I couldn't bear the thought of seeing him in the flesh and telling him in person because I was too ashamed of what I had done. I took the coward's way out and gave no thought to how he must have been feeling. I confessed to sleeping with Kyle and he was destroyed. He couldn't believe I could just shit on him like that. He thought I had more respect for him than to do that and, to be honest, so did I. In hindsight, I should never have agreed to be his girlfriend in the house but I didn't realise things could have progressed with Kyle the way they did.

After that phone call with Liam, he was still texting me, like anyone would. You would want answers and he deserved them too. But I childishly chose to ignore him.

I really regret the way I treated Liam; I'm genuinely sorry about it. If I could go back in time and handle it differently, I would do. It's probably the most horrible thing I've ever done to someone. The poor guy – who knows what he must have been feeling, knowing I'd finished with him for another lad.

Eventually, about two weeks later, I did end up meeting with Liam again to give him back all the things that he'd left at my house. We sat there and had a really long chat – the kind of chat I should have had with him as soon as I was out of the house. He cried, I cried and I just said that I wasn't in the right frame of mind for a relationship with him. He needed to be with a nice girl, who would treat him just as well as he was willing to treat them. He didn't need the head- or heart-ache that came with having a girlfriend from a crazy TV show. Eventually, he agreed and left. I still feel bad for the way I treated him and I just want to take this opportunity to publicly say how sorry I am.

It was August when we finished filming and Kyle stuck to his word by making the effort to come to Charlotte's to see me in the week I was there. I know this sounds crazy but I was absolutely terrified of seeing Kyle without the cameras. On the show we always had something to talk about because there was always some kind of drama, or producers would give us a topic to have a conversation about, but what if, in real life, we had nothing in common? Every time I was due to meet him, my heart would be racing and I'd be so nervous in case I said something stupid.

Then, when it came to the point where we would have to go back to Newcastle to film green screen, he asked me if I wanted to get some food. I said yes and I suppose you could say it was our first official date. It was nothing flash – we went to a Toby Carvery for an all-you-can-eat roast dinner, which totally sums up how down to earth we both are: classy. Another night he picked me up and took me round to his to watch a film and then dropped me off back home, which is really sweet of him considering it's a two-hour round trip to and from Middlesbrough.

Slowly but surely we began spending lots of time together. He introduced me to his mam and the rest of his family, which was a really big worry for me at first. I knew they had seen the show and I didn't want them to have pre-judged me from my stupid, slaggy antics on screen. But – I swear when I say this – I have never met lovelier people in my entire life. His mum Julie, dad Dale and his older brother Adam are absolutely amazing and made me feel so welcome right from the off. I've never really been close to a guy's family when I've been dating them but I instantly felt comfortable with Kyle's, to the point where sometimes he would go to the gym and leave me at his house with his mam on my own.

Apart from Kyle being drop-dead gorge, fit as fuck with a great-fun personality, behind that fluffy blonde hair is a very intelligent mind. When I realised he wasn't some 'himbo' who is all about his six pack, I really thought I'd struck gold: brains and beauty.

I only found out about the extent of his intelligence when we discovered we both have a love of war films. We watched the whole series of *Band of Brothers* and afterwards we would sit there debating the whole show in depth for hours. I know it's not something you would typically expect of two drunken lunatics from *Geordie Shore* but, like I've always said, there's much more to each and every one of us than you see on screen. Kyle is massively into history; you could ask him anything about World War I or II and he would know it. It really is refreshing speaking to someone who is knowledgeable about a fascinating subject.

Having said that, our guilty pleasure is *The Walking Dead*. We watch so many episodes of it in one go that we actually start looking like the zombie cast members. But we don't care. Just having the normality of being able to sit and slob in front of the box is what I look forward to in life. Being on a TV show is obviously so hectic and full of all these superficial people and places but the one thing I look forward to is getting into bed with him at night, putting on a box set and just chilling out. It's probably the one thing that most people take for granted but it's the one thing I cherish the most. It really does go to show that you can earn as much money as you want but just lying in bed, cuddling up to the person you care about most is priceless.

I was so comfortable with Kyle that I began staying over at his more and more but, even though we were spending all this time together, we weren't official. We hadn't had the conversation about if we were boyfriend and girlfriend. I mean, we weren't seeing other people but we weren't officially together either, which was a little confusing.

Soon enough, it was nearly time to go back to filming series ten of *Geordie Shore*. We'd had August through to November off and, in those three months, Kyle and I had spent so much time together. We'd been papped holding hands many times and even been on holiday, which had led everyone to believe that we were officially an item, but, like I said, we weren't.

It was like we deliberately hadn't spoken about it and, the longer it continued, the more confusing our relationship became. Why didn't Kyle want to have that conversation? Did he want a girlfriend or not? Was this a 'friends with benefits' situation? It was hard to know. Plus, I had just come out of a relationship with Liam and Kyle had only ever had one proper girlfriend in the past. So we didn't want to rush anything.

At the time, I didn't think we needed a label. It didn't bother me too much that we weren't official because I knew how close we were and that was all that mattered. I felt like, in time, everything would work itself out; we were strong enough to get through whatever the house could throw at us, so we just had to stick it out.

In the week leading up to series ten, Kyle and I did end up having many conversations about what we were going to do when we got back into the *Geordie Shore* house. At the end of the day, the last thing audiences want to see is a happy couple all over each other, just living like love's young dream. But our so-called 'relationship' was going so well before we entered the house that we didn't want to be arguing with each other just to create drama. We knew we would maybe have a few daft arguments because we do actually disagree on many things in real life but never have major rows. We are chalk and cheese in that respect. We have opposite views on everything and constantly bicker but I never expected anything to be as bad as it was when we actually got back into the house.

I can't say what did end up happening in series ten because, by the time this book is released, it won't have been on screen and I'm contractually not allowed to reveal what happens – plus, I wouldn't want to spoil it for everyone! But I can tell you it was the most emotionally draining series I have ever filmed. If you thought series one was bad, ten was – pardon the pun – ten times worse.

People say our show is set up and fake but I can tell you from the bottom of my heart that what happened between me and Kyle was devastatingly real. I put myself out there and it was tough knowing that audiences all over the world were now going to scrutinise what happened between us, even when I wasn't sure how we were going to pan out.

It's only now that I can fully appreciate how hard it must have been having a relationship in the house for some of my other past cast members. Kyle and I still hadn't had the discussion about us being together officially before filming and we came to the conclusion that we didn't want to commit to a relationship until we knew for sure if we could handle being on the show together. That house can break up even the strongest of couples. We wanted to see how strong we were and being in the house was the ultimate test.

It would make us or break us, that's for sure.

Like I've said, I can't say what happens in the series but I will say that I've seen a different side to Kyle – he isn't like the other lads in the house. I know that's what people expected of him; to be like them. He should have been shagging about and pulling girls and, in some ways, it might have been an easier choice for the both of us, rather than all the shit we've gone through. We had countless arguments in the house and they weren't your usual *Geordie Shore* pissed up rows. These were full-on, emotional car crashes. I found it very difficult to film but now I'm in a much better place than I've ever been. I can't say how Kyle feels about it all, mainly because he has too much bravado and he'd rather people think he was a total knob than a gentleman. But, whatever he thinks, I hope he is happy with the way everything has turned out.

Kyle wasn't quite my knight in shining armour. In fact, to me, he'll always be a dickhead in a leather jacket.

I have no idea where I'm heading right now but I'm happy

with where I've started and I'm excited to find out the rest along the way.

My life has been plagued by rejection, unrequited love and false hope but now I finally feel that, for once, everything is working out – with or without a boyfriend. And that realisation has been one of the greatest things I've learned this year. So if you're in the same boat as me, don't worry about a thing… whatever will be, will be.

Maybe this is just the beginning.

Or maybe this is my happy ending after all.

THANK YOU

This book has been amazing to write and I've had a great team of people behind me, who have helped me along the way. I do really appreciate all your hard work.

Firstly, to the most amazing mam in the world, I know I don't say it often but I really don't know where I would be without you. Thank you for always supporting me and giving me the best possible life, even when it was not always easy. I'm so proud to call you my mother and if I grow up to be just half the woman you are, then I'll be happy.

To my nana Olwyn, or should I say my second mam? I was lucky enough to be the first grandchild and have you all to myself for those eleven years. You always made sure we went on little adventures, even if it was just to the park or the swimming baths. Thank you for everything.

To my Dad, hiding under pub tables and sitting behind goal

311

posts is what I remember most from my times with you and I loved every second of it. Especially with a pint of Coke and packet of cheese puffs in hand while performing my dance routines to all your friends. I love how proud of me you have always been, even through the *Geordie Shore* times when my face was splashed all over the papers – you always stuck by me. I'll always remember the time you wouldn't let me go on the bungee trampolines in Clackton! I'm still upset about that! You're the funniest man I know and no matter how old I am I'll always be your Hunza Bunza. Love you, X.

To my granddad Barry: you're the most amazing granddad in the world. Thank you for always being there for me and always being so proud. Love you and Lol so much!

To Debbie: thanks for being the most amazing stepmam in the world.

To Joe – my little baby brother Joey, well, not so little anymore. Love you millions.

To John: thanks for putting up with me for all of those years when I was a stroppy teenager. I know it wasn't easy but I'm so glad that you did and that we have a better relationship now.

To Darci, my little beautiful nightmare of a sister: I hope after all the mistakes I've made I can teach you not to make the same ones. Love you all the world and back again.

To Nana Ann: I think I definitely got my wild side from you, Nana. I remember you letting me cut your hair because I said I knew how, even though I didn't because I was twelve years old! Watching *Spooks of Bottle Bay* with a cup of tea and a jar of biscuits, those were the days. Love you lots.

To the most amazing friends in the entire world: Tom, Leah and Christie. I know it's not always been easy being my friend, especially in the beginning, but even through all the grief you never let people change your opinions about me. We were friends before *Geordie Shore* and we will be friends for many years after. Thank you for always having my back, thank you for never treating me any differently, and thank you for always telling me that I'm 'just a freak' who barely has any friends! Haha! 'Boys will come and go but the four of us will always be there' – I wouldn't be who I am without you all.

To my friend and manager Luke Mills: thank you for believing in me and taking a chance on me when nobody else would. You work so hard for me, and I'm happy to call you a friend as well as a manager.

To the most glamorous and best ghostwriter in the business, Elissa Corrigan: thank you for all your hard work in helping me put this book together. All those hours in that Lanzarote hotel paid off!

To the MTV press team: Roberta Duman, thanks for always being on my side, you've helped me a lot. Lauren Goddard, thank you for being the friendliest person ever. I couldn't have done so many things, like travel to South Africa, without your help. Thanks to Hayley Hamburg for working behind the scenes a lot of the time and thanks to the now-departed Mandy Hershon. Also to Milly Gattengo at MTV Australia, who I hope to see for a drink in Sydney soon.

The wider MTV team: thanks to Adam Young, Marietta Constantinou, Vicky Godden, Jody Malam and David Morrish.

MTV senior executives, including Jo Bacon and Kerry Taylor: you've always taken time out when I needed you and I am incredibly appreciative.

MTV series producer Lauren Benson: you were the first

person I ever met when auditioning for *Geordie Shore*. With two pieces of material covering my nipples how could we not know I was the perfect candidate? We've been through a lot in the past three years and I have you to thank for my place in the show. Love you so much Benno.

MTV head of production Rebecca Knight: Rebecca, I've only ever met you once or twice, yet your name is never far from conversation. I know you deal with my management a lot, and it is with your help that *Geordie Shore* has become the show it is, and the cast the people they are. I can't thank you enough.

MTV talent manager Natasha Lewis: Tash, I'm saying both thank you and sorry to you, haha. For those who don't know Tash, she takes the brunt of all anger, upset, frustration, stupidity and much more from all of the cast members at MTV. Despite all our fall-outs, you're a really lovely person and I'm glad you're there, so for all of that, thank you. Also, thanks to Katherine Shenton, who worked as head of talent before you. And to Steve Regan and Craig Orr.

To everyone who has ever worked on *Geordie Shore* from runner to exec, I want to thank you for working so hard alongside us to make the best TV show on MTV!

Alexandra Bryant at Misfits Management: Thank you, Al, for picking up the phone, no matter what time of day or night. You're so organised and professional and you keep my diary in order.

Nuts Magazine associate editor Sam Riley: Sam, I hold you in the highest regard possible. It was your willingness to give me a chance and put me on the cover of *Nuts Magazine* that started a long relationship between *Nuts* and myself. I feel very much a part of the *Nuts Magazine* family and look forward to every single shoot.

The rest of the *Nuts Magazine* team, including the hugely talented hair and make-up artist Johanna Dalemo, photographers Zoe and Steve McConnell, stylists Lisa, Yusef, Liz, Tanee, Ashley, Steve and Karol at Big Bang. I'd like to thank you for keeping me busy with PAs, and putting up with everything that comes with that. Special thank you to Yusef for working alongside Misfits Management in pushing me so hard and I hope I always do you proud.

There's a lot of people in the press to thank, including Natasha Rigler, Jessica Boulton, Jen Crothers (love you, Jen), Rhiannon Evans, Olivia Cooke, Amy Brookbanks, Richard Innes, Damien McSorley, Jeany Savage (the legend), Nadine Linge, Dan Wootton, Clemmie Moodie, Nana Achempong, Hannah Shaw, Ashleigh Rainbird and Colin Robertson.

A few famous faces, including Chloe Sims, who's lovely and we shared management for a time. Sam and Billie Faiers, for being such sweet girls, along with your mother Sue and Auntie Libby and everyone at Minnies Boutique. Lateysha Grace, who's a lovely person, Jaiden Micheal, who's always given great advice, Amy Childs and your mother, Julie – you've both always been so lovely to me.

Commercial partners I've worked with over the years: I'd like to thank Coral, Lush Hair Extensions, Blue Banana, ONECM Onesies, Protein World and AskJerry, PE Events (Paulien Bolhaar), Joe Nemer at Illusive Australia. A big thank you to Lisa Fox at *TheFashionBible.co.uk*. With your help, Lisa, my range – Yours Faithfully – has grown from strength to strength and I'm incredibly excited for the future.

I'd like to thank Kate O'Shea for working so closely with Luke at Misfits Management. I love that you both work together when it comes to *Geordie Shore* and I know whatever you're working on, I can count on you, so thank you.

To Steve Cocky from In Demand Music and my record label All Around The World. Everything we've worked on has been brilliant and I look forward to the future with glee.

Photographer Danny Ryan, who's always lovely. I look out for you at every event, Danny, and sorry if I ruin your pictures by giving you a hug.

John Blake Publishing for commissioning this book! Thank you all, including John Blake, Chris Mitchell, Joanna Kennedy and everyone else I don't know. Writing this book has been a really fulfilling experience and I've enjoyed every moment of it. I thank you deeply for the opportunity and for believing in me. I'll never forget it.

Lisa Connell of Macauley Smith Solicitors: Lisa, you've worked so hard for me and never get any praise. I can't thank you enough – I really do mean that.

Mr Sultan Hassan of Elite Surgical who performed my breast augmentation so expertly. Thank you, Mr Hassan.

Gill and Dr Maurice of Harley Street Smile Clinic – you're both lovely people and put my mind to rest ahead of my veneers being fitted.

And finally my fans: thank you so much for supporting me through thick and thin because, without you lot, I wouldn't be who I am today. I am forever grateful.